Design Fundamentals for New Media

James Gordon Bennett

THOMSON

DELMAR LEARNING™   Australia Canada Mexico Singapore Spain United Kingdom United States

THOMSON

DELMAR LEARNING

Design Fundamentals for New Media
James Gordon Bennett

Vice President, Technology and Trades SBU:
Alar Elken

Editorial Director:
Sandy Clark

Senior Acquisitions Editor:
James Gish

Development Editor:
Jaimie Wetzel

Marketing Director:
Dave Garza

Channel Manager:
William Lawrensen

Marketing Coordinator:
Mark Pierro

Production Director:
Mary Ellen Black

Production Manager:
Larry Main

Production Editor:
Thomas Stover

Editorial Assistant:
Marissa Maiella

Cover Design:
Patricia Boffice

Library of Congress Cataloging-in-Publication Data:

Bennett, James (James Gordon), 1963–
    Design fundmentals for new media / James Bennett. — 1st ed.
        p. cm.
    Includes index.
    ISBN 1-4018-3779-4
    1. Multimedia systems—Design.
2. Digital media—Design. 3. Mass media—Technological innovations. I. Title.
    QA76.575.B46 2004
    006.7—dc22

                                2004007240

ISBN: 1-4018-3779-4

Notice To The Reader

This book is dedicated to two groups of people. The first group is made up of family and friends who have made sacrifices during the writing of this book, especially my wife, Lora; my daughters, Crystal and Audrie; my granddaughter, Anastasia; and my newborn son, James.

The second group is made up of the students who will use this book. In addition to this dedication, I also give this advice: *Always remember that it is the duty of every good student to build on what they have been taught and to surpass their instructors.*

Preface

Intended Audience

This book contains information that is essential for anyone who works with any of the emerging and evolving media. This includes Web sites, interactive CD-ROM presentations, electronic games, and a host of other applications. Too often, professionals in this field are forced into a race with technology. They must spend their time learning new software versions and techniques just to keep up, while design skills are left to be acquired on the fly. *Design Fundamentals for New Media* does away with this approach by explaining the elements of design as well as the psychological and visual processes behind them in a way that makes sense to the new media professional. This text may be used by introductory- to intermediate-level designers in a two- or four-year educational program as well as nondesign professionals who need a primer of design.

Emerging Trends

Nearly every day, there is some announcement about a new development or advancement that will further erode the lines separating the different methods we use to communicate with each other. Eventually, what is referred to as *new media* will become simply *the media* as it engulfs more and more of our traditional forms of communication.

On the surface, this trend might appear to make the designer's job easier since all forms of media seem to be moving toward a common ground, but instead, as each form of communication becomes assimilated, what was originally called new media adds to its ever-expanding list of properties and attributes those of the most recent addition. Instead of becoming easier, the concerns of the new media designer are becoming more complex.

This text addresses the problem by outlining many of the attributes associated with the different forms of communication in a way that will provide designers with the ability to recognize current and future issues as well as make informed design decisions concerning those issues. Not only is this text relevant to the present state of media, but the information presented here will serve designers through the changes that will inevitably come.

Background of This Text

Recently, educational institutions have seen a huge influx of a new kind of design student. These new students pursue an expertise in visual communication using technology and new media. Their paradigms and approaches to design are often different from those of the traditional artist and designer of the past. Because of these differences, textbooks that once enjoyed a reputation for providing a good foundation in design concepts are often found to be difficult for this kind of student. To make matters worse, the textbooks that are aimed at the needs of these new design students are usually concerned more with the use of a specific software application (e.g., Photoshop or Flash) and rarely address design concepts in a manner suited for their understanding.

From its inception, this book has been about presenting design essentials in a way that new media students can quickly understand and immediately put to use. Instead of merely defining an element of design and showing an example in the hope that a student will absorb the information on some intuitive level, this book defines the properties of a visual element, explains why it has the effect that it does, and shows how it can be used. In addition to this, any specifics about the visual element's translation to electronic media are covered in detail.

Because of the different approach in presentation, the research and information gathering necessary for this text included such diverse areas as aesthetics, cognitive psychology, physics, and technology. An accumulation of this research can be found in the pages of this text, but again, it has been presented in a manner that is sensitive to the learning style of the new media design student.

It is assumed that students using this text have at least a minimal experience with some imaging software, although this is not necessary. Beyond that, there are no prerequisites of design or technical experience for this book.

Textbook Organization

Each chapter includes the following:

- An introduction to the specific topic
- An in-depth body of text covering the topic
- Illustrations of topic concepts
- Examples of topic use in works of design
- Several hands-on exercises that address the topic
- Review questions addressing material covered

The textbook is divided into four sections. The first section is an introduction to the nature of new media and certain concepts that are essential to successful visual communication in a new media project. The second section is concerned with the elements of design, such as line, shape, and color. These elements are presented as building blocks and tools for the designer's use. The third section focuses on combining these elements to produce enhanced designs, using such concepts as balance, style, and emphasis. The fourth section covers nonstatic elements of design, such as motion, navigation, and importing other media. The material in each of these sections, as well as the individual chapters, builds on the understanding and skills acquired in previous sections so that students learn in a progressive manner.

In Chapter 1, students learn about the nature of the new media as well as its similarities to and differences from the more traditional forms of visual communication. In addition, they are introduced to successful working methods for designers.

Chapter 2 presents the design process for a typical new media project in a step-by-step manner. Each phase of the design process is defined and explained in detail. Special attention is given to how each step affects the steps that come after.

Chapter 3 begins the section of the book that covers the specific elements of design. In this chapter, students are introduced to the concept of space as the primary visual element and as the context for all design. Through the use of plain language and clear definitions, they will come to understand the use of space and its importance as the foundation for any design. Students will also learn about size relationships, negative and positive space, format, and illusionary space and be shown how these and other spatial concepts affect our perception.

In Chapter 4, students will read about the use of line in design. Here, students will also learn how line can be used to convey other visual concepts, such as contour, direction, volume, value, and texture.

In Chapter 5, students will explore the visual element of shape and how it can be used in visual communication. They will read and be shown examples of how our perception of the world is actually understood through the relationships of shapes. The content of the chapter deals with concepts such as identification and how humans interpret shapes. Other concepts that are examined are shape relationships, such as grouping and positive and negative space.

In Chapter 6, students will come to understand the visual element of value and the role that it plays in design. Students will learn that the principles governing light dictate value and about the influence that different values can have on the same design. Students will also learn how value can convey other visual elements, such as light and distance.

Chapter 7 covers the use of visual texture in design. Here, students learn how to use texture effectively and to avoid many of the pitfalls associated with this element. In addition to specific design considerations, this chapter also addresses the use of filters and other software-based applications that can be used to produce texture as a part of design.

In Chapter 8, students will learn a few of the more technical concepts concerning color. Topics include the visible color spectrum, color wheels, and the differences between additive and subtractive color methods. The chapter also covers the various properties of color, including hue, value, and intensity.

Chapter 9 continues the exploration of color as an element of design by concentrating on its use in visual communication. This chapter also addresses several other aspects of color usage, such as color relationships, color perception, and naming conventions. Students will also read about additional color concepts, such as color temperature, the association of color with emotions, and culture-specific symbolism.

Chapter 10 begins the section of the book that deals with combining the elements of design presented in previous chapters to create more complex and more effective design. This chapter addresses the concepts of composition through the use of layout and unity.

In Chapter 11, students will read about balance applied to the use of space as well as other design elements, such as color and value.

Chapter 12 serves as an introduction to the use of perspective as an element of design. Here, students will learn about fundamental techniques of perspective drawing and the rules that govern how we perceive perspective. This chapter also explains several of the different classifications of perspective, including one-point, two-point, and isometric perspective.

Chapter 13 addresses the use of repetition and rhythm in design. It also covers related topics that include creating emphasis through repetition and the alteration of a visual repetition. Additional topics in this chapter include grouping and association of visual elements as well as setting up a visual vocabulary of elements for continuity throughout an entire design.

In Chapter 14, students will learn about visual communication through the use of association. Topics include symbolic association, the association of the visual with other senses, and personal association on the part of the viewer.

Chapter 15 covers the use of abstraction in design. Several illustrations give the student a strong understanding of this concept and how a designer goes about the process of using abstraction.

Chapter 16 covers the use of style to facilitate even more communication through a visual medium. Students will learn that through the use of style, they can communicate abstract concepts, such as emotion, or call on symbolic associations for use in their design. This chapter also provides a visual glossary of several popular styles as well as the concepts behind them.

In Chapter 17, the use of emphasis as a visual element is explained. This chapter also covers several ways to create emphasis through the use of the other visual elements.

Chapter 18 begins by covering the basics of typography. After an introduction to the fundamentals of this design element, the chapter gives specific examples on the use of type and explores methods for its effective use. The chapter closes with a section on issues associated with type and new media presentations as well as how to compensate for them.

Chapter 19 begins the section of the book that deals with nonstatic elements of design. Here, students will learn about the concept of time as an element of design. Topics covered include evolution, transitions, pace, and motion.

Chapter 20 provides an overview of the use of interactivity as an element of design for new media projects. Here, students are introduced to several of the different principals that govern interactivity and how they can apply to the navigation of a new media project. Several navigation models are defined and explained as well.

Chapter 21 is concerned with the inclusion of additional media as a part of a project. Topics include basics on the use of sound and video, both as content and as a supportive element. This chapter also addresses common issues associated with the inclusion of other media within a project.

The glossary covers common words and phrases that are used in this book and in the world of the new media designer. This section will serve as a quick reference to terms and common jargon found in the professional field.

Features

The following list provides some of the salient features of the text:

- Richly illustrated text clearly explains the concepts that are vital to designing with new media—and shows them at work.
- A "Special Issues" feature highlights areas of concern for new media designers, especially when the conventions of traditional design differ from those in new media.
- Interviews and behind-the-scenes stories in the "A Designer's Tale" feature reveal the practical side of new media design.
- The concepts illustrated in the book make it a valuable resource for designers searching for inspirational ideas and practical advice.

E.Resource

This guide on CD-ROM was developed to assist instructors in planning and implementing their instructional programs. It includes sample syllabi for using this book in either an 11- or a 15-week semester. It also provides answers to the chapter review questions, additional exercises, PowerPoint slides highlighting the main topics, and other instructor resources.

About the Author

James Bennett has been involved with the marriage of design and technology for well over a decade. In 1991, he became associated with the highly experimental Arts and Technology Lab at the University of South Florida, where he developed screen graphics and computer-generated animation during the infancy of the new media explosion.

As a university instructor, he has taught at the University of South Florida and the International Academy of Design and Technology, where he now heads the departments of Interactive Media and Web Development. The subjects of his classes have included the history of film, drawing, design foundations, sculpture, professional portfolio, Web mastering, programming for the Internet, strategic Web design, and special problems of the Web. He has also participated in program and class development for other university-level curriculums as well as sitting on two selection committees at Ball State University.

Acknowledgments

When someone thinks about the production of a book, they typically envision a lone author sitting in a tastefully decorated study surrounded by mounds of papers and books. In this imagined scene, the author pecks away at a word processor until the last page is finished. The author then slips the completed text into an envelope and prepares to bask in the glory of being published. Although this is an attractive and romantic notion, it is far from reality. The author is only one of many people that pour professional sweat and expertise into the completion of a text.

In fact, there is a small army that mobilizes to produce this sort of book. On second thought, the term "army" might give the wrong idea. Rather, the group of people involved in a project such as this would be better classified as somewhere between a team and a tribe, a team because everyone works together to reach a common goal and everyone does their job, a tribe because over the length of the project the relationships of the people involved evolve into something more than anything that should be called a mere team. I would like to acknowledge a few members of the tribe who put a great deal of labor into this book.

It would be impossible to name everyone that has participated in this project, but I can at least mention a few of the major contributors. The first person involved was Jim Gish. Although his title is acquisitions editor, his role has actually been closer to that of guide, official encourager, creative counselor, and generally the man with the plan. It was Jim who believed in this project from the first phone conversation, and it is because of him that this project came to print.

Another important player has been Jaimie Wetzel. Much like Jim, her title of developmental editor is a misnomer. She has been the chief sounding board, the organizational glue that has kept this project on track, and my lifeline to the rest of the tribe. Without Jaimie, nothing about this project would have come together as well as it has.

Marissa Maiella, editorial assistant, has also played a major role. She has contributed significantly to making this project run smoothly.

The fourth major contributor from Delmar has been production editor Thomas Stover. Thomas is the conductor of an orchestra full of copyeditors, designers, and other unsung heroes of publishing. He is a master at taking a plain rock and turning it into a polished gemstone. I suspect that he is an artist at heart.

Other important contributors to this book have been the artists and designers who have generously allowed for their work to be reproduced here. I am indebted to Chris Collins, Robb Epps, Robert Cowie, and Chris Leventis for their time and effort in providing excellent examples.

Finally, I want to give recognition to those who taught me. Although there were many that contributed to my education, there were two who served as my chief mentors: John Gee and David Wright. They may not have been directly involved in this project, but years ago they passed on their own knowledge, much of which has found its way into this book.

Delmar Learning and the author would also like to thank the following reviewers for their valuable suggestions and expertise:

Cece Cutsforth
Visual and Performing Arts and Design Department
Portland Community College
Portland, Oregon

M. Elyse Diamond
Media Technologies Department
Community College of Southern Nevada
Las Vegas, Nevada

Tara Gray
Visual Communications Department
Allentown Business School
Allentown, Pennsylvania

Christine Holtz
Communication Technologies Department
University of Wisconsin, Platteville
Platteville, Wisconsin

Linda Rzoska
Center for New Media
Kalamazoo Valley Community College
Kalamazoo, Michigan

Walter Wimberly
Web Design Department
International Academy of Design and Technology
Orlando, Florida

Questions and Feedback

Delmar Learning and the author welcome your questions and feedback. If you have suggestions that you think others would benefit from, please let us know, and we will try to include them in the next edition.

To send us your questions and/or feedback, you can contact the publisher at:

Delmar Learning
Executive Woods
5 Maxwell Drive
Clifton Park, NY 12065
Attn: Graphic Arts Team
800-998-7498

Or the author at:

James Bennett
jbennett@academy.edu

Contents

Preface   iv

Section One: Design Overview   2

CHAPTER 1: The New Media Designer   4
CHAPTER 2: The Design Process   24

Section Two: Elements of Design   44

CHAPTER 3: Space   46
CHAPTER 4: Line   66
CHAPTER 5: Shape   88
CHAPTER 6: Value   102
CHAPTER 7: Texture   120
CHAPTER 8: Color   136
CHAPTER 9: Using Color   154

Section Three: Combining Elements   174

CHAPTER 10: Composition and Layout   176
CHAPTER 11: Balance   192
CHAPTER 12: Perspective   210
CHAPTER 13: Repetition and Rhythm   224
CHAPTER 14: Association   238
CHAPTER 15: Abstraction   248
CHAPTER 16: Style   258
CHAPTER 17: Emphasis   270
CHAPTER 18: Typography   280

Section Four: Beyond the Static   298

CHAPTER 19: The Element of Time   300
CHAPTER 20: Interactivity   308
CHAPTER 21: Incorporating Additional Media   318

Glossary   335
Index   341

SECTION

◊NE

The first section of this book begins by exploring a few concepts that are essential to the new media designer. Included in the list of topics are the origins of new media, where it has been and where it is headed, as well as what all of this may mean for the designer. Also found here are several special sub-sections that provide information that can be extremely useful for new media designers. These include an explanation of the basic differences found when comparing new and traditional media, as well as general advice on designer practices.

The second chapter in this section gives a detailed outline of the typical design process used to successfully produce a new media project. This is done through a brief overview of the entire process and then a detailed, step-by-step walkthrough.

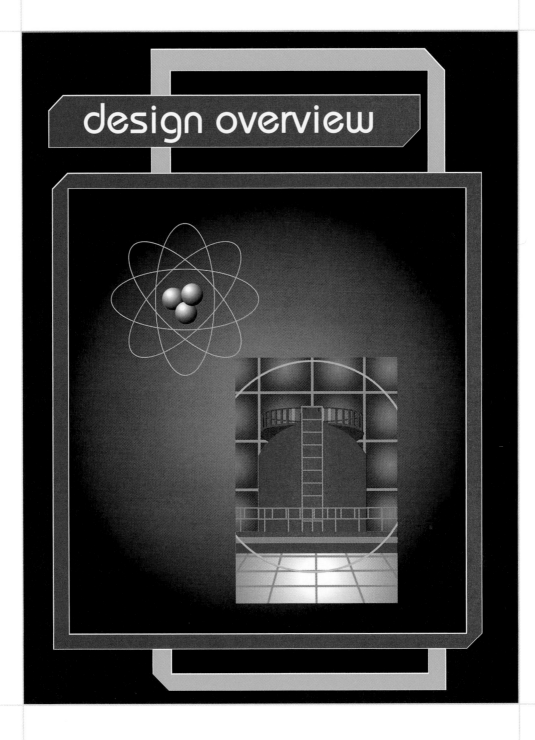

design overview

CHAPTER 1

The New Media Designer

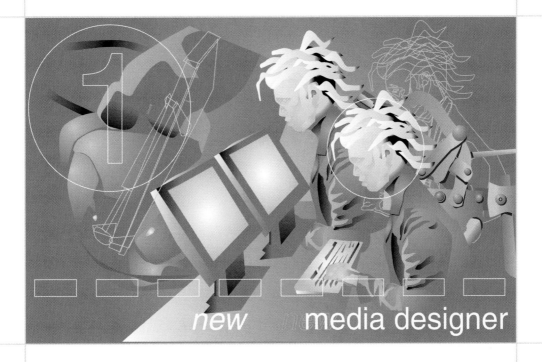

new media designer

For centuries, most people believed that the world was flat. This idea had to be rethought when it was proved to be completely incorrect. Today, new media designers are faced with the same sort of revolution of ideas. Several decades ago, it was proposed that the personality of a designer and that of a person who worked with technology were completely different. It was thought that the traits of each would rarely if ever meet in the same person. Even after scientific study proved otherwise, the idea persisted so that both the designer and the technophile are still believed to be locked into their own worlds with no hope for escape.

Since new media designers use both technology and design skills, the acceptance of this idea places them in an awkward position. In essence, it means that the new media designer does not exist.

There has been some good news, though, as recent studies have shown that people may be different in how they organize information, not in what they are capable of doing. This means that people are free to use technology or creativity whenever it suits them and are no longer limited by stereotypes. The world is no longer thought to be flat, and the new media designer has been placed in the role of Christopher Columbus to prove that the old ideas no longer apply.

Charting the Course

Even the journey of Columbus may have ended in disaster had he not first understood a few things about seamanship, such as principles regarding the nature of the sea and what it means to be a sailor. Likewise, this chapter covers a few things that are important to new media designers, such as principles regarding the nature of new media and what it means to be a designer who works with technology.

Key Points

▸▸ **Defining New Media**

▸▸ **The Evolution of Media**

▸▸ **New Media Differences**

▸▸ **Being a New Media Designer**

▸▸ **Practices for Success**

▸▸ **Issues with Technology**

What Is New Media?

What is **new media**? (If you can figure this out, don't bother writing it down because the answer might change by the time you get around to reading your notes a second time.)

A large part of the confusion over a specific definition of new media comes from the aggressive sales pitches of the various software companies. Each company will have their own version of what they claim to be the hot new media and they will try to sell it to you as fast as they can. Yet, each version of what is being called new media may be different from the next. If the people that develop the new media software can't agree on what it is, then perhaps it is better to look elsewhere for a solid definition.

The Evolution of New Media

Understanding what new media is can be gained by first establishing what *old* media is. The place to begin is with the word *media.* Media is the plural form of *medium,* which refers to some material or technique used for communication.

One of the oldest examples of a medium used to communicate are cave paintings (Figure 1.1). These pictorial works were created by humans using pigments and stains on cave walls. This method of communication remained basically the same for several thousand years. It is true that artistic styles evolved and that people started painting on things other than cave walls, but really little else was different: the medium was still a mark or pigment on a surface, and only a single medium of communication was used.

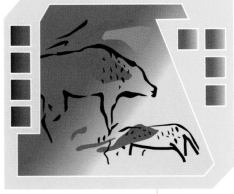

Figure 1.1

Figure 1.2

Eventually, advances in technology brought new methods of communication, and inventors began experimenting in areas that led to the development of photography, the telegraph, and recorded sound. Although these new methods revolutionized communication, each still relied on a single medium to send a message.

The single-medium barrier was finally broken with the introduction of motion pictures (Figure 1.2). This method was not limited to a single image but could show motion as well as tell a story over a period of time. These early films were also accompanied by live music played on a piano or an organ. In this form, several different mediums were being used simultaneously, and medium became media. It was only a short time until the recorded sound of music and voices was added to motion pictures. This was now a true media that existed on its own: it could be shown over and over without the need for a live performer to provide a portion of the communication.

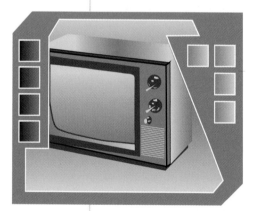

Figure 1.3

The next big development combined motion picture, sound, and broadcast to produce television (Figure 1.3). With television, it was possible to see things as they happened: people could watch and hear things that were going on far away as if they were occurring in their own living rooms. For the next few decades, the different media became more refined because of advances in technology, but little changed beyond the quality of the presentation.

The next big influence on what would become new media was the debut of the computer as a tool for the designer (Figure 1.4). Some of the first computers used for design were huge and expensive and looked like something from a bad science fiction movie. As imposing as these machines were, they were limited to performing the amazing feat of printing out a few lines of text on little scraps of paper. Even the simplest graphic illustrations were totally out of the question for these monsters, and to make the situation worse, the chemicals they used for printing smelled bad.

Eventually, computer technology advanced enough that it could be used to generate simple images, but the equipment was very expensive and the process time consuming. Thus, movies

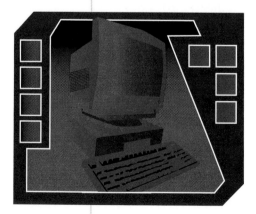

Figure 1.4

produced during this time used models and traditional animation to simulate any computer screen graphics that were needed as part of a scene. It was easier and cheaper to use motion picture techniques to produce what was supposed to be displayed on a computer screen than it was to make the display on an actual computer. It is ironic that film studios once used complex sets and hand-drawn animation to make simulated computer graphics but now use computer graphics to produce complex sets and lifelike animation.

The next big evolutionary step toward new media came when computers and devices like them became available to the general public. Until then, the technology had been used as a production tool for other media, like film and television, but now it could be used for presentation as well. With this new technology came a new quality: instead of being stuck in a passive role, the viewer could now interact with the media. This was the beginning of what would become known as new media.

What Defines the New Media?

So far, we have covered a brief history of the origins of new media but have not settled on a concrete definition of what it is now. A part of the definition of new media is that it is a blending of many of the old media in ways that enable new methods of presentation. An example of this is telecommunications. In its early form, this technology allowed two people, at either end of a cable, to communicate only through Morse code. But now the Internet can reach millions of people at the same time and can be used to communicate in much more interesting ways than a simple series of clicking noises.

Figure 1.5 is made up of two diagrams that represent several of the different methods of delivering communication and a few of the crossovers that create specific media. In 1983, media blending was relatively sparse, and television remained, as it had for several decades, the best example of combined media available to the general public. By 2003, the combinations and blending of the different media available had become so numerous that it was difficult to chart or even determine where one media left off and another began.

The Human Factor

If we stopped at this point in our definition of new media, it would be easy to suggest that it could be defined by the technology used to deliver the communication. It is true that technology does play a major role in what can be accomplished, but what matters more in defining new media is where

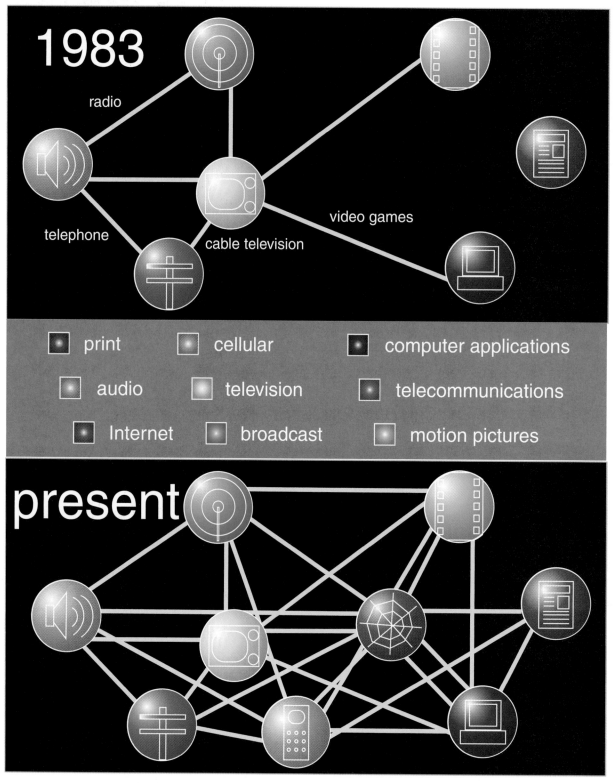

Figure 1.5

technology and humans meet—that is, what sort of experiences the media can provide and what a person can do with it. Figure 1.6 is a table that compares a few of these qualities in several different kinds of media.

communication	print	radio	television	Internet
portable	yes	yes	recent	recent
visual	yes	no	yes	yes
auditory	no	yes	yes	yes
real time	no	yes	yes	yes
motion	no	no	yes	yes
uses other media	no	no	recent	yes
two way	no	no	no	yes
interactive	no	no	no	yes
uses other media	no	no	no	yes

Figure 1.6

The New Media Difference

As shown in Figure 1.6, many of the different media share qualities that define the communication experience, but few possess all. In addition to these commonly held properties, there are several that set new media apart from other forms of presentation.

INTERACTIVITY

Interactivity is a term that can be used to cover several different concepts. In its loosest meaning, it is understood as the ability of the user to influence communication. In this sense, turning to the last page of a mystery novel and finding out who committed the crime before reading the rest of the book could be seen as interactivity, but to better define the qualities that set new media apart, a more specific meaning is needed.

In this case, interactivity can be thought of as the ability for the communication to change on the basis of direct input from the user. An example of this kind of interactivity is found in video games. Instead of sending the hero into the woods to search for a dragon, the player could choose to return to town and pick up more supplies. This cannot be done with something like a novel. No matter how much the reader skips around, only the order in which the communication is received changes—the story remains the same.

CONTENT EVOLUTION FROM USER INPUT

The evolution of content by the user can also be defined as a form of interactivity, but it is a specific kind of influence the user has on the media. In this instance, the user has the ability to create or alter the content of the presentation for oneself and for others. An example of this is an on-line bulletin board where visitors post messages and images about a specific topic. On a busy Web site of this nature, the content can change quickly as people add their own influence.

If this level of interactivity were compared to the previous example of the mystery novel, it would be as if several people were all writing the story at the same time, each adding their own ideas to what others had written.

ASYNCHRONOUS COMMUNICATION

Many forms of new media are asynchronous; that is, they are not dependent on the message sender and the message receiver being available at the same time for communication. The opposite of this is synchronous communication, such as a telephone conversation. For there to be a true conversation, both parties need to be on the phone at the same time.

An example of asynchronous communication is an e-mail or an on-line presentation. With this method, the sender can create a message at a time that is convenient. The receiver can then open the message and reply later.

GLOBAL ACCESSIBILITY

In the past, nearly any media seen by large numbers of people was produced by corporations or governments. Now it is possible for a person to shoot a video clip and distribute it for the world to see. Even some personal Web pages have a larger audience than many newspapers.

An obvious but still remarkable thing about global accessibility is that the communication flows both ways. Not only can individuals send their own messages out to the entire world; but they are no longer dependent on companies to provide them with communication, such as news and entertainment. Instead of watching a taped broadcast about something happening in a faraway place, a person can access the Internet and receive an eyewitness account from someone who was there or view live images sent via webcam.

Another quality that many forms of new media have is the ability to include a variety of presentation methods that blur the distinctions of each method into a single experience. An example of this is on-line gaming. Not only can the user receive communication about the game through sight and sound, but in some games players can speak or send text messages to teammates while playing.

These examples do not list all the distinct qualities that define new media, and even if they did, some new development would quickly make the list obsolete. Rather, these are a few of the things that differ from the attributes of what has come to be known as traditional media.

Being a New Media Designer

As you sink back into the fine leather seat of your new limousine, you watch the streetlights through the open sunroof; each light has the perfect flare effect as it passes by. After winding along darkened streets, you finally arrive outside the theater for the opening-night party. Stepping out of the car onto the red carpet, you are greeted by the squeals of adoring fans and a barrage of flashes from the cameras of the press.

Figure 1.7

You smile and wave to the crowd just in time to see a determined, young reporter break through the line of police officers. He quickly sidesteps your two bodyguards and shoves a microphone in your face. He wants to know what your next project is going to be. As your husky bodyguards toss him back into the crowd, you answer his question with something incredibly witty, and you see half a dozen other reporters quickly scribble down your words and dash off to make their deadlines.

If this sounds like your idea of being a designer, you might reconsider your career path. It might be a better idea if you learned to play the guitar or took acting lessons. On the other hand, if you are thrilled with the idea of using your imagination to create works that stimulate, excite, and challenge others, then you have what it takes to be a designer. The key is your creativity—nearly everything else is just practice. Your imagination is what sets you apart from everyone else, and it is your most important tool as a designer.

What follows are a few tips about being a designer. These are ideas that have worked for designers in the past. Use them or invent your own, but understand that no designer ever became successful by just sitting around and saying that he or she was a designer—it took a lot of hard work.

What to Expect

The first thing that you should know is what being a designer means. Often the terms **artist** and **designer** are used interchangeably, but there is a difference: an artist creates works for presentation, while a designer uses the skills of an artist to develop something of use beyond the aesthetic, be it an ad, a chair, or an automobile.

In new media, the job of the designer is even more specific: to communicate. It is true that the designer will create something to be used, such as a Web site or an interactive presentation, but the main focus of these kinds of projects is the communication of ideas. The ideas might not even be those of the designer but rather those of a client or an employer. Regardless of the source, the designer's job is to present those ideas in an effective way.

The second thing that you should know is that being a designer is going to take some work. No designer has ever walked up to one's tools, shot lightning bolts out of one's fingertips, and instantly created a brilliant work. Designers become successful because they spend their time working on their craft. This isn't all bad since design is often a labor of love.

For designers who choose to work with new media, practicing their craft is an even greater task because the tools and technology keep evolving. Usually, by the time a piece of software has been mastered, it is already outdated, and something better, faster, and more stunning has replaced it. The good news is that when something changes as fast as design in new media, there is plenty of room for exploration into uncharted territory. In contrast, there isn't much that an artist can do with a pencil that hasn't been done before. But with new media, designers have only begun to scratch the surface of possibilities.

A Few Practices for Success

At the most basic level, what designers do is take an idea, filter it through their imagination, and transfer it into something that other people can experience. How well they can do this is what separates good designers from mediocre ones. Almost all people have ideas, but communicating those ideas to others is the difficult part. What follows are a few ideas for improving the ability to communicate ideas through design.

Working on Your Skills

You should never stop developing your craft as a designer. No matter how good your last piece was, you should strive to make your next piece better. As a designer, imagine that you are running a race. But forget how far ahead of the other runners you are—you are trying to beat your own best time.

Feed Your Head

One of the best things that you can do as a designer is to look at the work of others. Their ideas will spark your ideas. This does not mean that you should try to make your work look like theirs, but there may be elements in their designs that you can bring into your own, or they may do something in a way that never occurred to you. Learn from other designers, as they can be your best teachers.

A DESIGNER'S TALE

Studying with the Masters

When I received the class schedule for my first quarter in art school, I was a little disappointed. I had a seat in all the classes that I wanted, but the schedule itself was going to be a hassle. Every day, I had a morning class and then another class late in the afternoon. This left a block of about three hours in the middle of my day with nothing to do.

Instead of wasting the time, I decided to spend it in the library looking at books on art and design. At first, I just wandered around the design section aimlessly pulling any book from the shelves that looked interesting, but after several weeks I developed a system. On Monday and Wednesday, I would look at books about specific designers and artists. On Tuesday and Thursday, I would read magazines on design. Fridays were reserved for special theme research, such as specific periods or a particular style of art.

I was actually happy when I picked up the schedule for my second quarter and found that I again had the empty block of time in the middle of the day. I felt that my daily trips to the library had become as important to my education in design as the actual classes were.

It wasn't long before looking at all the work done by successful designers and artists began to have an influence, and I could see that my own work was getting better because of it. I attribute those hours spent looking at art and design books as one of the important steps on my own path to becoming a designer, and to this day I still spend a good deal of time studying the work of others.

Recharging Your Batteries

Professional designers often have to be creative even when they do not feel like it; production deadlines and media releases are all hurdles that must be overcome, and they do not wait until the designer is in a creative mood. Trying to deal with them when you have "designer's block" can be exasperating. One way to avoid the frustration is to not allow yourself to become creatively dry.

How a designer keeps the creative batteries charged is a personal thing. Some travel, some read, and some go to the movies, but the one thing they all do is get some form of mental stimulation. As long as a designer keeps putting things into the imagination, creativity will flow. A designer's job is to pour out ideas, but if the idea jar is empty, nothing worthwhile is going to come out.

Keep Your Eye on the Target

During the design process, it can be easy to become distracted by some part of the project. Avoid this at all costs.

Attention to detail is both a blessing and a curse for the designer. The details of any piece are what separate the successful designer from the rest, but it is easy to get so caught up in details that the purpose of a project becomes secondary. Don't lose sight of a project's goal during the design process.

Develop Good Habits

For a designer, it is advantageous to develop work habits that produce quality and that save time. An example of a good habit for new media designers is making backup copies of all work. This may seem time consuming, but there is nothing that wastes time more than having to re-create a piece because of a corrupted computer file.

Another example is to always try to get the most out a design tool. Learning keyboard shortcuts and efficient ways to use applications can dramatically improve how a designer works.

SPECIAL ISSUES IN NEW MEDIA

THE DIGITAL GRAPHIC

At some point along the journey from the mind of the designer to the eye of the viewer, the new media project will pass through a digital realm. It is the designer's responsibility to plan how one's creation will fare in the sometimes hostile world of the electron.

The Digital Dance

New media projects and digital technology are so intertwined that it is often difficult to pinpoint where one ends and the other begins. Advances in technology facilitate new methods of communication; and new methods of communication drive advances in technology. The nature of technology can define the limits and present new possibilities for any new media element, especially for communication that relies on the visual.

The use of technology for visual communication can be thought of as a system that can be divided into three distinct areas:

1. The creation (how an image is made or converted to a digital format)

2. The delivery (how the viewer receives the image files)

3. The display (the method for making the image visible)

When considering these three areas and how they might affect a particular design, it is important for a designer to keep in mind that each one is greatly influenced by both the software and the hardware used as a part of the system. Figure 1.8 is a chart that shows a few components of the system for three different projects.

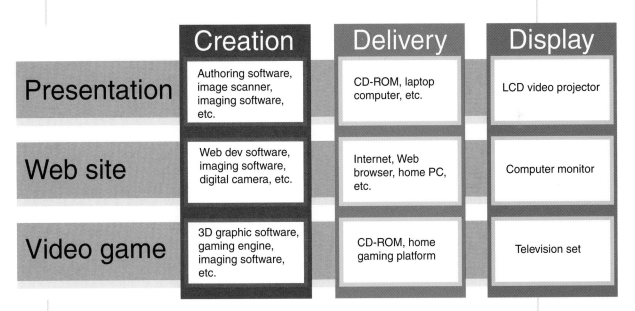

	Creation	Delivery	Display
Presentation	Authoring software, image scanner, imaging software, etc.	CD-ROM, laptop computer, etc.	LCD video projector
Web site	Web dev software, imaging software, digital camera, etc.	Internet, Web browser, home PC, etc.	Computer monitor
Video game	3D graphic software, gaming engine, imaging software, etc.	CD-ROM, home gaming platform	Television set

Figure 1.8

In this next section, certain characteristics of each area and their effects on an image are explored. The three areas of the system are presented in reverse order since it will be important to understand the nature of the display and the delivery in order to better comprehend the requirements of the creation.

The Display

The display is how the image will be shown to the viewer. It can be a monitor, a projector, or an LCD screen. To better understand how graphics and other design elements will appear through any of these devices, it is important to have a basic understanding of how these devices work.

The Problem with Pixels

Whether a designer's work is created on a computer and then sent to print, is an interactive CD-ROM, or utilizes any other kind of new media, somewhere along the line it is displayed on a video monitor or a similar device.

A simple way to think of a video monitor is as a surface covered with a large number of tiny dots. These tiny dots are called **pixels**. Any image that is displayed on a video monitor is created by the color of each dot. If an illustration consists of a series of white lines on a black background, each of the white lines is depicted with rows of pixels colored white, while the black areas are made up of pixels colored black. On a typical monitor, tens of thousands of these small dots, each with a single color, are combined to create an image.

Although a single pixel can be one of many different colors, the pixel itself cannot be divided into smaller sections. A pixel is either all one color or a different color entirely. In an image that depends on color shifts to show detail, like a photograph, the colors of each pixel will vary greatly over a small area. This helps reproduce subtle color shifts by placing pixels of different colors next to each other. If the pixels are small enough, the eye will see a blend of the two colors instead of two distinct dots of different colors. (For more on how monitors reproduce colors, see Chapter 8.) But in the case of a line or the hard edge of an image, single-color pixels can produce undesirable results. To better understand this, look at Figure 1.9.

Figure 1.9 shows two large pictures of the letter "T" and two smaller ones. The larger image on the far left is typical of what you might see printed in a book like this one. The lines that create the character seem to flow, and smaller details are visible. The larger image to the right is representative of the same letter made with pixels. In this illustration, each of the small squares represents a single pixel. As stated previously, a pixel cannot be

 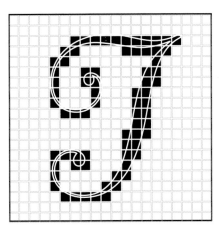

Figure 1.9

divided into two separate color sections. In this example, each pixel is either white or black. If a part of the image is rendered by a pixel, it can produce only one color in its entire area. As a result, details that are smaller than the area of the pixel cannot be shown. Instead, the entire pixel is filled with the required color. This makes the once-flowing lines of the character appear jagged, as if they were made from cutout squares. An exaggerated comparison of how the two "T"s might appear is shown on the far right. This comparison gives a clear example of the visual differences between an image that is displayed using a monitor and one that is not. This effect is less noticeable on a monitor with a higher resolution. (A monitor set at a higher resolution will have a greater number of smaller pixels across the screen.)

Size by Pixels

Images intended to be reproduced on a monitor are usually measured in pixels. Because of different screen resolutions, this can cause an image to appear in different sizes on different monitors. For example, if a monitor has a resolution of 80 pixels per inch, an 80-pixel-wide image will be 1 inch wide on the monitor. But if the monitor has over 100 pixels per inch, the same image will only be about three-quarters of an inch wide. This has nothing to do with the size of the monitor but is due strictly to its resolution. (For more on this, see Chapter 3.)

The Delivery

The delivery is the part of the system that is concerned with how the project or graphic will arrive at the display as well as the software and hardware needed to process it. The project can be on a disk or on the hard drive of a computer or transferred over a network. However, even though the files are available, there also needs to be the correct combination of components to deal with the project on the receiving end. The designer should keep the requirements of the delivery in mind while working on any new media piece.

One example of how much the nature of the delivery should influence the creation of images is found in the development of Web sites. At this time, Internet connection speeds are still relatively slow compared to the speed of a computer reading directly from a disk. Because of the delay in delivery time, images that would load fast from a disk can take a long time to download over the Internet.

At present, most Internet connections in the United States are still around 28k per second. (28k means 28,000 bits per second, not 28,000 bytes. A **bit** is only one-eighth of a **byte**.) On average, it would take an image that has a file size of 30 kilobytes over 8 seconds to download. If there were more than a couple images like this on a Web page, it is unlikely that the viewer would wait long enough for them to download.

Another delivery issue with any graphics sent via the Internet is the file format used. Only a handful of file formats work in displaying a bitmap image in a Web browser. (At this time, .jpg and .gif are the main formats supported by nearly all browsers. The .png format is increasing in popularity, but there are still several browsers that do not fully support its use.) If a designer did not convert an image to a compatible format, it would not be visible on a Web page. Of course, all this assumes that the viewer has a Web browser installed.

Many of the issues of delivery are specific to the file format of a project. Different kinds of projects need certain players, software plug-ins, or components for the viewer to be able to see them. As a designer, it is vital to either work with media that can be used with common delivery systems or provide a way for the viewer to get the necessary software additions quickly and easily. It's great to work on the cutting edge of technology, but if no one can see the project; the designer's effort is wasted.

The Creation

The creation is the making or the conversion of some part of a project into a digital format. As with the other areas of this system, the software used during the creation of a graphic can have an impact on the end result. Being aware of the characteristic traits of how images are created for new media will help you make graphics that will fully utilize the delivery and the display.

Raster versus Vector

In general, there are two kinds of imaging software: raster (or bitmap) based and vector based. The main difference between these is the method used by the software to create the images. A raster-based program makes an image on a pixel-by-pixel basis. For example, if a designer selects a paint tool, each pixel changes to the color assigned to the brush as the cursor moves over it.

This is different from vector-based software, which makes images by a mathematical process. For example, if a designer is creating a circle, dragging the cursor tells the software how big the circle will be and what properties it will have. If the image is displayed on a monitor, the software figures out which pixels to color and draws the circle to the proper size.

Because they are based on mathematics, vector images are scalable. That is, their sizes can be altered without affecting the details of an image. When a vector-based image is resized, the software computes the new properties and applies them. In the case of a resized vector circle displayed on a monitor, a different set of pixels are assigned to make the circle, and there is no distortion of the original image. This is not true for raster-based images. Because they are based on individual pixels, raster images can lose details if their size is changed. This is much like the example given in Figure 1.10.

Figure 1.10

Figure 1.10 is made up of three separate images. The image of the sun in the upper-left corner is the original and is shown at the size at which it was created. In the upper-right corner is a portion of the same rasterized image, but it is four times larger. Even at this small increase in size, the lines have become jagged squares and have lost a great deal of detail. At this larger size, what formerly looked like a smooth blend of colors has become solid blocks of single-color squares. In addition, the curved edges have begun to lose their shape. This kind of distortion is called pixelation. The bottom half of Figure 1.10 is a part of the same image made 16 times larger. As you can see, with each increase in size, the pixelation becomes more pronounced.

Which to Use?

In the past, it was easy to choose which kind of imaging software to use for your work. Vector images were especially well suited for print work, and since most computer image formats were raster based, the logical choice for an image that was going to be displayed on a monitor was one that used a raster format. Advances in technology have changed all that. Raster-based programs have increased in quality to meet the strict requirements of print media, and the scalability of vector imaging has become very useful for new media, especially when a new media designer may need to show the project in several different screen resolutions. The use of vector-based images can ensure that all the visual elements will have the appropriate proportions without pixelation.

In addition to these new features, the lines between the two kinds of software have become blurred. Designs made in vector software can be saved as raster images, and many raster-based software applications have adopted some of the best features that were formerly found only in vector tools. In some of the latest versions of imaging software, a designer can even mix the two in the same image.

Which Tool?

The rule used to be "the right tool for the job," but now so many different software applications can be adapted to other uses that it comes down to the designer's personal preferences. To meet deadlines, a designer often is better off working with an application with which he or she is familiar and then converting the image to the correct format. In choosing a particular brand of software, again it comes down to what the designer is the most comfortable with, as long as the software has the features the designer needs.

This does not mean that the designer should limit oneself to one particular brand of imaging software and ignore the others; some company is always going to come out with a new software release that will make the designer's job easier and faster. There are always going to be innovations in the visual effects that design software can create. It is a good idea to keep informed about new software without becoming obsessed over using every version of every tool available. The designer who falls into this pattern often spends too much time trying to learn all the tools but never masters any of them.

SUMMARY

This chapter focused on a few concepts that are important to the new media designer. Some of the topics covered were the evolution of media, the differences that set new media apart from other forms of communication, and an approach to being a new media designer. The next chapter deals with the design process for a new media project.

REVIEW QUESTIONS

1. Describe an attribute that can be found in new media that is not found in more traditional forms of communication.

2. What is interactivity?

3. Name two different types of media that can be included in a new media project.

4. What is the difference between an artist and a designer?

5. Describe each of the three areas of the technology/visual communication system. (What is the creation? What is the delivery? What is the display?)

6. What are pixels?

CHAPTER

2

The Design Process

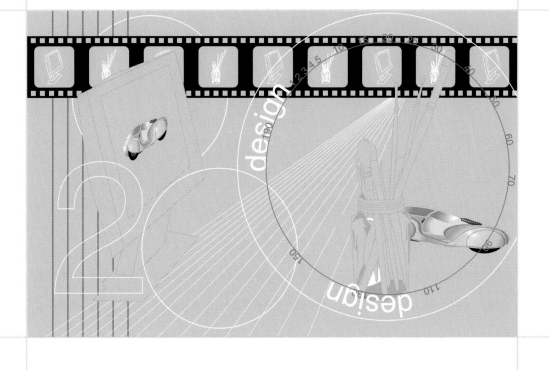

The term *design* is usually used to refer to one of two concepts. The first has to do with planning the construction of some new thing, such as a house, a bridge, or a piece of software. In this instance, the purpose of the design is to create something that fulfills certain needs, and a part of the design process is to plan ways in which the new thing will meet those needs.

For example, an engineer might be required to design an aircraft that does more than just fly. In the case of this hypothetical aircraft, it is also required to carry a large number of passengers over a long distance. To achieve this, the designer plans for larger fuel tanks (so that the aircraft can travel without stopping to refuel) and for more powerful engines (so that it can lift the combined weight of all the people and the additional fuel). How the designer solves each of these problems influences the end result. The word *design* is also used to refer to a work of art, so that an image or an illustration can be called a design.

Defining *Design* for the Media Designer

Key Points

▸▸ **The Design Process**

▸▸ **The Information Phase**

▸▸ **The Interaction Phase**

▸▸ **The Design Phase**

For the new media designer, both of the previously mentioned definitions are technically correct, but the meaning of the word design is actually closer to a combination of the two. A new media designer working on a project is concerned with aesthetic value but also with planning the creation of a new thing. This thing may not be an actual object that a person could ride in or sit on, but it is still a new thing. More often than not, this new thing is a communication. That is, the designer is using visual elements and design in the artistic sense to make something that can convey an idea to other people.

Just like the engineer who begins the planning of an aircraft, the designer must take into consideration additional needs that the creation will have to meet. Instead of being concerned with the problems of weight or fuel capacity, the designer will be dealing with issues such as who will be receiving the message and how that message will meet a client's needs.

A Designer Designs

Design can be looked at as a working progress, or as solving a problem to meet a need. The important part of that statement is *working progress.* Different designers work in different ways, but all plan and then adjust those plans along the way to complete a product. Some plan most of a design in their heads before ever starting, while others sit down and start drawing, working out the details along the way. Most media designers do a combination of both.

Pitfall of the Process

As a design evolves to provide solutions to specific problems, it may grow beyond the purpose of the original idea. This is an important part of the process, but a designer must be careful not to become so engrossed in the details that sight of the original purpose is lost. To return to the example of the aircraft, it would be as if the designing engineer became so concerned with the weight and fuel capacity of the airliner that the main purpose was forgotten. The result may be a jet that could hold plenty of fuel and passengers but that could no longer fly.

The Design Process

Figure 2.1 uses the development of a Web site to illustrate several steps in the design process, which is broken down into three different phases. The first of these is the **information** phase. During this phase, information is gathered about the site. The second part of the design process is the **interaction** phase, which is concerned with how visitors will interact with and navigate on the site. The final part of this process is the **presentation** phase, which determines how the site will look.

The Information Phase

1. The design of a Web site begins by determining the purpose of the site. The answer to the question "What is the site supposed to do?" will influence the design more than any other part of the process. For example, if the purpose of the site is to sell a product on-line, then the information and navigation should lead viewers to purchase items from an on-line shopping cart. If the intent of the site is to promote the company with a positive image, then the design of the site should reflect that purpose.

2. The second step is to determine who will be using the site. This is important because a site that appeals to teenagers will be different from one intended for business executives. The most important part of this step is to know your audience.

3. The last step of the information phase is to determine the content of the site. What information will be given? Will there be images? If so, of what? How will the information be grouped? The inclusion of content should fit the information gathered in the first two steps.

The Interaction Phase

4. The first step of the interaction phase should be to determine how a viewer will receive the Web site's content. In what order will the information be presented? Will visitors proceed through the site step by step, or will they be free to surf around the entire site? One of the best ways to work out this part of the design is to group the content by subject and work out a storyboard of how the information will be presented.

5. The second part of the interaction phase is to plan what kind of controls will be used by visitors. This is concerned more with what navigational elements are available on each page than with how they look. Where can a visitor go from each point on a page? Much of this is determined by the order of the content that was established in the previous step.

Project Design Process

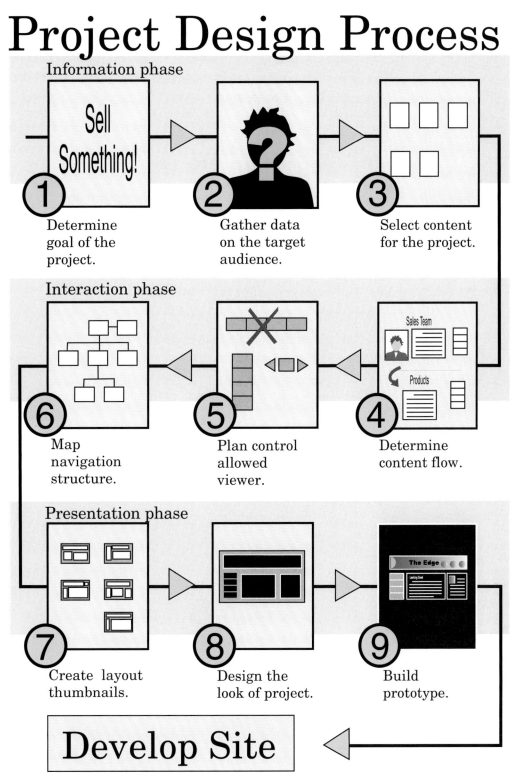

Figure 2.1 Step-by-Step Design

6. The final step of the interaction phase is to map out the entire site. To do this, a designer will already have determined how the content will be grouped (what content goes on which page), in what order the content will be presented, and how visitors will navigate the site. At this point, the arrangement of the pages should be relatively easy.

The Presentation Phase

7. The first step of the presentation phase is to design the general layout for each page of the Web site. This includes how the navigation and the content will be arranged on each page. The layout should be attractive and reflect both the purpose of the site and its target audience. The traditional way of working through the issues of layout is to make a series of thumbnails. This allows for experimentation and brainstorming.

8. The next step in the presentation phase is to design the style of the site, or how the site will look. This phase should rely heavily on the design influences of the other phase. The layout and navigation structure will play an important part in the style, but the purpose of the site and the target audience should also have a significant amount of influence on the design during this step.

9. The last step in the presentation phase is to produce a prototype. This should be a functional example of the site that can be taken out for a "test drive." It is during this step that overlooked issues may surface. After this has been completed, the bugs can be worked out, and the finished site can be produced.

The Design Process in Detail

In the following sections, each of the three phases of the design process is covered in detail.

The Information Phase: Close-Up

The information phase is the most important step in beginning the design of any new media project. Skipping this phase as the first order of business is the equivalent of deciding to go on a long trip but not planning anything. You don't know where you will go or how you will get there, nor do you pack any clothes or take any money; you just walk out the door and head off in a random direction.

Although this may seem like an interesting way to begin an adventure, it does not work well as a way to design a new media project. The measure of a successful project is how well it can communicate with a target audience. If a designer fails to establish what the message is or who the audience will be, the probability is high that the project will miss both.

ESTABLISHING THE PURPOSE

The purpose of the project is the first thing that must be determined when beginning the design process. Then every other part of the project should work toward that goal. It doesn't matter if the finished project will be a Web site, an interactive CD-ROM, or even a game—each component should be tailored to further what the project is intended to accomplish.

Establishing the purpose of a project can sometimes be difficult, especially if the client and the designer do not share the same idea of what the goal of the project will be. For example, clients may have no idea what they want from a Web site: their only thought is that they need a presence on the Web to remain competitive, or they are under the misconception that having a Web site will cause customers to suddenly flock to their doors. Although it is true that having a well-designed site can give a potential customer confidence in a company, it does not guarantee sales.

A DESIGNER'S TALE

Defining the Goal

As the ability of the Internet to handle more complex media forms increased, it seemed that everyone thought that they needed the fanciest Web site possible to represent their company. In their minds, entertaining Web sites became synonymous with profit. Because of this, I often found that I had to spend more time educating clients about the importance of having a goal for the project than I did designing their site.

One of these long education sessions began when I received a call from a successful midwestern manufacturing company. During the first conversation, I learned that they already had a company Web site but that they were interested in having a more professional design. When I asked about the purpose of the site, the person on the other end of the line had no clear answer.

After several phone conferences over the next week, I eventually spoke with the CEO of the corporation in an effort to establish the exact purpose of the Web site. His only thought was that he wanted the "coolest site on the Internet." I told him that I would be happy to work up a proposal, but I also asked him to think about how the "coolest site on the Internet" would benefit his business. A site like that would generate a lot of traffic, but it would have no purpose other than being "cool."

After about a week had gone by, we spoke again. His concept for the Web site had changed, and now he decided that he wanted the site to be the "best on-line reference for manufacturers," complete with charts and calculators. I again told him that I would complete a proposal for this new idea, but I also diplomatically pointed out to him that a site of this kind would be used mostly by the employees of his competitors, not by his customers. I also explained to him that the best way to go about developing the site was to first establish what he hoped to accomplish with it; later, we could work on what information would be included on the site.

For his business, the obvious answer was that he wanted new customers and more orders from established customers. We determined that one way to meet this goal was to provide an on-line catalog of his company's products. A catalog of products would lead potential new customers, searching for similar items, to his site. The catalog would also introduce additional products to current customers who were already using the site for ordering information.

By determining a goal that would be a benefit to the company, we now had a place to start. The end result was more profit from higher sales, even if it wasn't the "coolest site on the Internet."

What Is the Goal?

The following are a few of the possible goals for new media projects, but there are many more. Keep in mind that it is possible for a project to have more than one goal, but too many purposes in the same project can become confusing to the viewer (and the designer):

- Establish product benefits
- Provide company information
- Entertainment
- On-line ordering
- Education
- Information reference

Who Will Use It?

The second step in the information phase is to determine who will use the new media product that will be produced. Customizing the project to fit the needs of a target audience makes many of the other steps in the design process easier and will help achieve the purpose of the project.

The answer to the question *"Who is the audience?"* will influence everything from what information will be given to what it will look like. As an example, think of a situation in which you have been asked to design a CD-ROM presentation about a new line of software. If the presentation is intended for software merchandisers, it might focus on how popular the product will be and how much profit will be made by selling it. If the presentation is intended for end users, it would be better to show them how much they will benefit from the software and how easy it is to use.

During this step, it is also important to give some thought to how the targeted viewer will access the information. In an ideal world, the decision of how the product will be presented should not occur until this step; unfortunately, however, a designer is usually hired to produce a specific form of presentation first, such as a Web site, an interactive CD-ROM, and so on, and then all the details of the project are worked out.

Regardless of when the form of the presentation is determined, it is important to know the environment where the intended audience will see the finished product. Will it be projected onto a large screen in front of a group of sales associates, or will it be viewed by an individual on a computer?

How the project will be delivered should also be considered. For example, a new media presentation that requires a lot of interactivity might work well as a CD-ROM, but the same presentation would be slow and frustrating viewed over the Internet. The conditions under which your viewer will see the finished project are as important to defining for whom the project is intended as knowing their age-group or purchasing habits.

After the designer has come to know the target audience, it is important to allow their needs and what appeals to them to influence the rest of the design process. A simple rule is that the audience shouldn't have to accommodate the design of the project; rather, the design of the project should accommodate the audience.

WHAT ARE YOU GOING TO SAY?

After the goal of a new media project has been determined and it is known who the project is intended for, the third step is to plan out what information will be given.

The key to any decision about including specific content in a new media project is to put it to two tests. The first test is to ask this question: Does the specific content help achieve the goal? For example, the goal of a presentation given to new employees about a company would differ from one intended for potential investors in the same company. Although they might share some information, such as when the company was founded or what the company produced, the purpose of these two projects would require completely different content. Investors would probably not be interested in details about a company's sick-day policy, and new employees might not care about the fact that all the board members were also executives in other successful corporations. A safe guideline for the inclusion of content is that if the information does not further the purpose of the project, then it probably does not belong in it.

The second test for any content to pass is this question: Can this information be presented in a way that is easily understood by the intended viewer? For example, if the goal of a project is to show salespeople the benefits of a new computer system, proving its superiority over the competition might be a good idea, but attempting to do so with a long list of technical jargon would only put them to sleep. Instead, it would be better to present the technical highlights in a way that was clear to them.

Content in a new media project is not limited to text. It can also include images, video clips, and even applications such as calculators or some other program. These kinds of content can be the most difficult to omit from a project because of personal appeal. The same tests for content should still be applied. That is, no matter how impressive the video clip of the company picnic is, if it does fit the goal or the target audience, it probably doesn't need to be included in the project.

The Interaction Phase: Close-Up

After the three steps of the information phase have been adequately addressed, the second phase of developing a new media project can begin. In this part of the design process, the focus is on the interactivity of the piece, that is, what influence viewers will have over how they see the material.

How Will the Information Flow?

During the interaction phase, it is important to first determine the order in which (if any) a viewer should see the content. One way to understand how the order of content can affect a project is to think of the requirements for an interactive quiz. If the goal of the quiz is to test a viewer's knowledge, it might make sense to have the questions displayed first and the answers shown afterward. By reversing the order of the content, the purpose of the quiz would not be achieved.

How Much Control?

One of the first things to determine is how much control viewers will have over the order of the content they receive. For a Web site with just a few pages, it might be more important for the viewer to be able to directly access the information needed. In this case, the order in which the content is seen is entirely up to the viewer. But if the new media piece is similar to a slide show, it would be counterproductive to allow the viewer to navigate through the different parts of the presentation out of a specific order.

In practice, most new media pieces often use a combination of both loose and structured order. For example, visitors might have the choice of filling out an on-line registration form or seeing a list of new products first. But once they have selected to register, they are required to follow a specific order of steps.

Putting It All Down

One of the best ways to map out the content order is by using a storyboard (Figure 2.2). Using a system like this makes it easy to include mock-ups of the content for each section and to make notation for proposed navigation.

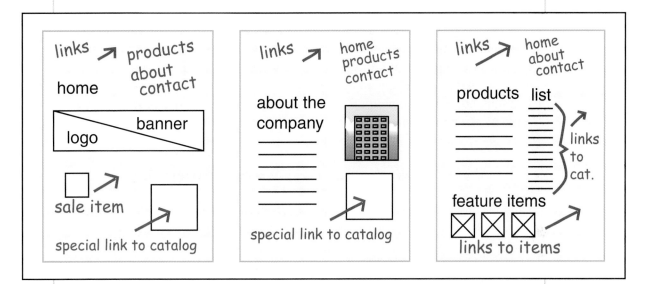

Figure 2.2

The storyboard system of arranging content flow helps the designer in several ways. It organizes the content into smaller units and also allows quick changes of the order during this part of the design process. After the order has been determined, the designer can refer to the storyboard to see exactly what needs to be included in each section of the piece as work on the layout of the individual pages begins.

The storyboard system aids the designer also by providing a key for the navigation design in the next step. By referring to the notes on the storyboard, the designer can see where a viewer might go from any part of the project.

By arranging the content in a storyboard, the designer can also get an idea of what the viewer will see in each section. If there is too much content or the information presented is a little confusing, a detailed storyboard can make this apparent.

Getting In and Getting Out

Another important part of this design step is to plan for a viewer to enter and exit the presentation. Too often these critical elements are included as an afterthought or ignored altogether. This can result in a viewer becoming trapped with no way to exit or no clear way to enter the piece. This can be frustrating and can ruin an otherwise outstanding new media project.

As a rule, the entrance and exit of any project should be given as much attention as any other part. It is the first and the last impression that anyone has of the presentation, and it can have a tremendous influence on their opinion of the entire piece.

Another issue that should be considered is what happens if the presentation is interrupted, especially if there is a large amount of content. Will viewers be able to leave the presentation from any point, or must they go to a specific place to exit? When they return, will they be able to start where they left off, or will they have to again view the parts they have already seen? A feature that allows the viewer to return to a specific point is important for lengthy presentations. Without such a feature, it would be like forcing a reader to reread every page of a novel rather than continuing from where one last stopped reading. Including a way to return to a specific point in the project can often determine if a viewer will return to the project at all.

DESIGNING THE NAVIGATION

After the order of the content has been established, the next step in the interaction phase is to design the navigation structure for each part of the project. This does not mean designing the visual appearance of the navigational tools but rather planning what kinds of interaction will be allowed and how the arrangement of the navigation will be made to appear consistent from one page to the next.

A part of this step in the design process is to determine how much control a viewer will have over the different elements of the project and how those elements will be accessed (Figure 2.3). An analogy would be to compare navigation and interaction with the controls on the dashboard of an automobile. Each knob or button is placed so that it is accessible to the driver, and only the needed amount of control is given. For example, in most cars it is easy to activate a turn signal, but it isn't necessary to adjust the color of the light that comes from the flasher. The opposite is true for a car's sound system; not only can a station be selected on the radio, but the driver needs

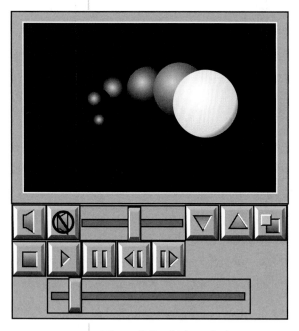

Figure 2.3 Although the interface for this video presentation gives the viewer a good deal of control, it is more than a little confusing.

to be able to control the volume as well. It is tempting to give a viewer too much control over the media project, but this can result in the viewer becoming distracted and the project falling short of its goal.

Too Much of a Good Thing

Once I was asked to consult on a very large Web site that was suffering from low use. The first page of the site was receiving plenty of traffic, but few of the visitors were going much deeper into the site or using the information that it provided. The first thing that I did was to take a look at the site for myself. What I found was that after only a few clicks, I was completely lost.

It would be easy to assume that the problem with the Web site was a lack of control over where I was headed. On projects that suffer from this design flaw, a click on the wrong link can send a visitor to an endless loop of pages, with no way out. But on this site, the problem was not too little control; it was too much control.

During the original construction of this project, the designers felt that it was important for the viewer to be able to navigate to any other part of this Web site as directly as possible. Instead of a single large navigation section, their solution was to place several different areas of links on each page. The result was that each page had between four and nine areas of navigation scattered throughout the content. The designers were so intent on leaving nothing out that each of the different navigation sections repeated most of the links to the major areas of the site. One page was so poorly designed that it contained seven links to itself. To make matters worse, because of the number of links, many of the buttons had similar labels (e.g., *Print Form* and *Print Forms*), and clicking on them did not always take the viewer to where they thought that they were headed.

For this Web site, the old adage that *more is better* did not hold true. The new version of the site was improved with simplified navigation, and the problems of low visitor usage disappeared.

MAPPING IT ALL OUT

With the other parts of the design complete, the final step of the interaction phase is to map out the entire project. This can look like a flowchart or a typical site map, with each unit of content represented by a rectangle and navigation paths shown through the use of connecting lines (Figure 2.4).

The map of the project should reflect the decisions made during the first two steps of this phase. It serves as an overview of the content storyboard and a quick reference to navigation flow. By mapping out the entire project, the designer can also spot any rough areas in the order of content or interaction.

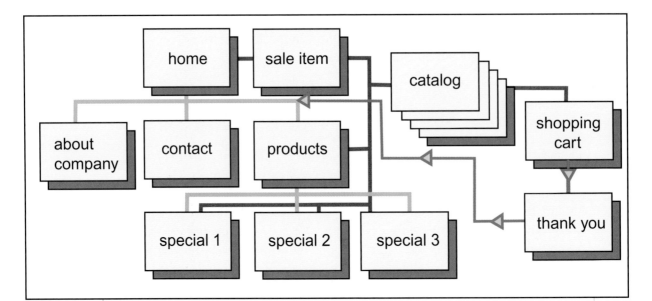

Figure 2.4

Mapping out a structure of the entire project completes the interactive phase. The next section deals with the last of the three phases in the design process.

The Presentation Phase: Close-Up

The last part of the design process is the presentation phase. Most of this phase is concerned with the appearance of the project. Although most new media designers won't be able to help thinking about how a project will look before this part of the process is completed, it is during this phase that the real work on the visual presentation begins.

THE CART BEFORE THE HORSE

Less experienced designers will often start with the presentation phase first and then attempt to force the content, navigation, and other elements to fit into what they have already envisioned. Starting the design with the presentation phase usually results in an inferior project and more than a few major design overhauls along the way. This can be prevented by allowing the work from the first two phases to influence the presentation phase.

THE LAYOUT

During this step, the designer works out the visual arrangement of the content and navigation areas on each page of the project. The layout can be thought of as the design of the area that will be presented to the viewer.

Designing Navigation with the Viewer in Mind

Make It Understandable

Viewers should be able to quickly understand which elements are the interactive controls and how they work. New media projects that require viewers to go through a long learning process to understand navigation are not usually effective. An example of this might be a project that uses buttons for navigation but also uses title graphics that look similar to the buttons. The viewer may think that the graphics are also part of the navigation.

The navigation design should also clearly indicate what the controls do or where they take a viewer. This can be accomplished through the use of descriptive labels and graphics. A project's navigation should not be a surprise or a mystery that must be solved by the viewer, unless that is the goal.

Give Feedback

Let the viewers know when they have activated some control. Whether it is by an audible sound, a color change, or some other indication, it is helpful to let viewers know that they have made something happen, especially if there is a delay for the next part of the presentation to load. When viewers click on some control and nothing changes immediately, they may assume that it didn't work.

Another good feedback device is to include mouse-over effects on controls. This lets the viewer know that they are in the correct place to trigger something.

Make It Easy

Viewers should not have to work at navigation. Keep the controls close together and in the same areas from page to page. If the navigation is spread all over the page or the controls are in a different place each time a new page loads, the project will become more about figuring out how to navigate than about its real purpose.

Make It Forgiving

Viewers who want to exit the presentation or who make a mistake in navigation should not be trapped. They should be able to get back quickly and easily to where they want to be. Allow them to change their minds. Also, making viewers perform some task before they are allowed to continue, such as answering a question correctly, is better suited for computer games than a media presentation.

Making Thumbnails

One of the best ways to approach the design of the layout is through the use of small drawings called **thumbnails**. By creating a series of thumbnails that explore different arrangements, the designer can narrow down layout possibilities to the one that works best for the requirements of a project. An example of this process is illustrated in Figure 2.5.

On the left-hand side of Figure 2.5, there is a larger rectangle that represents a page from the content storyboard produced during the interaction phase. This page shows the content that must be included in the layout.

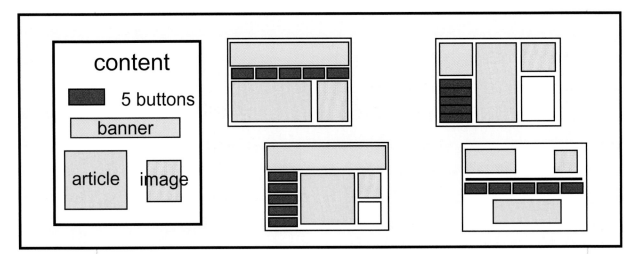

Figure 2.5

To the right of the larger rectangle are four thumbnails, each of which presents a different arrangement of the same content from the storyboard page.

Consistency in Layout

An important part of effective layout is to use a design that will appear consistent from one section of the project to another. A consistent layout allows viewers to know what to expect from any other pages of the piece. They will already know where the navigation is located, where the content is, and how to find what they are looking for. If the layout is inconsistent and each page is dramatically different, viewers will have to relearn where to find everything each time they navigate to another section. An inconsistent layout can effectively change the goal of the project from communication to a scavenger hunt for information.

Influential Elements The following chapters cover visual elements of design that have a significant influence on layout:

Space: Chapter 3
Composition and unity: Chapter 10
Balance: Chapter 11

Repetition and rhythm: Chapter 13
Emphasis: Chapter 17

THE STYLE

The next step in the presentation phase is to create the look or style of the project. It is during this part of the design process that the designer works on the graphics and visual details for the project.

In this step, it is important to keep in mind the target audience: a look that appeals to one group of people may not appeal to another. For example, an aesthetic style that is subdued and simple would be appropriate for a project intended to be viewed by businesspeople, but the same style would seem plain and boring to younger viewers.

The Project Looked Great, But . . .

One of the pitfalls in new media design is the temptation to use such stunning graphics and effects that they overshadow the purpose of the project. The classic example of this is the Web page that has so many animated images and scrolling text boxes that the content is lost in all the visual activity. Designers should be free to use the media to its fullest extent, but everything has its place. An effective way to approach the use of graphics and effects is the same as the use of content: if it doesn't further the goal of the project, then it may not belong in the project. On the other hand, if it doesn't interfere with the purpose of the piece and it will enhance the viewer's experience, feel free to impress them.

THE PROTOTYPE

The last step in the process of new media design is to build a prototype. This is a working example of the entire project that can be tested to find any areas that need to be adjusted. The prototype presents the piece in the way that the viewer will see it, and any problems that were missed during the earlier design phases will become apparent.

It is often during prototype testing that any technical issues will arise. For the designer, it is much better to deal with these problems while still in the design phase than while producing the final product. Putting any technical issues off until later often results in the designer looking for a quick fix instead of a real solution to the problem.

Completing the Design

After the three phases of the design process have been completed and the bugs have been worked out, the production of the actual project can finally begin. By covering each step of the design process in order, the tasks are made easier for the designer, and the final production can be as simple as putting the finishing touches on the prototype.

SUMMARY

This chapter provided an overview of the design process. The process was broken down into three major phases: the information phase, the interaction phase, and the presentation phase. In turn, each phase was divided into three steps and details were given for each.

REVIEW QUESTIONS

1. What are the three phases of the design process?

2. What is the significance of determining the target audience? How can the target audience influence the other parts of the design?

3. What are the two tests to determine if a certain piece of content should be included?

4. Name a concept from the section "*Designing Navigation with the Viewer in Mind.*"

5. Why are the entrance and exit of a project important?

6. Define a *layout* as it applies to a new media project.

7. What is a *prototype?*

NOTES

SECTION

TWO

One of the reasons that new media has such a strong appeal is because it allows for the combination of different communication methods in a single presentation. Although the use of multiple media forms can create a rich sensory experience, humans still receive more information through sight than any other of the five senses. For the new media designer, this means that visual design is one of the most effective ways to communicate.

Because of the importance of visual communication to their audience, it is advantageous for new media designers to develop skills in creating graphics and using aesthetics to convey concepts. Without these skills, the designer must choose to either ignore the strongest form of communication available to them or leave most of the presentation phase of a new media project to someone else. The next section of this book is dedicated to helping the new media designer obtain the skills needed to avoid making that undesirable choice altogether.

To ease understanding, each of the different elements of visual design has been broken down into building blocks that can be combined with other elements to produce effect layouts and graphics. These elements of design are the same used in graphic design and fine art, but the approach of this text is to present them in a way that is understandable and to explain how they can be used in new media projects.

The first elements presented are the basic fundamentals of any graphic or illustration. They include topics such as the use of space, line, and shape. Later chapters cover how these elements can be combined to create more complex visual communication through concepts such as composition, perspective, and rhythm. The final chapters of this section address other elements of new media communication, including motion and interactivity.

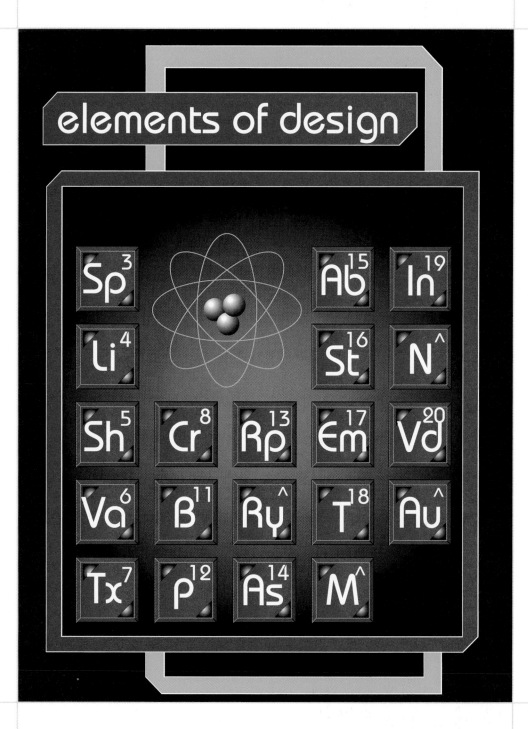

elements of design

3

Space

When someone says the word *space* most people think of rockets, planets, and telescopes, but when it comes to design and visual communication, *space* is actually something even bigger. Space is the universe in which a design exists.

When a designer first begins to work on the visual components of a piece, usually all that exists are a few ideas of what it should look like. Whether the designer starts with a white sheet of paper or a blank computer screen, space is important because it forms the context of the design and can be used to communicate to the viewer as much as any other part of the layout can. A good designer will use space in a way that dramatically enhances the communication. If the designer is a master, space will become so much a part of the design that any change in it will alter the piece entirely.

Three Kinds of Space

The term space, as it applies to design, is often difficult to define because several different visual elements are lumped together under this same term. Space could refer to the actual presentation of a piece of work. This includes the scale or size of the work and how it relates to its surrounding. Space could also refer to the area of a design that surrounds the main objects. The word space could also be used to discuss an artificial or illusionary space that has been created in an image through the use of certain visual techniques. In this chapter, the different approaches to using space as an element of design are covered in detail with visual examples.

Figure 3.1 was made with the following concepts in mind:

- Format (space as size, scale, and presentation)
- Positive and negative space (space as the relationship between the objects of focus and the area around them)
- Illusionary space (space as a perceived third dimension)

Key Points

▸▸ **Format**
▸▸ **Positive and Negative Space**
▸▸ **Illusionary Space**

Figure 3.1

Space as Format

The first thing that a designer must consider before creating a piece is the **format.** In the past the concept of format was usually concerned only with the physical dimensions of an image and how the space within those dimensions would be used. Now, because of technology, the same piece may be viewed on a wide variety of media, and different people may see entirely different versions of the same work as a result. Because of this, new media designers should determine during the information phase the conditions under which a project will be displayed or design the project so that it may be viewed in a variety of formats.

Format = Size

The first concern with format is often size. This is the width and height of whatever will be used to display the project. The format could be a 17-inch computer monitor or projected onto a huge screen. The format used by a designer has a great deal of influence on how a viewer sees the work. Because of this, the designer must make decisions on how to best use the format space (or multiple formats) in a design. To better understand the importance of format, think about watching a movie that has a lot of visual effects. Would you rather view it on a tiny television monitor or on a huge theater screen? On the large screen, details are visible and the effects impressive, while on a small television monitor, much of the visual impact is lost, and details are all but invisible.

Know Your Format

Several examples of format issues in new media can be found in Web design. Web designers will often work on high-quality computer monitors and the newly created sites may look great to them, but most of the people visiting the site will probably not have spent the money on an expensive monitor. On an inferior monitor most of the designer's efforts may be lost. To make matters worse, computer monitors often have different screen resolutions. An image that fills the screen in a powerful way on one screen may appear small and insignificant on another screen. Because of this, the entire effect of a design could be ruined (Figure 3.2).

It is important to understand the nature of the format in which your work will be displayed. The following are a few things to consider about format before beginning any new media design that may be displayed on a monitor:

1. If the viewer will look at the design using a monitor, what will be the size of the monitor? What are typical monitor sizes? Be aware that as the technology available to consumers evolves, the answer to this question will change.

2. What is the screen resolution of the monitor? Think of this in terms of pixels across the screen. Most monitors today are set at a resolution of 800 by 600 pixels, but this is rapidly changing to higher numbers as new models come on the market. Just a few years ago, the typical screen

Figure 3.2 Simulated screen shot on the same monitor set at two different resolutions

resolution was only 640 by 480. At this setting, an image that was 400 pixels wide would fill almost the entire screen. At a screen resolution of 800 by 600, the same image would cover only about one-quarter of the screen area. On a monitor set to 1280 by 1024, the 400-pixel-wide image would be limited to a small corner of about one-ninth of the total screen width. Keep in mind that this has little if anything to do with the actual size of screen. Two computer monitors that both measure 15 inches could have completely different resolution settings.

In addition, the advent of new media also means that the same design may be presented in multiple formats. It is possible that a designer who has been hired to create a graphic for a corporation's advertising campaign would have to develop an image that would look good in a company publication, on a Web site, on a billboard, and even in a television commercial.

Using the Format Space

After the designer has determined the specifics of the medium that will be used to display the piece, the next big decision is how to fill the space. Throughout the ages, art and design "experts" have proclaimed strict codes for the use of format space. Some have claimed that a good design must use all the available space and that any imagery should completely fill the entire format to the point that it bleeds off the edges. Others have maintained that good design needs borders of empty space to give viewers a place to rest their eyes. Some have even argued the extreme view that the use of the format for any design should have very specific dimensions (i.e., the Golden Mean: the ratio of the height to the width of any piece should be 1:1.68).

Contrary to what many have said, there are no absolute rules for using format space; there are only different effects and the influence that the use of space has on the overall piece. Keep in mind that the opinions of the so-called experts are usually derived from the fashion and style of design popular during their time, so don't be afraid to bend a few of the proclaimed rules.

Bending the Rules

An example of how bending the accepted rules of format space can influence the success of a piece is a drawing that I made while still in graduate school. The piece was on an enormous 9- by 12-foot canvas that I had constructed with the intention of making a painting that would overwhelm the viewer by its sheer size. My thought was to use the scale of the format to make a dramatic impact, but I never got around to painting it, and the unused canvas leaned against the wall of my studio for a long time. One day, I looked at the big empty canvas and drew two little black lines, at about shoulder height, on the left side. The drawing was no more than 9 inches high, and the two lines looked tiny and lost in all that open space. Whenever I looked at the piece, I would remember the voice of a professor from my undergraduate days admonishing freshman art students, "Use the whole sheet of paper when you draw! The drawing should go to the very edges of your paper! What is this a drawing of—a little doll on a waterbed?" Even though I personally liked the little drawing on the huge canvas, it went against what I had been told. Because of this, I still intended to paint over the drawing when I found the time.

A few months before I made the drawing, I received an offer for a solo exhibition at a local gallery. As the date of the show drew near, I began to become concerned because I wasn't certain that I had enough new work to fill the large galley. Out of desperation, I loaded up everything that I had in my studio and took it to with me; this included the huge empty canvas with the two little lines. Just as I suspected, the gallery still looked bare after I had brought in the majority of the work. With more than a little reluctance, I hauled the giant canvas inside and half expected the gallery director to laugh at the piece when she saw it or, worse, refuse to let it hang in the show. Instead of making any negative comments, she stood silently, looking at the piece. After what seemed an eternity, she quickly directed the assistants to hang it in the most prominent part of the gallery, where it would be the first thing seen by anyone entering the room.

I admit that I was a little nervous about having the piece in the show, but I was so happy to have been invited to have a solo exhibition that I had decided not to worry about it.

In a few days, the show opened, and nearly everyone I met wanted to talk about the big canvas. People would stop me on the street and say things like, "Hey, I saw your show. I loved the big canvas with the two little lines. It was really powerful!" The show had about 10 large pieces in it, but all that anyone wanted to talk about was the big canvas with the little drawing. Later in the week, I opened up the art section of the newspaper and saw a full-color, quarter-page photo of the piece. The photographer had taken the picture with a person in front of the piece to show the scale of the drawing. In the photo, the size of the canvas dwarfed the person and really illustrated the way in which the format of the drawing had been used. What did people find so interesting about the piece? Was it how well I had drawn those two little black lines? Was it the colors used? No. What made the piece interesting was how the space and format had been used to create a dramatic effect. The contrast between the actual drawing and the space in which it was presented made the work much more interesting.

In Figure 3.3, two different images with similar subjects are placed together in a diptych. In the image on the left, the cow is small compared to the overall area. This gives the viewer little else to look at and forces the cow to be the main focus of the image. In the image on the right, the bull fills the entire picture plane, and the eye of the viewer tends to wander around, looking at specific details.

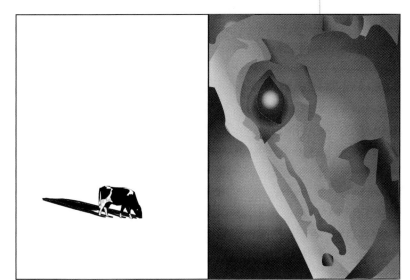

Figure 3.3

Positive and Negative Space

Another design element that is also referred to as space is any area that surrounds an object that is the main subject of a visual work. This concept divides all the parts of any design into one of two kinds of space. The first kind of space is *positive space.* This term usually refers to the elements of a design that are understood to have implied volume, such as an object. The positive parts of an image are anything that is perceived to be a solid or that is the main focus of the design. Everything else in a design is seen as *negative space.* This concept can be a little tricky to pin down since any negative space in a design can be filled with objects that are in the background or that are less important than the main objects.

To better understand this, imagine that you have a blank sheet of paper. If you were to draw a doughnut in the center of the paper, the doughnut would be considered positive space. All the empty area around the doughnut, as well as the hole, would be negative space. If the doughnut were erased and redrawn in a corner of the paper, the design would be completely altered. In the second drawing, the shape of the doughnut did not change, but the use of the negative space did. The same sort of thing would happen if the doughnut were drawn larger. Again, it is the relationship between positive and negative space that has changed. Even if the doughnut were drawn sitting on a countertop, it would still be the negative space that changed. Even though the negative space has now been filled with a positive element (the countertop), it is still seen as negative space (Figure 3.4).

Figure 3.4 In each of these images, the basic form of the main object remains the same. It is the space surrounding the object that changes.

The Power of Positive and Negative Space

One of the reasons that the use of positive and negative space is such a powerful design tool is because it is one of the ways in which humans perceive the world. We are able to recognize the contours of objects because of the negative space around them. Even the words on this page are understood as a result of this. If there were no negative space around each of the letters, you would not be able to read them. It is the combination of positive and negative space that gives the characters their shape and allows us to identify them so that we can associate a meaning with the letters and words.

Working with Positive and Negative Space

Now that positive space and negative space have been defined, we will look at several examples of how they can be used in an image. The main thing to keep in mind while working with positive and negative space is the relationship between the two. One always defines the other. This is demonstrated in Figure 3.5.

Illustrations such as Figure 3.5 are usually presented as an optical illusion, but for our purposes, we will examine it with the concept of positive and negative space in mind. In this image, there are the outlines of two blue faces, but the space between the faces forms the shape of a red vase. Whether one part is seen as positive or negative space depends on how the viewer chooses to see it.

Figure 3.5

PLAYING WITH THE UNEXPECTED

The use of the relationship between positive and negative space in an unexpected way can also generate interest in a design, as seen in the Figure 3.6. In this image, what would normally be seen as the positive space of the figure has been left empty, while the negative space of the room behind the figure has been rendered in detail.

NEGATIVE SPACE IS NOT THE LEFTOVER

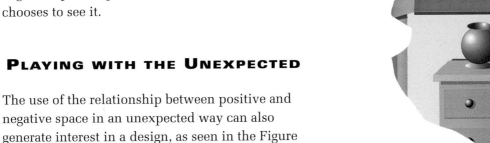

Figure 3.6

As a designer, it important to keep in mind that negative space is not wasted space. The area that makes up the negative space can be filled with elements that add interest and information to an image, or it can be completely empty. In either case, it is as much a part of the design as the positive elements. The negative space may not be the main focus of an image, but it should enhance and emphasize the important parts (Figure 3.7).

Although the relationship between positive and negative space can be a strong element on its own, it can also be used to include other elements of design, such as balance and rhythm. (For more on these, see Chapters 11 and

13, respectively.) As you explore the other elements covered in this text, think about how positive and negative space can be used in these other ways.

SPECIAL ISSUES IN NEW MEDIA

PREJUDICE AGAINST THE NEGATIVE

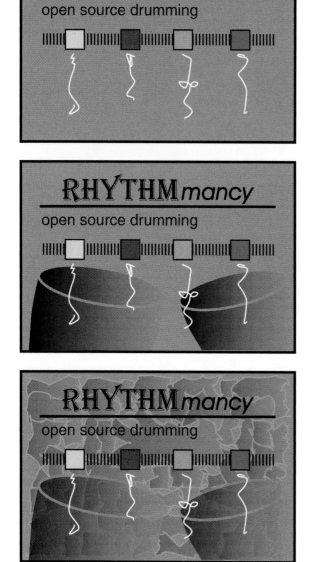

Figure 3.7 This illustration demonstrates how the negative space of an interface can be used to increase its visual appeal.

When it comes to new media, the relationship between positive and negative space is often one of the most overlooked elements. Because of space limitations associated with most electronic media, designers often concentrate only on the main subject in any image. In addition, designers who work with new media are often concerned with file size. As a result, they concentrate on the most important parts of an image and look for ways to shave off resource-hogging details, and attention to the negative space is often the first thing tossed out the window. Designers do themselves a disservice by using this approach. With a little effort, the negative space in any design can be used to dramatically improve the appearance without adverse affects to the media, but this takes some planning on the part of the designer. Whether the designer works with the negative space or not, it will still be present in any graphic or layout. By giving attention to the negative space, the designer makes use of a valuable communication resource that would be otherwise wasted (Figure 3.8).

Illusionary Space

There is another kind of space that is used as a primary element in visual design. This element is called **illusionary space**. This concept refers to the creation of the illusion of a third dimension (depth) on a two-dimensional picture plane. If your work is in print or on an electronic screen, the physical dimensions of the work are usually only height and width, but through the use of several different design techniques, the illusion of a third dimension can be created. The effect can be made through the relationships among the sizes of objects appearing in the image, through comparison of the relative positions of objects, or by using much more complex applications like perspective. (See also Chapter 12.)

Nearly every technique that can be used to create the illusion of a third dimension simulates the properties of human vision. For a designer, it is often easier to use these techniques effectively after they understand why they work. In this next section, each of the different techniques is presented along with an explanation of the property of vision that they imitate.

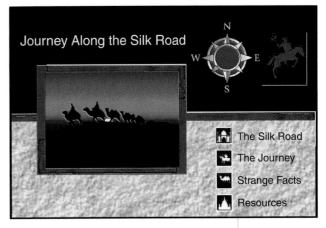

Figure 3.8 The negative space on this Web page was made more interesting by filling the bottom half with a texture. If the texture had been created using one single large graphic, the page would take significantly longer to load. To solve the problem, the Web designer used a much smaller image and allowed it to tile, or repeat, to fill the space. This approach saved on file size and used the negative space in the layout without adding too much to the download time of the Web page.

Vision in Stereo

Because we have two eyes, we can perceive depth. A way to better understand this is to first examine how our brains process sound. We are able to detect the direction from which a sound comes because we have two ears. If we shut our eyes and a person to our right claps his hands, we can determine the position of the person in relation to us through our hearing. Because the person clapping is closer to our right side, the sound reaches our right ear a fraction of a second before it reaches our left ear. The sound of the clapping is also slightly louder to our right ear than to our left. Our brain processes this information, and we are able to determine the location of the clapping person by the differences of elapsed time and volume that we perceive between our two ears. (This is pretty incredible when you consider that sound travels at around 750 miles an hour and that we can detect a difference of only a few feet.) Our ability to visually perceive depth works much the same way. An object will appear in a slightly different position in the vision of one eye from where it appears in the other. Our brain then sorts out the difference, much like it does with sound and our

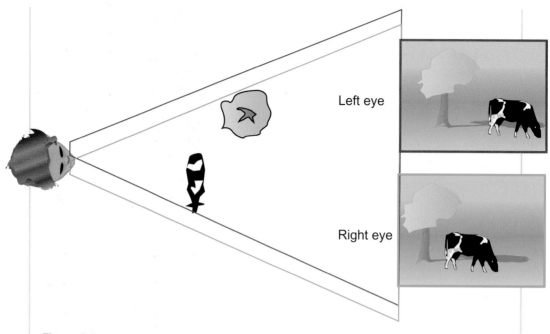

Figure 3.9

ears, and we are able to determine the object's distance from us and its position in space (Figure 3.9).

Designers have been aware of how this works for some time. In the nineteenth century, artists made use of a novelty device called a stereoscope. The device had two lenses set in something like a pair of goggles that a viewer would hold up to the eyes. Attached to the goggles was a mount that would hold an inserted card. Printed on the card were two different versions of the same image. Each image had slight variations in the positions of objects on the picture plane. The result was that a viewer's brain would interpret the two images as a single one, and the viewer would see the differences of position as depth. The same principles that governed the effect of the stereoscope were later applied to toys and 3D movies; currently, it is being used in some virtual reality-based media.

In projects or games that use virtual reality, the illusion of a third dimension is produced through a set of goggles that sends a slightly different image to each eye. The result is that the brain processes the information generated by a computer as if it were the real world. Applying this principle to a standard two-dimensional image is nearly impossible, but as the technology used to present new media evolves, this concept will become increasingly important. Virtual reality has already been introduced in theme park attractions and more expensive computer games, but if this technology follows the path of nearly every other form of new media, it will become more common in a short period of time. When it does, it will be the new media designers who use it as a part of their craft.

Size Matters

Another principle that affects our perception of depth relies on the relative size of objects. Our brains often automatically interpret objects that appear larger as being closer to us. This is because things that are closer to our eyes fill more of our field of vision. In reality, two viewed objects may be exactly the same size, but the closer object will look larger and dominate a scene.

In each of the three images of Figure 3.10, the street sign appears to vary in distance from the viewer. In reality, nothing in the images has been changed except for the size of the sign. A viewer who did not perceive distance in this manner might think that the sign in the last image was as large as the buildings. Instead, it is understood that the sign is closer than the other objects in the scene. The same technique is used to create the illusion that the buildings at the end of the street are farther away. For a designer, the use of size is an invaluable tool to convey illusionary space, and ignoring this method of perception can cause problems for the viewer. In an image where size relationships between objects do not make sense, distances can seem distorted and even disorienting.

Figure 3.10

Lower = Closer

In addition to size, a designer can also use the position of objects along the vertical axis to convey illusionary space. Objects that are closer usually appear lower in a person's field of vision than objects that are farther away. In the Figure 3.11, the lone soldier appears closer in the image because it is presented lower in the image.

Figure 3.11

The Properties of Light and Distance

There are several other closely related techniques that can be used to enhance the effect of illusionary space. Although these are usually more subtle than using size or position to give the illusion of a third dimension, they can still be very effective, especially when combined with the other methods.

One of these techniques is applied by making objects that are in the foreground brighter while making objects that are farther away from the viewer darker. A different way to utilize this same technique is to use colors that are closer to a "pure color" for objects that are in the foreground and to use muted or subdued colors for objects in the background of an image. (For more information on color, see Chapters 8 and 9.)

Figure 3.12 is made up of two halves, each containing a similar image. The difference between the two halves is that some of the objects on the right

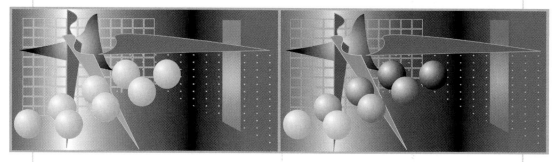

Figure 3.12

side of the image are slightly darker than their counterparts on the left. By darkening the objects that are behind other objects, the illusion of depth is enhanced. This is especially evident with the gray spheres. On the left, each of the spheres is exactly the same, but on the right, each sphere is a little darker than the one that appears to be in front of it. The result is that the rows of spheres seem to recede in space.

We are able to see objects by perceiving any light reflected off of them. If an object is close, it appears brighter because more of the light reflected from it reaches our eye. Objects in the distance appear dimmer because less of the reflected light enters our pupils.

Another technique that can be used to create the illusion of depth is by simulating an effect that is often referred to as **focus.** Objects that are close will often seem to be in sharper focus than objects that are in the distance. An object that is near the viewer will seem to have hard edges and stand out from the background, while an object that is far away will appear slightly blurred and may even seem to melt into the background.

This effect is due to the atmosphere that surrounds everything we see. In the air around us, there are countless tiny particles. These particles diffuse the light that is reflected from an object and make it look less sharp. In a fog, objects appear dim and blurry. Things are difficult to see because the reflected light is scattered by all the vapor particles in the atmosphere. Objects that would normally appear well defined seem out of focus.

An example of the extreme opposite of this effect can be seen in photographs from the moon landings. On the moon, there is no atmosphere to diffuse reflected light. Even objects that are a good distance away from the camera still appear in sharp focus. Because of this, it is difficult to determine how far away an object might be. What appears to be a small mound behind an astronaut might actually be a huge mountain miles in the distance.

How all this affects our perception of depth is directly related to how much atmosphere is between the viewer and an object. If the object is close, there is little atmosphere to diffuse the reflected light. The greater the distance between the viewer and the object, the more atmosphere the reflected light must travel through before it reaches the eyes of the viewer. In a comparison between two objects, the object that is farther away will seem to be more blurry.

SPECIAL ISSUES IN NEW MEDIA

TOO SHARP

Although some software applications that are designed to produce 3D images will automatically compensate for atmosphere, most programs do not.

Because of this, any distant objects in a graphic will be as sharp as the objects that are to appear closer. If the image is left this way, it will have an alien look; as if the laws that govern vision have no effect. To solve this problem, the designer will often have to apply some technique to soften the edges of distant objects in order to make them appear more realistic. An example of this can be seen in Figure 3.13.

Figure 3.13 contains two images of the same illustration. The image on the left is the original and has been left as it was rendered by the imaging software. In the image on the right, objects in the distance have been softened through the use of an application filter. This makes the image appear more natural than the original.

Figure 3.13

SUMMARY

In this chapter, several techniques concerned with using space in design were covered. You read about format and how the size of a piece can dramatically influence the effect of a design as well as the impact that the use of that space can have. You also read about the concept of positive and negative space and learned that the negative space is as important as the positive space in any design. In the latter part of the chapter, the creation of illusionary space was covered, and several techniques for creating the illusion of a third dimension on a two-dimensional space were shown.

EXERCISES

1. Use format to make an image more interesting. (Examples of this would be making a small image in a large space or filling the entire space with a cropped image so that it appears to go beyond the boundaries of the format.)

2. Do a series of three thumbnail sketches using variations of size and object placement to give the illusion that the same object appears far, near, and in between in each of the three images. For an example, see Figure 3.14.

3. Make an image, but leave the primary object or objects of focus in the image blank. That is, draw only the area around the object as if you were reversing the positive and negative space. For an example, see Figure 3.15.

4. Create an image by repeating the outline of an object several times, creating at least three distinct layers. Color each layer different to give the effect of depth. For an example, see Figure 3.16.

Figure 3.14

Figure 3.15

Figure 3.16

1. What concepts are referred to by the term *format*?

2. What is positive space?

3. What is negative space?

4. What is illusionary space?

5. If two objects are the same size but one of them is closer to the viewer, which one would appear smaller?

6. Would an object closer to a viewer normally appear lower or higher in an image?

7. Would objects in the distance usually appear lighter or darker when compared to objects that are closer to the viewer?

8. Would objects that are closer to the viewer appear to have sharper focus than those in the background?

NOTES

CHAPTER 4

Line

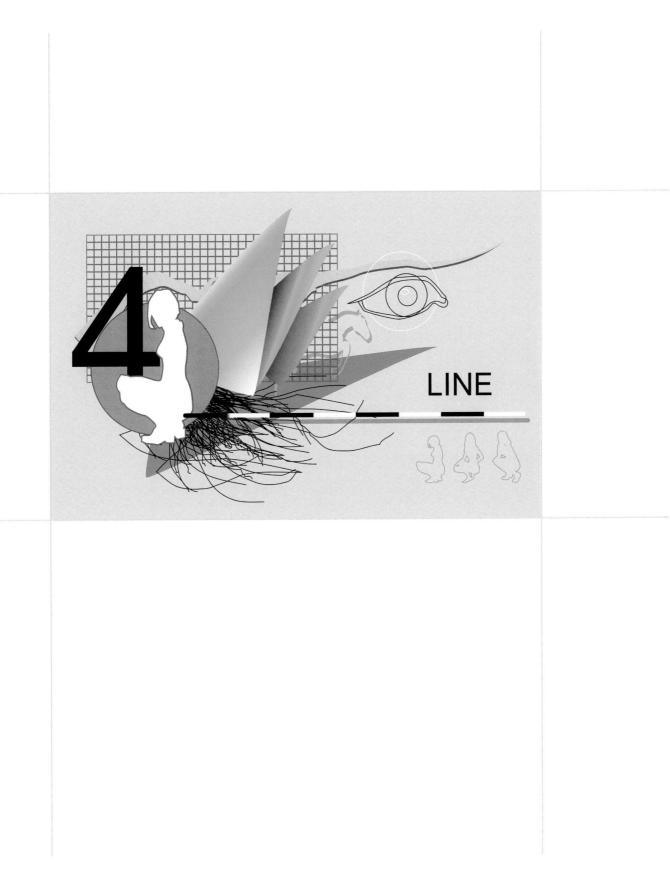

4

LINE

Among the different graphic elements that are covered in this text, the use of *line* as a design tool is probably the most diverse and very likely the strangest. A line can be one of the simplest elements used in visual communication, and it can also be the most expressive of all in a designer's vocabulary of visual elements. Line can convey a great deal of information, or it can be very subtle. It can define the visual details of an image, or it can be used to convey emotion and other psychological concepts within a design.

What Is a Line?

A line is typically thought of as any mark that is longer than it is wide. Although this definition is technically correct, line as an element of design can be a great deal more. In essence, it is line that defines nearly all the other elements in design. For example, the previous chapter contained information about the use of positive and negative space. It is the line that separates the two kinds of space by forming the contour of an area and defining the edge of an object. That is, it is a line that determines where one object ends and another begins.

Key Points

▸▸ **Contour**
▸▸ **Volume**
▸▸ **Expression**
▸▸ **Direction**
▸▸ **Value**
▸▸ **Texture**
▸▸ **Motion**
▸▸ **Special Issues with Line**

Lines Don't Exist

In reality, lines rarely occur in nature. They are more of a construct of the way humans see things. In short, we interpret the world as being made up of lines even though they are only a construction of our perception. We may see a twig as a line, but it is a three-dimensional object that has volume. Because we are so accustomed to visually interpreting the things around us as lines, a few simple marks with an ink pen can easily be seen as a drawing of the same twig.

This way of seeing is clearly illustrated in the drawings of children (Figure 4.1). Younger children who draw people usually start with a circle for the head, but the body, arms, and legs are all made with simple lines. They do not draw people this way because they see the world as being populated with stick figures but rather because the line is enough to represent what they are trying to portray.

As young artists become more skilled, they begin to use more than just a single line to represent each of the different body parts. An arm or a leg might be drawn with two or three lines to fill it out more. This is due to the artist's desire to provide detail and to make the person being drawn more realistic. Even though the main body parts now have some volume, the budding designer may still fall back on the use of single lines to represent small details, such as fingers and hair.

As an artist's skill matures, lines will be used to describe the form of a person in space

Figure 4.1

as well as specific details instead of using lines to simply represent a portion of an object. With this approach, line can be used to convey folds of cloth, muscle tone, and even the shape of intricate facial expressions.

Considering the drawings of children, we might think that an image can be made better simply by adding more lines. It is how the lines are used, not how many lines there are that gives the most visual information about a design. This concept is evident in Figure 4.2.

In Figure 4.2 only two lines have been used to convey a great deal of information. Because we interpret the outside edge of a three-dimensional object as a line, this image is recognized as a drawing of a horse. Not only can the horse be seen, but also, because of the shape defined by the two lines, the horse appears to be rearing or jumping. Slightly changing the lines can make it appear as if the horse is walking or standing in one spot.

By understanding that we use the imagined concept of line to interpret what we see, designers can use this knowledge to dramatically impact their own work.

Figure 4.2

Line: What Is Covered

This chapter is divided into two sections. The first section deals with the use of line as an element of design. The second section covers special issues with the use of line in new media.

Figure 4.3

Line as Contour

One of the main uses of line in design is to define **contour.** The simplest way to think of contour is as the outside edge of an object. A typical contour drawing is made up of lines that follow the outline or silhouette of the object being portrayed (Figure 4.3).

In Figure 4.3, the outline of the person's face is portrayed by lines. Facial details are shown by including lines that convey the edges of a few interior areas, like the cheekbone and eyes. Because of the way our brain interprets lines, this image is easily recognized as a representation of a person. In reality, the illustration is nothing more than a few marks on a page, but anyone who knew the person would probably be able to recognize her from the arrangement of these marks.

Although any illustration that merely re-creates the outside edges of an object could be considered a contour drawing, well-done images of this kind are usually more than just a silhouette. In a contour drawing more information can be conveyed by including edges other than the outermost ones. Depth and detail can be added to simple contour drawings by including a few lines that indicate the edges of additional areas of mass.

When making a contour drawing, one might find it difficult to choose which lines to include beyond the obvious outline. One guide is to draw a line wherever the surface of an object is separated from a background area or changes direction. Using Figure 4.3 as an example, the surface of the woman's face is definitely separated from the background and would be a good place to start. Another obvious place to add a line would be around the bottom of the nose. Here the surface changes direction where the cheek and the upper lip come in contact with the nose. Other surface areas may have more subtle changes in direction, but they can be drawn to make the image look better. An example of this is the eyes. Although there is little perceivable difference in the surface of the eyeball from the iris and the pupil, without lines to separate those areas the eyes would be empty and the drawing would look strange. For another example of how lines can be used to define the contours of a three-dimensional object, examine the drawing of the robot in Figure 4.4.

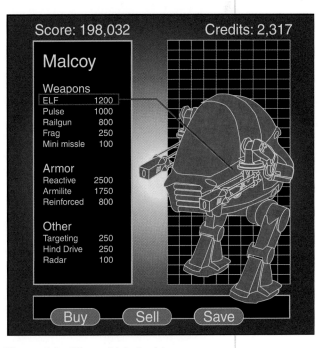

Figure 4.4 The vehicle in this game interface was created using only contour lines. The lines give enough information to define the form in detail.

Using Line as a Design Element

Recently, I was faced with a project that had more than its share of design constraints. The solution to the problems came in the form of the simple line and a little "out of the box" thinking.

I was tasked with developing a Web site for a class that I was teaching on Web design. Not only was the site to be an on-line reference, but it would also serve as an additional text for the class. This meant that students needed to be able to download the entire site and keep it with them as a sort of e-book. In order to accommodate everyone, the site needed to be less than 1.4 megabytes in size so that it could fit on a single floppy disk.

After I finished with the content phase of the design process, I estimated that the site would be about 40 separate pages. This was not a huge site but one that was still pretty large considering the file size constraints. I knew that I could easily keep all the content under a megabyte if the entire site used only text, but much of this class was concerned with design aesthetics; it would not set a very good example if the class Web site were plain and boring.

I struggled with the dilemma for several days but did not come up with any satisfactory ways to produce a decent-looking Web site that fit the requirements. Most of my attempts involved creating very small graphics and using them several times on each page, but no matter how much I tried, the site was still over the file size I needed.

Eventually, I hit upon the idea of using line as the main design element of the entire site. But instead of using large raster images as graphics, I would create the lines using nothing more than HTML (Figure 4.5).

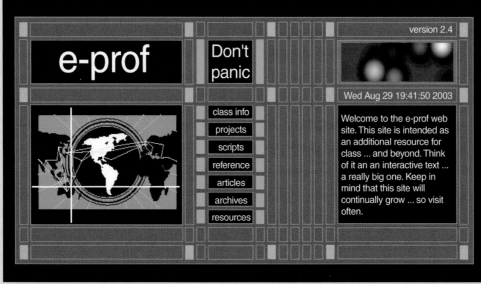

Figure 4.5 The majority of the graphics on this Web page are made from lines created through standard HTML.

For the look of the site, I used a style that was made popular by the architect Frank Lloyd Wright. This fit my target audience (design students), and I found that I still had enough room left to incorporate a few standard graphics.

The end result was a Web site that was more than plain text but small enough to fit on a disk.

Using Line to Convey Volume

Up to this point, the use of line has been examined as it defines the edge of an object. In this section, we begin to explore what can be done with a line by varying its width.

Beyond defining an edge, a line can produce the illusion of **volume** in space. By applying different thickness to a line over its length, a designer can make certain parts of an image appear as if it takes up three-dimensional space or even has weight. In Figure 4.6, notice how some sections of the drawing have thicker lines, while other sections have thinner, faint lines.

Figure 4.6 *The Markets of Al' Allaath Ngun,* by Robb Epps (a cell from *The Mestari* series).

The areas that are defined by the heavier lines appear to have more volume and are closer in space. This occurs partly because of a visual phenomenon that was explained in the last chapter. Remember that one of the techniques used to convey illusionary space was to use brighter colors for objects that were to appear closer to the viewer. One way to make a specific object seem brighter is to make the elements around it appear darker. (This concept is explained in detail in Chapter 6.) Making the line that defines an edge of an object thicker makes it appear as if there is more darkness around the object. Our eyes see an object that is coming out of a darker area as lighter and therefore closer to us in space. Varying the thickness of line width in a drawing adds the illusion of three-dimensional space.

Too Much of a Good Thing

Although this technique is very useful for portraying illusionary space, there are a few things that a designer should be aware of before using it. The first is that using any variation of line thickness is completely relative. That is, the only reason that a line may appear heavier is because there are other, thinner lines near it. This may seem obvious, but it is important to understand because once variations of line thickness have been incorporated into a design, they may dramatically influence the other portions of the image.

 The other area of concern is that even though a slightly thicker section of line can be used to create the illusion of volume, overdoing it can have the opposite effect. If a line is too heavy, it becomes a solid border around the object. The thick border visually reduces the object to a flat shape, almost as if it were cut out and laid on the background. There is no simple rule to avoid this, but size, shape, and even the subject of the drawing can determine what is too much. The only way to judge how thick the line should be is to use your designer's eye. If the lines look too heavy, then they probably are.

 In Figure 4.7, there are two separate drawings. They are almost the same except for their line thickness. In the drawing on the left, a thin line follows the main contours, but thicker lines have been used around the areas of the drawing that are to appear forward in space. In the drawing on the right, the line thickness is the same in relation to each other, but all the lines are heavier. Notice how this lessens the dimensional qualities of the image and makes it look flat.

Figure 4.7

Line as Expression

As an element of design, line can be used for far more than depicting how an object appears. Lines can also be used to bring the expression of ideas or emotions into a design. This is probably one of the most difficult artistic techniques to master. What makes expression through line so difficult is that there are no rules. Any effects that are achieved by using the form of a line are based purely on the perception of the viewer.

Deep from Our Psyche

We humans interpret much of the world around us through our emotions. Because of this, we have a strong tendency to anthropomorphize inanimate objects. That is, we often lightheartedly imagine that common everyday objects have personalities (e.g., a cantankerous old car or a malicious computer that is bent on defeating us). We also frequently apply human emotions to objects when describing them (e.g., happy wallpaper, tired shoes, or an evil-looking tree). This is due to our methods of communication with each other. We are not limited to only words for conversation but also rely on facial expressions and body language to convey meaning. (Some psychologists claim that up to 80 percent of our personal communication is expressed with our bodies, not by the words we use.) Humans are so accustomed to reading the body language of others that we tend to project this form of communication onto other objects.

Because of this tendency, designers can convey far more information in an image than merely producing a visual representation. The use of line can be one of the most effective ways to accomplish this.

In Figure 4.8, there are a series of lines. It is easy to imagine that each line has a different personality or conveys a different emotion. One line may seem relaxed and wandering, while another seems agitated or excited. Much of this is left up to the interpretation of the viewer, but a skilled designer can at least narrow the interpretation down to give the viewer a few hints. Most of these hints come from different

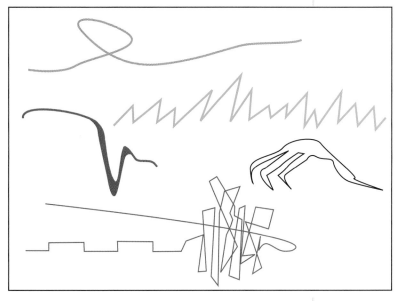

Figure 4.8

experiences that usually have very little to do with the drawing itself. For example, note the jagged line in Figure 4.8. It conveys a sense of excitement. It may even appear angry or dangerous. This is because of outside associations that we bring to the image. The jagged line might remind us of something sharp like a saw blade or a row of knives. It is argued by some psychologists that our associations may be even more primitive and that we see a line such as this as hostile because of instinct (i.e., we subconsciously interpret the sawtoothed line as a representation of the hairs that stand up on a predator's back just before it attacks or as a row of sharp teeth). Whatever the reason, the use of human interpretation of forms can be a very effective design tool.

Creating a design is not always as simple as including a single line to convey expression, but by applying the same qualities to several of the lines in an image, the designer can achieve the desired result. In each of the images found in Figure 4.9, the subject is the same, but different lines have been used to add a variety of expressive qualities. In the first drawing from the left, the dog seems melancholy. Because humans project emotions onto other objects and creatures, basset hounds already seem a little sad to us. This can be attributed to their drooping features. (Think of human faces when they frown.) This sense of sadness is made even more obvious by drawing the dog with lines that seem to droop and hang.

In the center image, the lines are sharp and jagged. Although you may not be able to determine what breed of dog this is, it is clear that the drawing is not of a friendly puppy. This dog is angry and irritated. The associations that we bring to this image are the same as the threatening ones discussed earlier.

The image on the far right is yet again different from the other two. This image is made by using thin, graceful lines. These lines seem to accentuate the motion and speed of two greyhounds running a race.

What Kind of Line Conveys Expression?

In some instances, it may be difficult to choose what sort of line would best convey a particular expression. A useful approach is to think of the

Figure 4.9

stereotype qualities associated with whatever it is you would like the line to convey and then draw a line that exaggerates those qualities. If the image is of a soldier standing at attention, straight, stiff lines would enhance the effect. In a graphic that depicts calm water, soft, flowing lines would work better than lines that are jagged and sharp.

Some of the best examples of how line can be used to convey expression can be found in comics and cartoons. These can be excellent resources for studying this technique.

Line for Direction

In the introduction of this chapter, it was explained that a line is actually a human construct and rarely occurs in nature. The next section covers how our tendency to see lines can be used to influence a viewer's experience of the entire image.

Composition and Line

Several times throughout this text, you will encounter descriptions of ways that different design elements can be used to enhance **composition.** In design terminology, the word composition is commonly used to refer to how the different elements of an image work together. (See Chapter 10 for more specific details on this.) If a designer makes good use of composition, every part of a design will work to enhance the piece.

One method of improving the composition of a piece is to use the elements of a design to encourage the viewer to look over the entire image while occasionally pausing to focus on specific areas. One of the most powerful tools for directing the viewer's gaze around an image is the line.

When we perceive a line (whether it exists or not), our eyes tend to follow it to its end. If there is another line nearby, our eyes will then follow that one. A designer can use this phenomenon to guide a viewer around an image from one point of interest to another. In this technique, the lines create a sort of a roadway and guide for anyone looking at the image.

Three Kinds of Line

There are three different types of lines when it comes to using them as directional elements for composition. The first is an **actual line.** An actual line is drawn and is like the lines that we have covered so far in this chapter. It is solid and is a mark of some kind that has a beginning and an end.

The second kind of line is an **implied line.** This is a line that is made up of elements other than an actual line. It can be formed by the edge of an object or from a combination of elements in a design that are perceived as a line. An example of an implied line is an image that contains a row of railroad cars along a track. A designer might draw the track itself as a thick line (an actual line), but the railroad cars also form an implied line. Even though there is an open space between each car, the viewer's eye will follow along the tops of the cars as if the artist had drawn an actual line.

The third kind of line is an **imaginary line** (also referred to as a **psychic line** or a **psychic wire**). This line is even more subtle than the implied line and is often created without any part of a line at all. For example, to create an imaginary line, a designer might have a figure in an image looking or pointing in a specific direction. The viewer's eye will naturally follow the direction that the figure is indicating. Because of our tendency to see lines, an imaginary line need not be created in such an obvious manner as a pointing finger. A leaning object, the direction of a shadow, or even the use of positive and negative space can all be used to create an imaginary line.

In Figure 4.10, each of the three types of line is present. The most obvious are the white and yellow horizontal lines that stretch across the image. These lines are solid and are easily recognized as actual lines. In the upper part of the image, there is a row of three circular shapes. Because these shapes are arranged in a row, the viewer's eye will move along each of them, forming an implied line. There are also two examples of imagined lines in this image. The first is made by the arrow in the large circle area. This arrow points toward the car and leads the viewer to look in that direction. The second imaginary line may be a little more difficult to recognize because it is based on what we know about the real world instead of a visual element. This imaginary line is made by the car and the empty space on either side of it. Because we associate cars with motion, we imagine that the car might be moving along some road that we can't see. The empty space behind the car implies a path that stretches from the edge of the image to the place where the car is now. The space to the left becomes where the car is headed.

Now that we have defined the three types of lines, we can examine how they can be used to move a viewer's eye around an image. In Figure 4.11, the

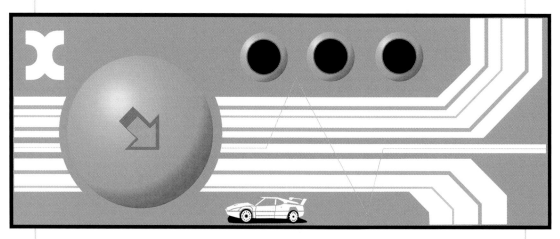

Figure 4.10

Figure 4.11

most prominent part of the image is the large moth in the upper-left corner. This figure attracts the viewer's attention and provides a place to begin the visual journey. Notice that the shape of the moth's antenna and wings forms arrows that direct the viewer's eye downward toward the bottom of the image (Figure 4.12). The path of the viewer's eye in this direction is also reinforced by the runs of paint streaming down from the colored bar.

Once the gaze of the viewer has been led to the bottom of the image, attention will be attracted to the dominant shape of the helicopter. Again, an arrow shape is made by the blades of the helicopter's rotors. The arrows formed by the shape of the moth and the helicopter create an imaginary line that guides the viewer's eye to the lower-right corner of the picture.

Beginning in the lower-right corner, there are a series of actual lines that lead across the bottom of the image. They start near the helicopter and run to the left-hand side of the illustration. These lines are made by the form of the landscape and horizon (Figure 4.13).

After the viewer has made the visual journey across the bottom of the entire image, the light-colored shape in the background forms an implied line that leads the viewer back up the illustration. These end near the upper-right side of the image, where a small spur forms implied lines that point back toward the moth (Figure 4.14).

Figure 4.12

Figure 4.13

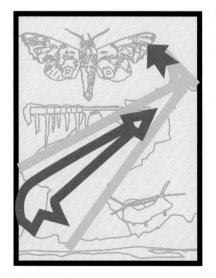

Figure 4.14

The entire path is now complete, and the viewer can either start the journey over or go back and revisit the parts of the image that were found more interesting. Through the use of different kinds of lines, the viewer is sent on a visual scavenger hunt around the entire image. At each point of interest, the viewer may pause a moment and study a specific element, but eventually the eyes will continue along the paths that have been laid out by the designer.

One of the more common ways to promote unity in new media projects is by aligning the different elements along implied lines. Figure 4.15 shows two examples of the same Web page. The first image shows the page as it would appear to a viewer, while the second image maps the various implied lines. These lines create a series of visual connections between the different parts of the layout. This approach is covered in greater detail in Chapter 10.

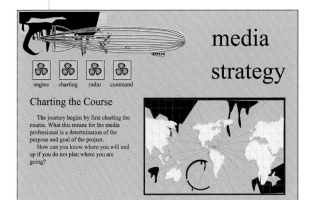 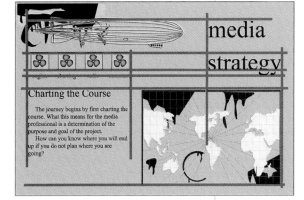

Figure 4.15

Other Uses for Line

In addition to the techniques that have been covered, lines can be used several other ways. This section explores a few of those.

Line as Value

One of the more common uses for line beyond what has already been covered is to simulate the value of light and dark areas on an image. Although the concept of value is covered in detail in Chapter 6, it is important to at least introduce it here for the purposes of studying the uses of line. For now, think of value as the shading used to more accurately depict the darker and lighter areas of an image.

The use of line to create shading is distinctive enough to have several names. The generic term for this technique is **hatching** (sometimes called

Figure 4.16

hashing). Hatching is the use of a series of lines, drawn close together, to create a darker area on an image or to imply volume through shading. To create darker areas, the basic rule is the closer the hatching lines are to each other, the darker the area.

In Figure 4.16, notice that the basic contour of the chair is depicted with a line but that details and darker areas are created by using smaller lines. Although the darker areas are not like the uniform blend that a designer would get by applying a solid color, the addition of the small lines is enough to change the value of the area. Notice also that many of the hatching lines follow what would be the contour surface of the chair. Making hatch lines in this way not only brings out the darker areas of the drawing but also conveys the details of the shape of the chair.

This technique probably developed as an attempt to give more details to images that were created by using hard materials. This method of shading was especially useful for the metal plates used in early printing. Since then, developments in technology have made printing much easier, and computers have made adding value to an image as simple as clicking a mouse. Nevertheless, the style and look of images made with hatching have remained popular, so much so that many computer software programs used for creating graphics have features that can automatically convert areas of a drawing into hatching. Although using a computer program to instantly create hatching may not be as accurate or as detailed as doing it by hand, it does have the advantages of speed and ease.

In addition to this simple form of hatching, there are several other kinds. Each of these techniques is defined by the type of stroke used. Figure 4.17 presents three different examples.

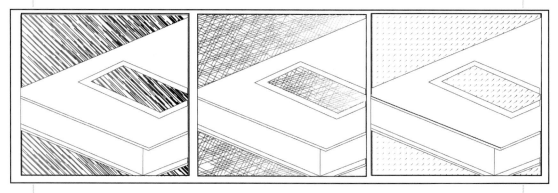

Figure 4.17

Using Line to Create Texture

Hatching can also be used to create extreme details, such as **texture.** The use of texture as an element of design is covered in greater detail in Chapter 7, but here it is briefly addressed as it can be conveyed through the use of line.

As previously discussed, line can be used to outline the contours of something being drawn. This is not limited to the larger parts of an object but can also be used to create very small details. If a detail is small enough, it can communicate how an object might feel to the touch; this is its texture. An example of this can be illustrated with a scrap of cloth. If a few lines are depicted on the surface of the drawing to show the weave of the fabric, the viewer is given visual information about the cloth's texture.

Figure 4.18

Figure 4.18 is significantly different from the kinds of line drawings that have been previously given as examples. In most of the other drawings, continuous contour lines have been used to outline the form of the object being represented. In this drawing of a cat, a larger number of much smaller lines have been used to simulate fur. Individually, each line seems to represent a single hair, but together they create the form of the cat's head. The collection of lines not only portrays the cat but also visually creates the texture of the cat's fur.

Line to Depict Motion

In Figure 4.19, lines have been used to represent **motion.** This technique can be most effective when the lines used to depict motion originate near outer contour edges of the moving object. In this illustration, all areas of extreme contour—head, hip, elbow, and shoulder—have lines showing motion.

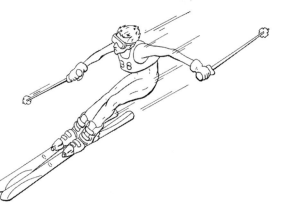

Figure 4.19 *Skier,* by Robb Epps

As mentioned in Chapter 1, pixelation can occur with some visual elements when they are displayed on a monitor. This is especially true for lines. As long as any line is strictly vertical or horizontal, there is no distortion, but if a line curves or varies from the straight perpendicular, it can appear jagged.

In Figure 4.20, there are two examples of interface buttons with a simulated enlargement of each. In the image on the left, the buttons are rectangular and the lines either horizontal or vertical. In the enlargement there appears to be no pixelation because the lines follow along the same pattern of the monitor's pixels.

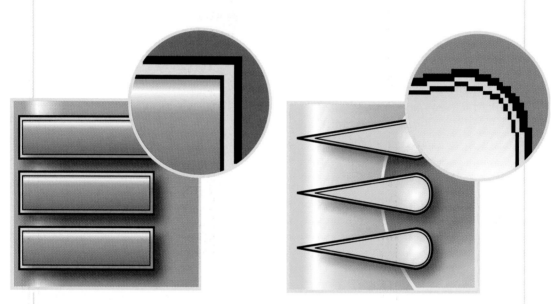

Figure 4.20

In the image on the right, the buttons are an irregular shape that is made by combining a triangle and a semicircle. In the enlargement, the curved lines do not appear smooth but rather look as if they have been made by a series of smaller lines arranged in a stair-step fashion. This is caused by the curve of the line crossing more than one row of pixels over a short distance. On monitors with higher resolutions, the distortion of curves and angles will not be as obvious because the pixels are smaller. (A detailed explanation of this was given in Chapter 1.)

Fixing the Problem

There are several solutions that the designer can use to deal with this issue. The obvious way would be to use only graphics that are rectangular, but this would be extremely limiting. A more realistic approach would be to pay close attention to the areas of a graphic that might be prone to problems of distortion and adjust the shape to minimize the effect. This can be a little tedious, but the end result can be worth the time and effort.

ANTIALIASING

Another method that is not as restrictive or as labor intensive is the application of *antialiasing* filters to problem graphics. But, like the other methods, this also has a few drawbacks.

In its simplest explanation, antialiasing is the color conversion of pixels surrounding a line in an effort to relieve some of the jagged edges produced by raster images. For an example, see Figure 4.21.

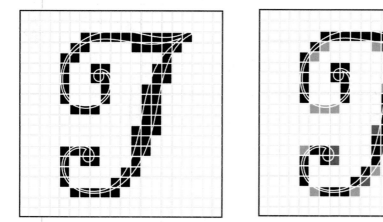

Figure 4.21

In Figure 4.21, there are two larger versions of the letter "T" and two smaller versions for comparison. The illustration on the left is the same as the raster image in Figure 1.9 from Chapter 1. It has the same problems with jagged edges as discussed in that chapter. The illustration on the right represents the same character with antialiasing applied to it. In this example, notice that several of the squares representing pixels are not exclusively black or white but rather a shade of gray. These gray pixels have been colored by the software used to apply the antialiasing.

Antialiasing uses several colors that are in increments between the colors of the foreground object and the color of the background. When antialiasing works, our eye naturally fills in the differences between the pixel colors, and we perceive a less jagged edge. When antialiasing doesn't work, an object will look fuzzy and out of focus.

Many of the more advanced imaging software packages will allow an artist to adjust how much antialiasing is applied. This can help prevent some of the extreme blurring. But be cautious when using this technique, and always check the final look of your piece before you commit to it.

THE VANISHING PROBLEM

The good news about pixelation is that it is becoming less of a problem as better monitors are produced. With each new generation of display devices, the resolution improves, and the jagged edges produced by pixelation become smaller. It is hoped that pixelation will not be a problem for much longer.

SUMMARY

This chapter covered the nature of line as well as several different ways that it can be used as a design element. Some of the specific areas that were addressed were methods for using line to create representational images through contour drawing and hatching as well as volume and using line as an expressive medium This chapter also presented the use of line in composition and gave step-by-step examples of using line to lead the viewer's eye around an image. Finally, the issue of pixelation and its effect on the line as a design element was addressed.

EXERCISES

1. Choose a photographic image and reproduce it as a drawing, using only line. Include as much detail as possible but do not include any shading, only contours.

2. Fill a drawing space with a series of lines each of which conveys a different emotion (e.g., an angry line, a happy line, and a sad line).

3. Make a drawing that includes each kind of line: actual, implied, and imaginary.

4. Create a drawing using a hatching technique to imply value.

5. Make a drawing that uses only lines to create texture. Good subjects would be cloth or fur.

REVIEW QUESTIONS

1. What is a contour drawing?

2. How does variation of line thickness affect a drawing?

3. What are the three types of lines in regard to composition?

4. What is hatching?

5. How can pixelation affect a curved line displayed on a monitor?

CHAPTER

5

Shape

SHAPE

I t has often been said that one of the best ways to understand a culture is to study its language. Many anthropologists believe that the words and phrases of a language will provide key clues to the things that are most important to a group of people. An example of this way of thinking is this overused bit of trivia: *Eskimos have over "X" different words for "snow."* (I know that I have personally heard this statement dozens of times, but each time I hear it, the number represented by "X" is different. I have heard numbers as low as seven and as high as in the forties.) Regardless of how many different ways an Eskimo can say "snow," there does seem to be some merit to this idea. It stands to reason that if something is important to a group of people, they would probably use many different words to designate variations of the same thing. If all this is true, then our own culture must be obsessed with the concept of shape.

When it comes to shapes, we have names and descriptors for nearly every kind and variation. A shape with three sides is called a triangle. A shape with four sides is called a rectangle. If the four sides of a rectangle are of equal length, that shape is called a square. The list of names goes on and on.

What Is Shape?

Every object has a shape, but it is rarely limited to the neat mathematical ones that we are taught about as children. In its simplest definition, shape is the basic outline of an object formed by a line (real or imagined) and the area enclosed by that line. In essence, shape can be thought of as the combination of line and space. For a visual example of this, look at Figure 5.1.

The image in Figure 5.1 has several shapes. Each shape is defined by a line that forms its outer edge. The space inside each shape has been filled with a solid color that sets it apart from the others and from the negative space of the background. Notice that the triangle does not have an actual drawn line forming its outer edge but rather uses the concept of an implied line to define its area. Even without an actual line, the shape of the image is easily identifiable.

Figure 5.1

Shape in Two Dimensions, Volume in Three Dimensions

As just mentioned, a shape is generally thought of as having only two dimensions: height and width. By that definition, a shape is flat and thought of as existing only in the two-dimensional world of paper, canvas, and the electronic screen. In the real world, objects are never actually flat but have three dimensions.

True to our practice of using many different words to identify variations of shape, a whole new set of names and terms are used to refer to an object that also has the third dimension of depth. For example, a square that also has depth and has all sides equal is called a cube. A three-dimensional object that has 12 sides is called a dodecahedron. Even a 20-sided object has its own name (icosahedron).

Even the term *shape* is replaced when it comes to three-dimensional objects. In referring to the three-dimensional area that an object takes up, we use the term **volume.**

Compare the two images in Figure 5.2. The first is a flat shape on the two-dimensional plane of this page. The second image is a representation of a three-dimensional object and how it fits into the space around it. In the second image, depth is added to the shape, and it fills a certain volume in space. An easy way to think of volume as it relates to a three-dimensional shape is in terms of how much space it contains. A designer may imagine that the object depicted is actually a hollow vessel, such as a vase or an aquarium. How much liquid or air would the object hold? That is its volume. This concept is important when an artist is conveying illusionary space or is using three-dimensional modeling programs to create images.

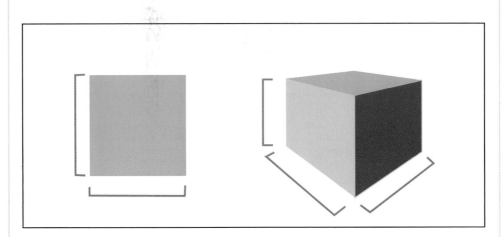

Figure 5.2

Shape Concepts Covered

Initially, the concepts of shape and volume might seem extremely simple, even taken for granted. But it is an important design tool that, like the other elements covered in previous chapters, has its roots in how we perceive the world. Ignoring these concepts can dramatically affect a designer's work. However, if a designer uses them to their advantage, they can greatly enhance any piece.

The remainder of this chapter explores several of the fundamentals of shape and how these fundamentals can be used in design.

Identification and Shape

A casual glance across the room can result in a tremendous amount of information for our brains to process. For example, visually scanning a room, you may see the outline of a small chair in a corner. Without studying any details, you recognize the basic outline and mentally classify it as a chair. This process also works in the world of design. When it comes to perception, humans are quick to simplify what they see and accept the simplified version as a symbol representing the original object. Because of this we can easily recognize something devoid of detail, such as a silhouette or a simple shape, as a representation of the original object (Figure 5.3).

Figure 5.3   This image is an example of how well humans can identify shapes. The purpose of each button is identified through shape alone.

Figure 5.4

Our identification of objects through their shape is not limited only to simple images. In Figure 5.4, there are dense layers of many objects, each with a large amount of detail represented through the use of shape alone. Even in this complex illustration, it is easy to recognize the dinosaur running through the jungle.

This way of seeing is so much a part of the way that we look at the world that, like the concept of the line, we tend to impose identification through shape on everything. It is not unusual to recognize shapes in things that have nothing to do with what we are actually looking at. A good example of this is when we look at clouds. Clouds are nothing more than vapor suspended in the air, but people will often say that one looks like a dog or another looks like a person. Designers have made use of such perceptions as far back as prehistoric times.

These early designers would recognize the shape of a horse or some other animal in the natural formations of a cave wall and then add pigment to bring out even more details.

A designer can use the human tendency to see and recognize shapes in some fairly creative ways. In Figure 5.5, the words of Edgar Allen Poe's poem *"The Raven"* are laid out inside an imagined outline. Because of the arrangement of the text, the shape of the raven is apparent. Not only can the viewer see the outline of the bird, but because certain letters are in a bold type, additional darkened areas of shape add detail to the illustration.

Figure 5.5

Final Notes on Identification of Shape

It cannot be emphasized enough how often we make associations with shapes. Developmental psychologists insist that this may be one of the first ways in which newborn infants use visual information. Since newborns are unable to focus, they visually recognize the things in their world through blurry shapes. The process of associating shapes with actual objects stays with us into adulthood and becomes part of the way we take in visual information. We become so good at it that we can recognize objects by shape alone regardless of our point of view. Most people rarely consider this and actually take the ability for granted. An example of this can be seen in Figure 5.6.

In Figure 5.6, there are several different views of a coffee cup. Each cup is recognizable by shape regardless of its position. The process that allows us to do this is fairly complex and at present is beyond the ability of all but the most sophisticated computer systems, and even these need a controlled environment to do so.

Figure 5.6

The Subtle Use of Shape

Because we are quick to associate shapes to some object or meaning, another effective way to use shape as a design tool is to include it in an image to enhance the main subject. That is, the shape itself is not the main image; rather, some shape or shapes included in the image make the piece even stronger. This can be either readily apparent or subtle.

In Figure 5.7, the main subject of the illustration is the figure of a man in a martial arts stance. The image could have been made with the man alone, but instead the designer chose to add a triangle behind the figure. Not only does the added shape make the figure stand out from the black background, but the corners of the triangle help move the viewer's eyes around the design. In addition to this effect, the triangle shape also contributes to the balance of the image.

Figure 5.7

In the example in Figure 5.7, the blue triangle is not very subtle, but since it is not the main subject of the design, it becomes part of the background. The use of shape in this way need not be as obvious. A designer could choose to use more subdued colors that would cause the shape to fade into the background or could even arrange the negative space of an image so that it formed the desired shapes. Many designers push the use of subtle shape so much that it begins to function on a subliminal level. An example of this is given in the following section.

The Power of the Subtle Shape

Early in my teaching career, one of the first classes I taught was on the history of filmmaking. As research for this class, I spent a good deal of time watching some of the earliest films. I was especially interested in the silent movies because they had to rely exclusively on visual communication to convey a story.

There was one group of films that I found particularly intriguing. These were the early films that were produced in Germany. A number of these films were some of the first horror movies, and even though they were very tame compared to today's standards, many of the scenes had a disturbing effect. As I watched these scenes, I could not find anything specific that made me uncomfortable; but I definitely had a general feeling of uneasiness.

This disturbing feeling interested me enough that I did more research into the techniques of these filmmakers. What I learned was that many of them had worked at making shadow plays before their careers as filmmakers. These shadow plays were made by holding cutout shapes in front of a bright lamp. The light behind the shapes would cast shadows onto a screen, and the shadow players would move the cutouts around in different scenes to tell a story. The pioneer filmmakers had brought with them their old techniques and applied them to the new technology. They would often cut shapes like they had used for the shadow plays and place them over the lights used in shooting a scene. These boards would cast shadows of the shapes onto the actors and the scenery behind them.

After I had found this out, I watched a few of the films again, this time keeping an eye out for unusual shapes. Sure enough, they were there—harsh angles, odd shapes, and even strange shadows resembling claws. After I had become aware of the subtle use of shapes as light and dark areas in these early films, I realized that this technique had not died out with the silent movies. I began seeing shapes used in the newer movies, especially in the films of contemporary masters, such as Ridley Scott and Francis Ford Coppola. It wasn't long before I began adopting this subtle use of shape in my own images.

Getting the Most Out of Subtle Shape

The subtle use of shape is not limited to background and negative space. It can also be used as part of the subject. In Figure 5.8, the upper part of the image contains the figure of a woman kissing a man. At first, this may not be apparent, but attention to the different areas reveals that the shape of the man is alluded to by the other parts of the image, such as the woman's face, her hand, and a portion of the background.

Figure 5.8

In Figure 5.9, the opposite effect has been achieved by making the triangle area on the man's face more prominent through the use of color. In this image, the man appears more dangerous because of a shape that we see as threatening: a knife blade.

Subtle shapes can also be used to separate visual elements in an unobtrusive way. An example of this can be seen in Figure 5.10. Here are three versions of the same screen from a media presentation. In the first image, the text is lost against the background and is nearly unreadable. Although the text can be clearly seen in the second image, the solid oval blocks most of the background. The problem is solved in the third image by making the oval more transparent. Here the slightly different area of the oval has worked to make the text readable.

Grouping of Similar Shapes

Earlier in this chapter, several different ways of using shape were discussed. Until now,

Figure 5.9

Figure 5.10

most of these applications have been related to the use of a single shape. In this section, a new element is introduced—that of shape association. It has already been pointed out that humans tend to recognize shapes and will even go so far as to make mental connections between shapes and objects that have nothing to do with what they actually are, as when a person sees the shape of a face in a wood-grain pattern.

In regard to shape, humans have another tendency. Not only do people attempt to assign meaning to a shape by associating it with some object, but they will also automatically group similar shapes together mentally.

An example of this might be found in the left-hand side of Figure 5.11. Even though the objects are scattered about in a random pattern, most people will mentally group the different objects by shape: circles with circles and stars with stars. The right-hand side of the figure illustrates that even our strong inclination to group objects by color can be overpowered by shape association. The tendency to group objects by shape is so prevalent that the triangles can even be seen to form a larger triangle out of the three smaller ones.

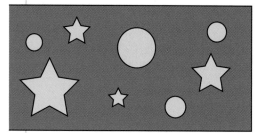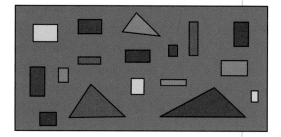

Figure 5.11

Bringing the Shapes Together

Shape association can be used by a designer not only to group different parts of a design together but also to move a viewer's gaze around a composition, much like line. (See Chapter 4.) The use of shape is an excellent way to create implied or imaginary lines specifically for this purpose.

An example of this can be found in Figure 5.12. In this illustration, there are four separate images consisting of the main image at the top and three smaller versions below. The smaller versions show the elements of the larger image in regard to shape association. The first two smaller images show how the elements of the illustration form the shape of two triangles. These two triangles point in opposite directions and form imaginary lines that lead the viewer's eye up and down the image. A person looking at this illustration may not consciously see the two triangle shapes or realize that they direct the eyes in a way that calls attention to the fact that the figure of the man is suspended in the air.

The third of the smaller images shows the repetition of a series of oval shapes that are arranged in a vertical row. These shapes become sort of a measuring device on a subconscious level and give the viewer a mental standard by which to measure the height the man has ascended. These ovals are also arranged in an implied line that would lead the viewer's eye up and down the image. If the viewer's eye wasn't guided by the triangles, the series of ovals ensures it.

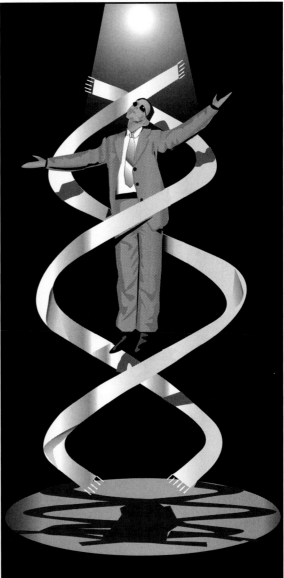

Grouping within a Shape

Another way that shape can be used to bring unity is by forming an enclosing border around different elements. An example of this can be seen in Figure 5.13.

Figure 5.13 shows two versions of the same Web page. If the image on the left was published as is, Web site viewers might find the arrangement of the content confusing. This problem is solved by grouping different parts of the content with shapes. In the image on the right, not only are the

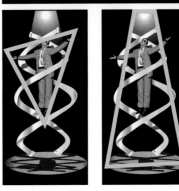

Figure 5.12

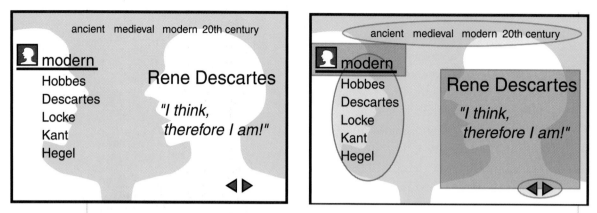

Figure 5.13

different elements contained in local areas of shape, but the different shapes also provide additional information to the viewer. In this case, general content is contained in rectangles, while navigational elements are inside ovals.

SUMMARY

This chapter presented several ways to use shape as an element of design and introduced concepts concerned with the perception of shape. A few of the topics covered were the tendency to group similar shapes together and using shape as a container for other elements. The use of shape to create other visual elements, such as an implied line, was also shown.

EXERCISES

Figure 5.14

1. Make an illustration using only solid shapes with no internal details. The shapes should be recognizable as the objects they represent. For an example, see Figure 5.14.

2. Make an image that uses the shape of the negative space to enhance it.

3. Illustrate a poem or song by arranging the text into a shape. An alternative exercise would be to repeat the same word over and over in the shape of the object that it names, such as an image of an apple made up entirely of the word apple repeated over and over again (see Figure 5.5).

REVIEW QUESTIONS

1. Shape can be thought of as a combination of what two design elements?

2. What is the term for the shape of a three-dimensional object?

3. Can shape alone give enough visual information to allow for the identification of an object?

4. How can negative space be used to form a shape that enhances an image?

5. Can the parts of an image be mentally grouped together through shape association?

6. Can separate objects be arranged to form specific shapes?

Value

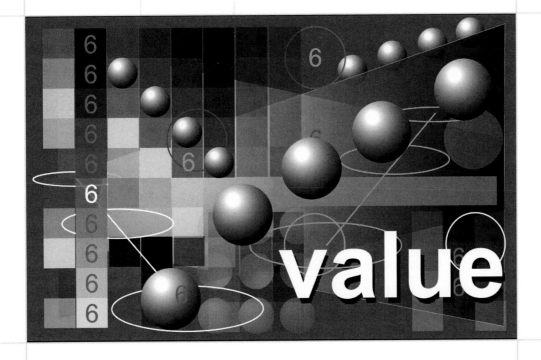

W hen we look at something, we usually tend to assign a general color to the entire object without taking the time to observe any subtle variations. For example, if a person asks, "What color is that car?" we might simply respond, "Red." But if we looked at the car with more attention to detail, we would see that it appeared to be several different reds because of the lighting around it. On the parts of the car that were well lit, the color of red would be somewhat lighter than in other areas. On parts of the car that received less light, the red would appear to be darker. This variation of the same basic color is called *value.*

The Nature of Value

In its simplest definition, value can be thought of as the variation of light and dark areas within a design. This concept can be applied to a monochromatic image (an image that uses only a single color) or to an image that uses many colors. In the case of a monochromatic image, areas of different values are lighter or darker variations of the same color. If the image uses more than one color, the same rule applies with the exception that each colored area uses a lighter or darker version of itself to convey value. An example of this can be seen in Figure 6.1.

Figure 6.1 shows several pieces of metal that have been attached using Phillips-head screws. A portion of the metal has been painted with an American flag. Notice that it is the variation of value that makes each screw head appear rounded. On each of the bare metal screws, there is a highlight of reflected light that is almost white. Radiating out from this point, the value becomes an increasingly darker gray color until it is almost black near the edge of the screw. The same effect occurs on the screw heads that are covered with paint. On the screws where there is blue paint, the highlight is a pale blue. As the value shifts over the surface of the screw head, the blue becomes darker. Again, the same variation of value occurs on the screw heads that are red or on the areas that have portions of white stars on them, except that the values are lighter or darker versions of the area's original color. In this image, the concept is not limited to only the screw heads. The same sort of variation of lighter and darker colors is used to show the edges of the metal plates and the screwdriver slots on each screw.

Key Points

▸▸ Defining Value in an Image
▸▸ How Light Creates Value
▸▸ The Relativity of Value
▸▸ How Value Can Be Used to Create Mood
▸▸ The Use of Value with Other Elements of Design

Figure 6.1

Figure 6.2 *Beautiful DNA,* by Robert Cowie.

The Strength of Value

The element of value can convey a great deal of information in an image. This is apparent in Figure 6.2. Here, the number of colors used is extremely limited, yet because of the range of values, the image appears very dense and full of details. In fact, most of the objects that are visible in this image are portrayed through value alone.

To better understand how much visual information can be conveyed by value, examine Figure 6.3. Here, the same image is repeated several times. Each of the four images contains the same objects, but a greater range of value has been applied in turn. With each increase in value range, more details become apparent. In addition to greater visible detail, the objects in the illustration also begin to appear more dimensional with every increase of value range.

In the first of the four images in Figure 6.3, there are only two values present. These two values are black and white and represent the extremes of the entire value range. Because there are only two values, the first illustration appears as flat shapes, and it might not be apparent that this is an image of a boat.

In the next image, two values of gray have been added. These grays are about halfway between the entire range from black to white. In this quarter of the illustration, the additional values add some detail to the picture, but it still remains relatively flat.

In the third image, several more values of gray have been added. These values are both lighter and darker than the middle values. In this picture, details have become evident, and the image of the boat is beginning to take form.

In the last of the images, nearly the full range of values has been added. This image is full of detail, and the differing values give a great deal of visual information about the light in the scene and how the boat exists in the three-dimensional world.

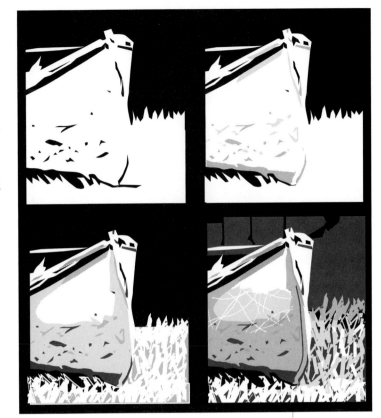

Figure 6.3

This exercise could be continued by adding additional values to the image until the entire range, from black to white, was present. With each increase in the number of values present, the image would become more and more realistic until it appeared to be a high-quality photograph. However, there is a limit to how far this could go. It has been determined that humans can detect only about 40 different values in a full range. Because of this, any number of values beyond 40 would not be visible to the viewer. Instead, they would appear to blend into the other areas of similar value and be lost. (This should not be confused with the ability to detect differences in color, the number of which would be in the hundreds of thousands.)

Value Concepts Covered

Value can be used in design to convey a tremendous amount of information about an image. The remainder of this chapter further explores the properties of value and how they can be used in design.

Defining Different Areas of Value

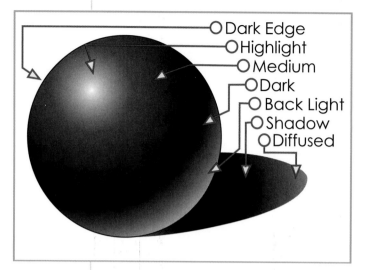

Dark Edge
Highlight
Medium
Dark
Back Light
Shadow
Diffused

Figure 6.4

One of the keys to using value as an element of design is to understand how it works in an image and how to apply it. Simply making areas of an image lighter or darker is not a good use of value. Attention to the detail in the variations of value is required, as is knowing how to convey those details. Part of this comes from being able to see subtle differences in value. In Figure 6.4, each major variation of value has been labeled to provide a reference of what to look for.

Figure 6.4 shows a sphere on which seven different areas of value have been labeled. The first is a **dark edge** around the outside of the sphere. Although this thin dark line has the smallest area when compared to the other sections of different values, it is what makes the sphere stand out from the background. It may be difficult to see, but this outer edge is actually the darkest part of the image. The second designated area is called the **highlight**. The highlight is the lightest value of any area on the sphere. This is where the greatest amount of light is reflected off the object toward the viewer's eye. (More about the influence of light on value is covered later in this chapter.) These two extremes are the lightest and darkest values in the image.

The next area in the list is labeled **medium**. This is referred to as the **midtone** and is the middle value of the entire image. This area would normally be the closest to the actual color of the object. Notice that there is not a sudden jump from the lighter value of the highlight to the midtone area, but there is a gradual fade from one value to another.

Outward from the midtone area, the value on the surface of the sphere becomes increasingly darker as it nears the area referred to as **dark.** Again, the shift in value from one area to the next is made by a steady increase in the darkness of the value.

After the dark area, the value begins to become lighter again where the surface of the sphere reflects light that is coming from a secondary light source (in this case, light bouncing from the surface on which the sphere is resting). Notice that this area becomes gradually lighter as it gets closer to the source of the secondary light. This area is called **backlight.**

Under the sphere is another dark area representing the **shadow** of the object. Even the shadow is not one solid value but rather is made from a variation of value like the sphere. This is evident on the outer edge of the shadow where a lighter area is labeled **diffused.** The lighter areas within shadows are caused by ambient light entering into the dark of the shadow.

Light and Value

In art and design, the use of value is described by the term **chiaroscuro.** The meaning of this word covers more than just the variation of values between the light and dark areas of an image. It also takes into account how light influences the appearance of an object's shape in three-dimensional space.

Light Defines Value

It is the lighting depicted in an image that dictates the properties of value. The parts of an object that receive the most light will have the lightest value, while areas that have little or no light will be dark shadows. The areas between these two extremes will have a variation of value, depending on how much light they receive.

 Like most of the primary design elements, how light defines value is rooted in how our vision works. The way we actually see objects is by observing reflected light. Light originates from some source, such as the sun or a lamp, and bounces off an object. The reflected light then reaches the eye of the viewer, and the object is seen. An example of this is found in Figure 6.5.

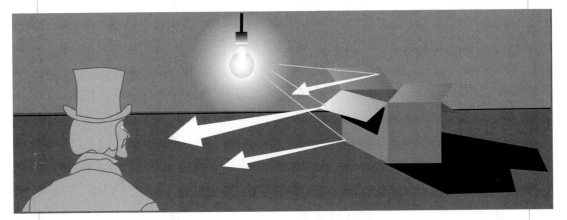

Figure 6.5

 In Figure 6.5, there is an image of a cardboard box that is illuminated by a lightbulb. There are also several arrows that represent the direction of light as it is reflected off the box to the eye of the viewer. On surface areas where more light is reflected, the arrow is wider.

This image illustrates how we see different values on the surface of the same object. If a specific area receives more illumination from a light source, it will usually reflect more light. Because of the greater amount of light reflected, more light reaches the viewer's eye, and that area seems to have a lighter value. The opposite is true of the darker areas. Less light reaches that portion of the object, and less light is reflected. To the eye, that area has a darker value. Shadows exist because the light is blocked entirely by some object, and almost no light is reflected from that area.

Position of the Light Source

In Figure 6.6, there are nine globes arranged in a pattern with a small red circle representing a light source. Differences in value can be found on each globe because of its position relative to the light source. Several of the differences are listed next. While reading the list, look at Figure 6.6 for illustrated examples of each.

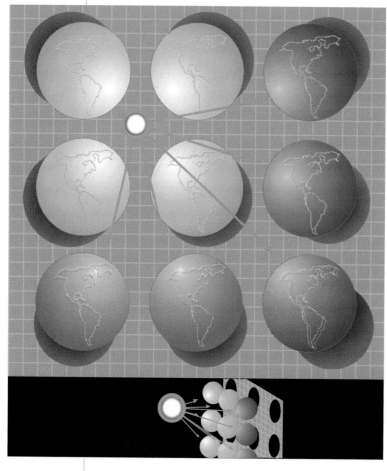

- Objects farther away from the light source will appear darker than objects that are closer to the light source.
- Any objects closer to the light source will have a greater range of values than objects farther away.
- Objects that are closer to the light source will have larger shadows than those farther away.
- As an object moves away from the light source, the position of the shadow may change.

Figure 6.6

Choosing the Position of the Light Source

When a designer is working from a photograph or a still life, the light source is usually determined by the lighting that is already present in the image source. But if a designer understands how light affects the range of values on an object, the light source can be altered in the image. The same is true if the image is made up entirely from the imagination. The designer can choose the light source and use its location to define the form of an object (Figure 6.7).

Figure 6.7 Even though this media player exists only as a virtual object, the designer has created the illusion of solid form through the use of value.

With three-dimensional imaging software, positioning a light source is often as easy as placing it where you want it. The software will then render objects with the appropriate lighting. But if you are working with a tool that doesn't provide such a feature, you will need to determine how an imagined light source will affect the value of surfaces in an image and apply the values manually.

Light Source Effects

The positioning of a light source can be used in powerful ways when it comes to creating images. In order to best use this technique, a designer should understand a few of the following concepts.

Direction

The first rule that a designer should be familiar with applies to the direction of the light. For some reason people seem to be most comfortable with images in which the light comes from the upper-left corner. If the light comes from a different direction, a sense of tension seems to be added to the image. In part, this may be because our major light source (the sun) usually appears overhead, but this explanation alone does not account for why we prefer the light to come from the upper left.

This is not to say that the direction of the light should always come from the upper left; rather, it is important to be aware that moving the light

Figure 6.8 An amount of tension and emotion is conveyed in this image by placing the light source below the subject.

source from this area can have an effect on the image. If the image is intended to convey comfort and familiarity, then place the light source in the upper-left corner. But if the image would benefit from tension and drama, then an alternate choice for lighting direction might be better (Figure 6.8).

Light Source Consistency

Another light source preference has to do with consistency. In images, people seem most comfortable with lighting that has a consistent direction. This means that once the direction of lighting has been determined, everything in the image should be illuminated by the same source. Much like the position of the light source mentioned previously, this is not an absolute rule but rather a technique that can be used to influence a design. A designer should be aware that departing from a consistent light source can dramatically alter the appearance of an image. Good examples of how this rule can be effectively broken are found in the work of fantasy artists. In many fantasy types of images, there may be several objects in the same illustration, each with a different light source. This gives the scene an alien quality and makes things seem as if they belong to another world.

Lighting Values

In nature, there is usually a gradation of light to dark values caused by the amount of light that is reflected from an object. If all the surfaces in an illustration appear to reflect the same amount of light with little variation in value, the image may have a dreamlike quality. The same effect can occur if the variations of values on objects are not consistent within the same image. These are a few of the lighting techniques that have been used by many surrealists to give their images a strange appearance (Figure 6.9).

Light and Value Summary

It cannot be emphasized enough how important it is for a designer to understand the role that light plays in determining the values present in an image. Whether the lighting is true to an image source or something that has come

Figure 6.9

from the imagination of the designer, it is the property of the lighting that defines the different values in an image. To best use value in images, a designer should understand these principles and apply them or know the rules and bend them with purpose.

The Relativity of Value

Although the nature of light dictates a great deal of how value is used in an image, it is not the only thing that affects how we see variations of light and dark. Another major property of value is its **relativity**. That is, the value of an area may seem to be altered by other values that are nearby. This is called the **adjacency effect**.

For example, an area that is dark in value will appear even darker if it is placed next to a lighter area. The opposite occurs for the lighter area. The value of the light area will seem to become lighter near the dark area. This is seen in Figure 6.10.

In Figure 6.10, there are two separate panels. The panel on the left

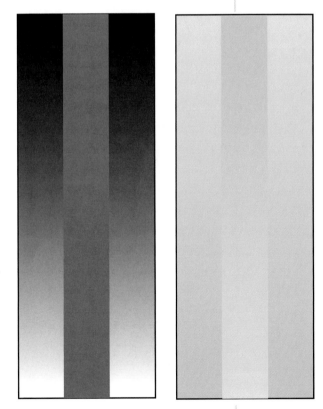

Figure 6.10

has a gradation of value from black to white. Running down the center of the panel is a strip of gray. This strip is the same value of gray along its entire length, but it appears lighter next to the darker section of the panel. At the bottom of the panel, the strip seems to darken next to the white area.

The panel on the right has a gradation of only three different values of yellow, with the lightest value at the top. In this part of the illustration, the center strip has the same gradation of value but is applied in the opposite direction. Just like the image on the left, the areas of the strip appear darker or lighter, depending on the value of the panel. But the middle section of the strip fades entirely into the panel because the values are the same.

The Way It Ought to Look

As I stared at my drawing, I could feel my frustration begin to get the best of me. I had drawn, erased, and drawn again several times, but no matter what I did, the image still seemed dull and lifeless.

The drawing that I was working on was an assignment in an art class that was dedicated to accurately portraying objects through value and perspective. The professor who taught the class was a wizened old artist who had made a name for himself by creating incredible photorealistic paintings. It seemed to me that he would choose the most difficult things to paint: glass bottles, old cars, and so on—anything highly reflective. He would paint them with such skill that they looked as if they were giant photographs. I can still remember the amazement that I felt when I found one of his paintings in a museum. The painting was of an old car from the 1930s and had so much detail that I could see the reflection of a man in the chrome around the headlight. I looked closer and saw that it was my old professor, long since retired, looking back at me in the mirrored surface of the chrome.

In the classroom, he must have sensed that I was having trouble because he came over to my table and looked over my drawing.

"Hmmm . . . ," he began. "You are trying too hard to draw what you think it looks like."

"What do you mean?" I asked. He then told me about the relativity of value, how a light area next to a dark area will appear lighter. I have to admit that I didn't believe him.

He must have seen the disbelief in my face because he then pointed to a corner of the room where the walls met the ceiling.

"Look right there. See how the darker wall becomes even darker in the corner next to the light wall?" I looked, but all I saw were two white walls and a white ceiling.

"Try squinting your eyes," he said.

Even though I was beginning to think that this guy was suffering from some hallucination, I decided to humor him. Once again I looked at the corner of the room and squinted. It took a few seconds for my eyes to adjust, but I clearly saw exactly what he was talking about. I then opened my eyes wide and squinted again several times to make certain that it was not some trick or that I had not caught whatever he had. Each time it was the same.

With a smile on his face, he walked away from me and for emphasis repeated his earlier advice: "Don't draw things the way you think they look. Draw them how they ought to look!"

Contrast

The relativity of value can be used by a designer for more than merely rendering an object. There are several other influences that a range of values can have on an image. Many of these enhancements have to do with the contrast of the values.

Contrast can be thought of as the difference in values within an image. An illustration that has mostly light and dark areas is said to have high contrast. If an image has a large number of different values in about the same range, the image does not have very much contrast. Like many of the other attributes of value in design, contrast is relative. A single bright area in an otherwise dark image will have a high contrast even though the rest of the image may contain values that are very close in range.

In Figure 6.11, an illustration of a shark has been sectioned into separate areas. In each section, different levels of contrast have been applied in a variety of ways.

Figure 6.11

Figure 6.12

Mood with Value

Value can also be used to bring an emotional quality to a design. If an illustration is to be playful or convey some positive emotion, generally lighter values will help convey that. Negative emotions, such as suspense or a sense of brooding, can be added to an image by using darker values. Figure 6.12 contains two different treatments of the same illustration.

In the image on the left, the values used are more toward the lighter end of the range. This illustration of a child's toy seems lighthearted and friendly. In the image on the right, the darker values give the same clown a completely different mood.

SUMMARY

In this chapter, information on the use of value as an element of design was given. The topics covered included how light defines value and how value, in turn, defines the shape of objects. Also included were specific details on the subject of light sources and the effects they can have in an image. Additional topics in this chapter were the relativity of value, contrast, and how value can be used to convey an emotional quality.

EXERCISES

1. Draw a series of 10 squares in a row. Make the square on one end as dark as you can and leave the square on the other end white. Fill in each of the squares so that there is a steady gradation of values from light to dark. For an example, see Figure 6.13.

2. Choose a simple three-dimensional object, such as a sphere or a cube, and make an image of it by using value only.

Figure 6.13

3. Make a series of drawings of the same object. Somewhere near each of the objects, make a small circle that represents a light source. Place each light source in a different relative position. Create the values on each of the objects in a way that represents the specific light source. For an example, see Figure 6.14.

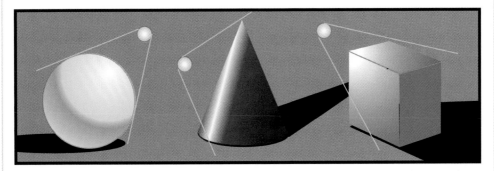

Figure 6.14

4. Create a detailed drawing that uses value to portray a complex object, such as a face, or a car. For an example, see Figure 6.15.

5. Make an image that uses value to convey a mood.

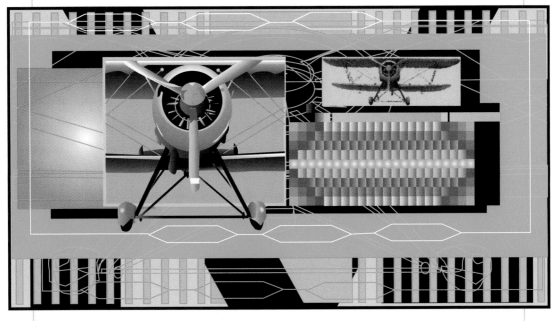

Figure 6.15

REVIEW QUESTIONS

1. What is value as it applies to design?

2. How does color affect value?

3. Does a greater range of value generally increase or decrease detail in an image?

4. What is chiaroscuro?

5. How does the position of a light source affect value?

6. What is the preferred direction of light in an image?

7. How does relativity affect value?

8. If a darker area of value is shown next to a lighter area, what happens to the appearance of the darker area?

9. What is contrast?

7

Texture

TEXTURE

7

n the physical world, we generally think of *texture* as something that is felt by our sense of touch. The texture of an actual object may be rough or smooth, soft or hard, and how it feels to the touch is how we classify it. Design can also include texture, but since the viewer will be unable to feel the texture, the designer must rely on visual information to convey how it might feel. This makes the use of texture one of the more peculiar elements of visual design. When using texture, a designer is substituting the sense of sight for the sense of touch.

When looking at an object, one can usually make a good guess as to how it might feel to the touch. This ability may be based on past encounters with objects that appear the same way or due to our ability to see things in such fine detail that we can distinguish small surface differences. The result is that when we look at a texture, our brains can translate the appearance of a surface into how it might feel to our sense of touch. To explore this further, look at the rows of different textures in Figure 7.1. Imagine how each would feel to the touch if it made up the surface of an object. As you can see, it is relatively easy to determine how something might feel through visual information alone.

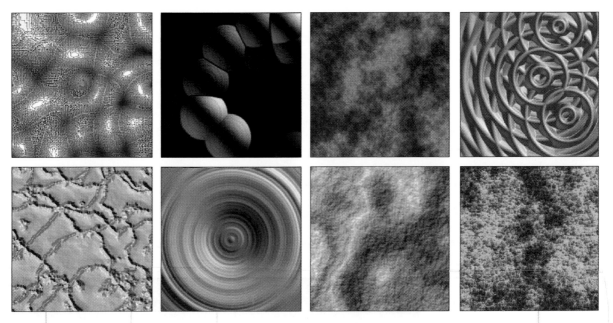

Figure 7.1

The Magic of Texture

As an element of design, texture can be used in some remarkable ways. It can transform a plain image into one that is full of richness and detail, or, without altering the composition of the piece, texture can be used to fill empty areas of an image. It can add depth to space, create detail in an illustration, or define the style of an entire project. There is so much that texture can do as a design tool that it almost seems to be magic.

For the new media designer, the use of texture as an element of design can be simple. Most imaging software includes applications that allow a designer to create interesting textures with just a few clicks of the mouse. If the texture isn't quite right, it can be instantly removed and replaced with a different one just as easily as the first. For a designer who works with brush, pen, or pencil, the creation of texture is one of the most tedious and time-consuming tasks, but for the new media designer, it is one of the quickest and easiest elements to incorporate into a piece.

Key Points

▸▸ **Uses for Texture**
▸▸ **Creating Texture**
▸▸ **Using Filters**
▸▸ **Texture Issues**

Uses for Texture

The different ways in which texture can be used in design are as numerous as there are design ideas. This section identifies several of the major ways that texture can be used in imagery, but how you will use texture is up to you. This will provide a firm foundation for you to build on in your own work.

Texture as Detail

One of the most common uses of texture is to provide detail within an image. Designers and nondesigners alike can appreciate well-crafted detail in any image. Some artists and designers have made careers of creating images that capture and reproduce the finest of details of objects that exist in the real world. Used this way, texture makes the image more realistic and brings the association of touch to an illustration.

In the image presented in Figure 7.2, the artist has put a great deal of effort into accurately portraying the details of a flower, so much so that it looks like a high-quality photograph. In this image, the smooth texture of the stalk and petals can be seen, as can beads of moisture that have collected there. Because of the amount of detail, it is not difficult for the viewer to imagine how it would feel to touch the different parts of the flower. To use texture for detail, a designer must pay close attention to how the actual texture of an object appears and then render it as accurately as possible. Using texture to create this effect is not a technique by which a designer can cut corners or save time. The process can involve a great deal of time to get the correct effect.

Figure 7.2 *Iris,* by Chris Collins.

Texture as Space

When texture is used to provide detail, its purpose is to enhance the image of any objects that are portrayed, but texture can also be used as an element of design to fill in empty space.

In design, one of the most difficult issues can be how to fill empty space in a way that makes it interesting for the viewer. If there is some environment present in the image, such as a landscape, then the problem may already be solved. But if the elements in a graphic seem out of place and isolated, the

Figure 7.3

imagery may need an environment in which to exist. Texture can be a way to fill in empty space and make it more visually appealing to the viewer.

In Figure 7.3, there are two illustrations of an ant. The first image has a solid color as a background. This image appears flat and relatively plain. The second image has a texture added as a background. Even though the texture in this image is mainly the same color as the background in the first image, it adds richness to the illustration, making it more interesting. The texture also gives a degree of illusionary space for the ant to exist in. Texture used as a background is one of the easiest ways to make the space of a new media project more appealing.

Texture as a Separate Component

Another way to use texture is as a visual element that exists for compositional reasons. Instead of simply adding a plain shape as a part of a design, consider filling in the shape with a texture that will enhance the visual appeal of the overall piece. In Figure 7.4, there is a central image surrounded by four smaller images. The four images are actually simple shapes that have a texture applied to them. Although the central image might be interesting enough to stand on its own, the additional areas of texture add to the composition by drawing attention to certain parts of the illustration. For example, the added areas magnify the "X" created by elements in the central image and expand the implied lines beyond the boundaries of the illustration. This could be done by using simple flat areas of color, but the texture makes the image more interesting by giving the viewer something to compare with the central part of the image.

Figure 7.4

Figure 7.5

Texture as Simulation

Another way to use texture is to create an effect that simulates a surface that is found in the natural world. For example, an artist might want to make an image that appears as if it were drawn on a scrap of old paper. Using a texture that simulates the surface of the paper would help convey this.

Figure 7.5 is a drawing of a bull that is intended to look like cave paintings found in western Europe. Adding a simulated texture to the background not only makes the image more interesting but also makes the bull look as if it were drawn on the surface of a rock wall.

Creating Textures

In its simplest form, texture can be created by using value to describe extreme surface detail. This technique works best when the surface is rendered more realistically. Figure 7.6 is a drawing that uses value to define a series of small rods arranged in a pattern. Because of the way light is reflected off each rod, the rods appear slightly metallic and rounded. The detail in value makes it is easy to imagine how the rods would feel to the touch.

Another way to create texture within an image is by the repetition of some element of design. This way of creating texture involves taking a visual element (or multiple elements) and repeating them within an area. The elements can be arranged in a pattern or can be placed randomly, depending on the effect the designer is trying to achieve. For an example of these two ideas, look at Figures 7.7 and 7.8.

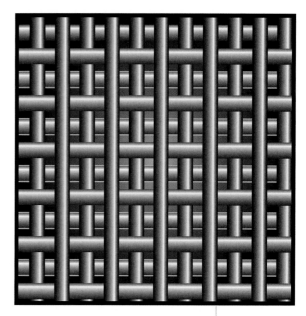

Figure 7.6

In Figure 7.7, blades of grass have been added in a seemingly random pattern throughout the space. The large number of grass blades and their repetition create a texture effect in the illustration. This texture is in contrast to the smoother areas of snow. (In Chapter 6, the concept of contrast was introduced as a relationship between light and dark areas of value. A similar idea is applied in this image, but in this case the contrast is between two different textures as well as their values.)

The texture of the grass also enhances the image by creating a layer that gives the image more visual depth, with some parts of the illustration behind it and other parts in front. This technique is usually more effective if the elements that are used to make the texture are small. This is because the viewer sees them grouped together in much the same way one would see similar shapes

Figure 7.7

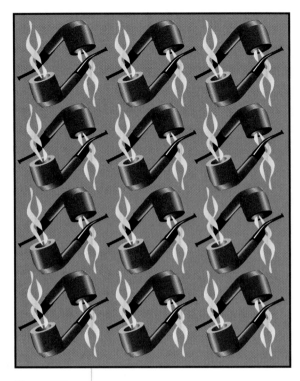

Figure 7.8

grouped. In this drawing, if the blades of grass were larger, they would cease to act as a texture and would become individual elements of the drawing on their own.

In Figure 7.8, a series of pipes have been arranged in a pattern. As in Figure 7.7, the repetition of a smaller element forms a texture. By creating patterns such as this, a designer can bring other visual elements of design into an image. For example, in this image the rows of pipes form implied lines that enhance the composition of the illustration and keep the viewer's eye moving around the entire drawing.

Flat Texture

Texture is generally thought of as having some subtle dimension, but in design a flat pattern can also be used in the same way.

Although a patterned area may not have a tactile quality, it can still be an effective way to create a texture to fill space.

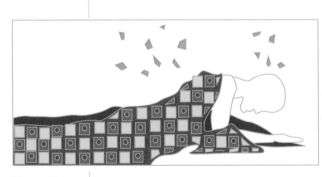

Figure 7.9

In Figure 7.9, the pattern in the background has been created by repeating a series of flat shapes in the space. This pattern forms a sort of stylized texture that has been used to fill space.

Another way to create flat texture is by using text. In Figure 7.10, text has been added to the background behind the door. The text, combined with the grid pattern, forms a texture that makes the black space around the door more interesting.

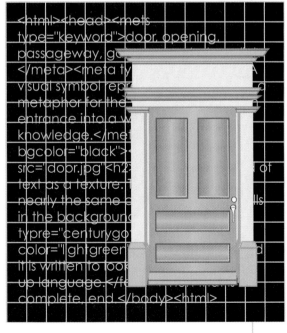

Figure 7.10

TEXTURE FILTERS

Because computers have become more integrated as a design tool, many of the tasks that took a great deal of a designer's time and skill in the past have become quicker and easier to accomplish. As mentioned earlier in this chapter, one of these tasks is the creation of textures.

Most professional imaging software has features that create textures at the click of a mouse button. Generally, this is called "applying a filter," but different software applications may call the process by a different name.

In most software applications, the process of creating a texture is similar. A designer selects the image to which one wants to apply the filter and then chooses the specific filter from a menu. The software does the rest of the work, and the chosen textural qualities are automatically added to the image. Creating the same sort of textural effects manually might take hours of altering an image a few pixels at a time. But with this process, it takes only as long as the time needed for the computer to generate the new image.

Figure 7.11 consists of an unaltered image and the same image with a few of the more common filters applied to it. Try to imagine how much effort a designer would have to put forth to create these same effects by hand. Each tiny detail would have to be added and made to work with the areas around it. This would probably take a great deal of time, but it takes only a brief moment for the software to perform the task.

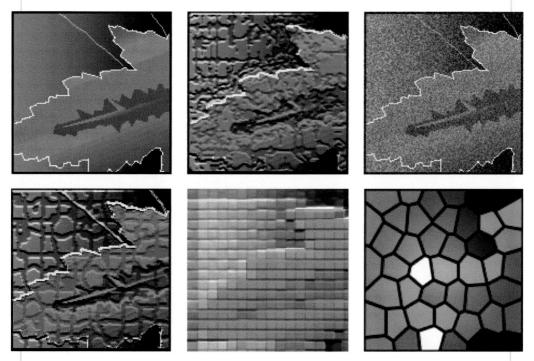

Figure 7.11

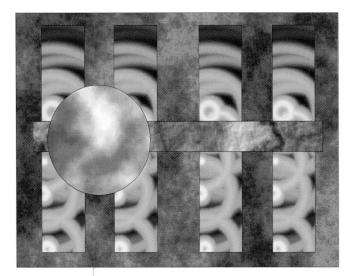

A Few Drawbacks to Using Filters

Although the use of filters can make a designer's task considerably easier, a new set of problems can arise with their use. Because applying filters is so easy, some designers might be tempted to overuse them. When there are too many different textures in an image, the viewer can get caught up in comparing them to each other while ignoring the rest of the design. In such a case, the competing textures actually detract from an illustration instead of enhancing it (Figure 7.12).

Figure 7.12

Another problem with the use of filters can occur when two different designers use the same software to produce their images. If each designer applies the same filter to an image, what should have been two original illustrations will look very similar. With hundreds or even thousands of designers using the same filters, the problem is compounded. In fact, the default filters get overused so much that veteran designers can often look at a piece and tell what brand of software was used to create it just by the characteristics of the filter applications.

The best way to avoid this problem is to go beyond simply applying the default settings of a filter. Most professional-quality software applications allow the designer to adjust the properties of each filter. It is a good practice to experiment with the effects that can be created this way. The result will be that any textures you create not only will be unique but also may be better for your work than the standard effect created by the software's default settings.

Another good way to create original looking effects is to apply more than one filter to the same image. Keep in mind that the image can be dramatically altered by the order in which the filters are applied. For example, a designer could create an image and apply a filter that would make the picture look dry and cracked. If the designer then used a filter that added a rippled-water effect, it might look as if an old and peeling image were underwater. But if the filters are applied in the opposite order, it might be the surface of the water that appears cracked, not the original image.

In Figure 7.13, there are several versions of the same image. The first image is presented without filters. The second is presented with the standard default filter, and the next two show what the image looks like with several alterations to the filter's properties. The final image is the same as the others but has two different filters applied to it.

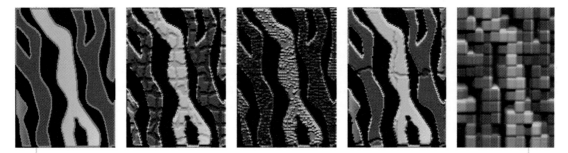

Figure 7.13

Texture Design Problems

Texture can be used in many different ways to enhance an image, but there are a few issues that a designer should avoid. What follows are a few of the problems a designer may encounter when adding textures to an illustration.

A Matter of Scale

If a designer is using texture to bring detail to an image or to make an area of a design more interesting, it is important to make certain that the texture is an appropriate size. For example, if an illustration contains a brick wall, the texture used to portray the bricks should be the correct scale for the wall. If the bricks are too large or too small, the use of texture to create detail will interfere with the effect the designer is trying to achieve.

In regard to image detail, issues of scale can also exist when applied to design areas. An example of this can be seen in the two images shown in Figure 7.14.

Figure 7.14

In Figure 7.14, the same background has been used, but the scale of the texture has been changed. In the first image, the squares used to create the texture are smaller, and the figure of the football player is easily distinguishable from the background. In the second image, the same texture has been used for the background, but the scale of the pattern is much larger. This change in scale causes portions of the football player to become lost in the pattern of the texture.

Too Much Information

Another problem that can arise when using texture occurs when there is too much visual information. This is closely related to the issue illustrated in Figure 7.14, but is not limited to the scale of the texture. For example, the background texture can be too busy, or the other objects in an illustration can become indistinguishable because of the pattern of the texture. This potential problem can be seen in Figure 7.15.

In Figure 7.15, there is almost too much to look at, and the viewer can become overwhelmed with the task of taking in all the visual information. Another problem illustrated in this image is a lack of distinction in that the objects that share the same hues as the background do not stand out very well.

A way to avoid this is to use colors that strongly contrast with those in the background texture. In Figure 7.15, the rail in the foreground stands out

Figure 7.15

because of the dramatic difference between the yellow and all the blues in the rest of the image.

As a designer, it is important to keep in mind that it may be difficult to find a color that contrasts with a background texture since textures are often made up of both light and dark areas. The best way to prevent this is to choose textures carefully and avoid the problem altogether.

Text and Texture

Another common issue related to the visual interference that can occur between an object in the foreground and a textured background is the placement of text over a texture. Because of the visual details that need to be present to distinguish one character from another, text does not work very well over a background that also has a

Figure 7.16

lot of texture. In situations like this, words and letters can become almost impossible to read. An example of this is shown in Figure 7.16.

In Figure 7.16, the text is difficult to read because it tends to blend into the background texture. Just like when a foreground image and a background texture conflict, this problem may be overcome by using a text color that contrasts with the background, but the text may still not be as clear as the designer would like. Generally, it is a good idea to avoid placing text over a texture. When this cannot be avoided, a designer should take special care to choose a font that can be read over the texture. By using a larger, bold font, the designer can also increase the readability of any words or characters placed over a texture.

SUMMARY

In this chapter, you learned about texture and some of its uses as an element of design. Also covered were several different methods to make texture in an image. The last section of this chapter dealt with using imaging software to create texture and several special issues in applying filters.

EXERCISES

1. Make a small drawing of something that has a good deal of texture. Look closely at how the texture actually appears. Draw the texture as realistically as you can using value. Good subjects are shoes with laces, the seams of a pair of blue jeans, or a cracker.

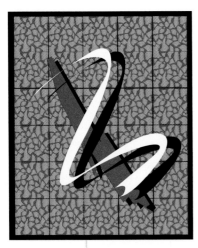

Figure 7.17

2. While using a good imaging program, experiment with altering the attributes of the default textures. Create textures that look like the surfaces of things, such as water, carpet, or the soil of an alien planet.

3. Create an interesting texture by repeating some small image in a pattern. An example of this is shown in Figure 7.17. In this illustration, the area on the right was created using an illustration program. It was then repeated to fill in the area of the main image to form a background texture.

REVIEW QUESTIONS

1. What is texture as it applies to design?

2. How can texture be used to show detail?

3. How can texture be used to simulate a surface?

4. What is one of the main visual elements that can be used to create texture?

5. What are filters in imaging software applications?

6. What are some common issues with filters that should be avoided?

7. How can the scale of a texture affect an image?

8. Can a flat pattern also be thought of as a texture?

_____
_____
_____
_____
_____
_____
_____
_____
_____
_____
_____
_____
_____
_____
_____
_____
_____
_____
_____
_____
_____
_____
_____
_____
_____
_____
_____
_____

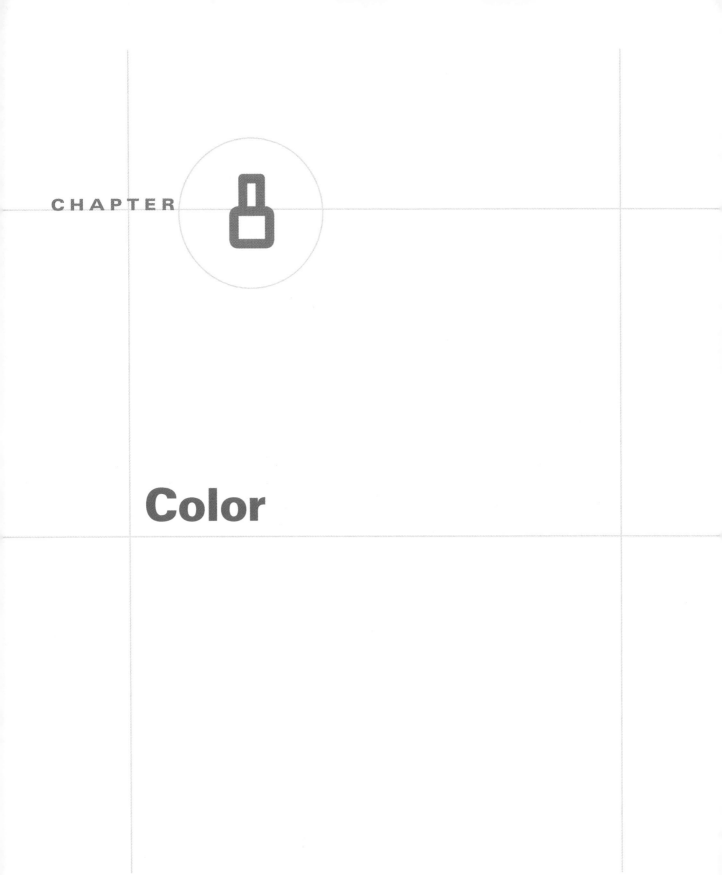

CHAPTER

Color

There is no other element of design as complex as color. Its use in visual communication is influenced by scientific principles, cultural symbol association, and even fashion. There is so much to know about color and so much yet to be understood about it that many artists and scientists have dedicated their careers to discovering the properties of color and how we perceive it.

Understanding Color

For many of the elements of design, after a designer learns the basic principles, the use of that element becomes almost a matter of intuition; the designer will use an element without spending too much analyzing how it works. The element of color is different. Although a designer can rely on some artistic instinct when it comes to color, it is rare that one can ever entirely get away from the necessity of understanding the principles that govern color. Knowledge of how color works is so critical to design decision making that it is nearly impossible to choose the correct color combinations without it. For new media projects, this is even more important because of specific color limitations under certain circumstances. As a new media artist, it is vital to know which colors can be used and how to use them.

Key Points

▸▸ Additive and Subtractive Color Systems
▸▸ Color Value
▸▸ Hue
▸▸ Color Intensity

What Is Color?

Few people think about color beyond how it looks. They simply look at something, such as a red ball, and know it is red. As a designer, it is important to understand the true nature of color in order to use it most effectively.

Why an object appears to be a certain color is based on the principles of physics. Color is how we perceive different wavelengths of light. A good way to understand this concept is to think of it in terms of sound. Like light, sound travels in waves. If a sound wave is long, we hear a low noise, such as the bass line in a song. If a sound wave is short, what we hear is a high-pitched note, such as the sound made by a flute. The pitch of a note is how we perceive different wavelengths of sound.

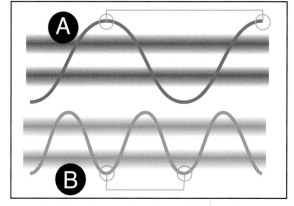

Figure 8.1

Light is a part of the electromagnetic spectrum and travels in waves, much like sound. But instead of seeing light as being high or low in pitch, we see different wavelengths of light as different colors (Figure 8.1). The electromagnetic spectrum extends far beyond the narrow band that we see. It includes infrared, ultraviolet, X-rays, radio waves, and many others. The wavelengths that we can see are referred to as the visible spectrum.

Figure 8.2 is an illustration of white light passing through a prism. The white circle in the upper-right corner represents a light source of white light.

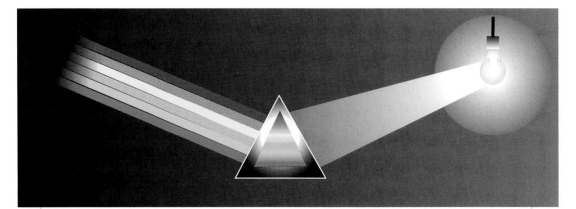

Figure 8.2

The white lines represent the light coming from the source and entering the prism. As the light passes through, the prism separates the light into different colors, each of which has a different wavelength.

Note that the separated colors are in a specific order. This order is due to the wavelength of each color. The bands of color start with the longest waveform of the color red and change with each shorter wavelength until finally the shortest wavelength of violet is separated from the rest.

It is no coincidence that this pattern of colors resembles a rainbow. This is because rainbows are created in the same way as depicted in Figure 8.2. When light from the sun passes through water particles in the atmosphere, the different wavelengths are separated, and this color banding appears as a rainbow.

What about Black and White?

Although black and white are commonly thought of as specific colors, they are really not a part of the color spectrum. We see the color white when all the colors of the spectrum are present in light. It is the mixing of the different wavelengths that our eyes and brain interpret as white. Black, on the other hand, is the absence of light. (This concept is covered in greater detail later in this chapter.)

What Is Covered in This Chapter

There are many things to know about color in order to get the most from it, so this chapter is broken down into several sections. Each section deals with color from a simplified approach and concentrates on the specific properties as they affect that approach. In many cases, a few of the properties will overlap from one topic to another, but they may be treated differently. As a designer, it is important to understand that using color a certain way does not mean that the other concepts do not apply. A good designer will keep all the different approaches to color in mind while creating a piece. These different approaches are merely a way to understand and manage a vast topic.

Two Different Color Methods

In design, there are two different models for producing color: additive color and subtractive color. Their names are derived from the way in which the color is produced.

Additive Color

Of the two methods, **additive color** is the most important to designers who work with any of the new media because this is the way that computer monitors and television screens produce color. In reality, it is the way in which colors are produced in the natural world, but it can also be the more difficult of the two to understand. Figure 8.3 is a simple illustration of how color is seen through the additive method.

In the additive color method, a light source produces specific wavelengths of light. A viewer sees the light, and the different wavelengths that make up the light are interpreted as colors. At first, this may seem easy enough to understand, but the process of producing colors through the additive method can be quite complex.

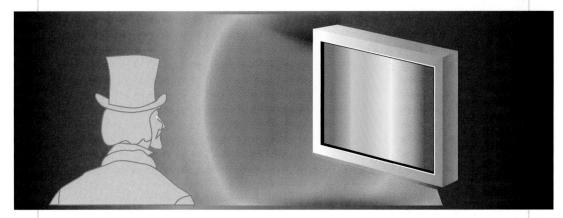

Figure 8.3

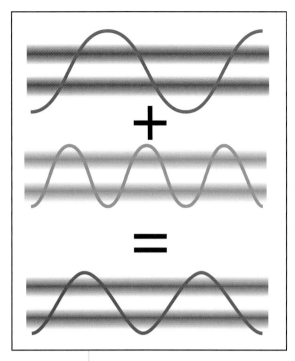

Figure 8.4

COMBINING WAVES

As stated in the introduction of this chapter, light is made up of different wavelengths of energy. The color of light is determined by its wavelength. But if two or more wavelengths are combined, a different color is produced. An illustration of this principle can be seen in Figure 8.4.

In Figure 8.4, there are three different waveforms that each produce a different color. The first waveform represents light that is the color red. This wave is by far the longest of the three. (Note that waves are measured by the distance from one peak to the next.) The second waveform represents blue light, and its wavelength is much shorter than the first. The bottom waveform represents what would happen if the two different colors of light were combined to produce magenta. Notice that the length of the wave in this example is now longer than the blue but shorter than the red. Here, the waves of the two different colors have been combined to form a completely new wave with a new wavelength that would be seen as a color different from the first two. If this new wave of light were passed through a prism, the waves would be separated again into their original colors.

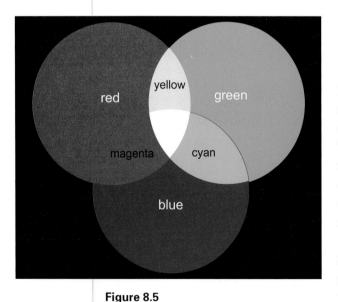

Figure 8.5

PRIMARY AND SECONDARY COLORS OF THE ADDITIVE METHOD

In the additive color method, different amounts of red, blue, and green light are mixed to create additional colors. The mixed light is seen by the eye and interpreted as a different color. Figure 8.5 is a representation of the different colors produced through the additive method.

To better understand this illustration, think of the red, blue, and green circles as light sources. The viewer sees the light coming from each circle as the color that it produces, but in the areas where the beams of colored light overlap, a secondary color is created. Red and green combine to make yellow. Green and blue combine to make cyan. Blue and red combine to make magenta. In the center of the three light sources, all the colors combine to make white.

In this illustration, the secondary colors are produced by mixing equal amounts of the primary colors in the form of light, but other colors can be made by varying the amount of light from each primary color.

In Figure 8.6, there are three squares. In each square is a rectangle that is a specific color. To the left of each rectangle are three colored bands that represent the amount of each primary colored light that is mixed to produce the specific color.

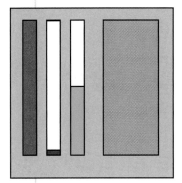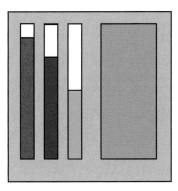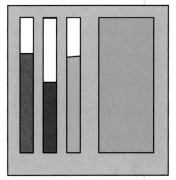

Figure 8.6

NEW MEDIA COLOR

Additive color is also known as RGB color (RGB stands for the primary colors red, green, and blue) and is the system that most new media imaging software uses to mix colors. RGB is also the main color system used for output to a monitor or video signal. For the new media designer, this color system will be the one that is used the most. Even if a design originates in a different color system, it will have to be converted to RGB for display on an electronic device.

Subtractive Color

The second color method is referred to as subtractive color. It relates more to how color is used in print or painting. Because these mediums are more common, the properties of subtractive color are more widely known. How subtractive color works is illustrated in Figure 8.7.

In Figure 8.7, the surface of the square has been painted in a way that makes it appear blue. The reason a viewer will see the square as the color blue

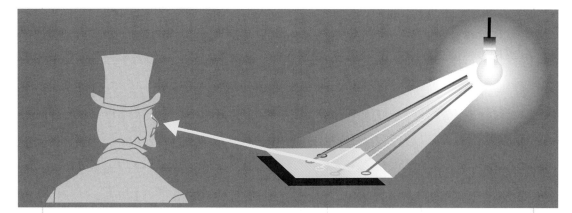

Figure 8.7

is because the paint absorbs all the other color wavelengths. In the image, light comes from a source that produces all the colors of the visible spectrum. If the viewer were to look at the light, it would appear white, though it is made up of all the colors that can be seen by humans. When the light strikes the surface of the square, only the blue light is reflected. The wavelengths of the other colors are absorbed by the paint. This is why it is called the *subtractive* method—because certain visible wavelengths are removed from the light before it is reflected.

If the square reflected all the light from the source, it would appear white. If the square absorbed all the light, it would appear black. In the subtractive method, the rule is that the darker a color, the more light is absorbed. This is why something painted black will become hot if left sitting in the sun. The black paint absorbs most of the energy from the light, and the energy makes the object warm to the touch.

SUBTRACTIVE PRIMARY COLORS

Because the subtractive color system produces different colors by removing specific wavelengths from white light instead of mixing them together, the primary colors are different from the red, blue, and green that are found in the additive method.

Figure 8.8 is what is known as a color wheel. Because this wheel

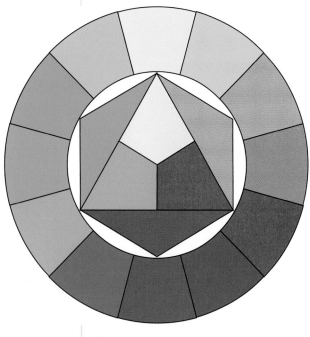

Figure 8.8

deals with the subtractive method, the primary colors are red, blue, and yellow. In reality, the primary colors of the subtractive method are very close to the secondary colors in the additive method (magenta, cyan, and yellow), but traditionally red and blue have been substituted for magenta and cyan.

Notice that midway between each of the primary colors along the wheel is another set of colors: purple, green, and orange. These are the secondary colors, which are made by mixing two pigments that would reflect both of the primary colors on either side of their location on the wheel. Red and blue make purple. Blue and yellow make green. Yellow and red make orange. On either side of the secondary colors are other bands of color that are called **tertiary colors.** These colors represent incremental steps between the secondary colors and a primary. They would be colors like red-orange or yellow-green.

PUTTING IT ALL TOGETHER

For hundreds of years, the subtractive color method and its associated color wheel served artists and designers well, even though it was not completely accurate when it came to mixing colors. Most of the problems in accuracy were overcome by trial and error or by relying on the experience of the designer, but as different forms of media became more popular, the need for an accurate color system became evident. Because of the apparent inconsistencies between the use of color in the additive and subtractive systems, a new color wheel has been developed (Figure 8.9). This wheel has 10 steps in place of the original 12. It includes the primary and secondary colors of the additive

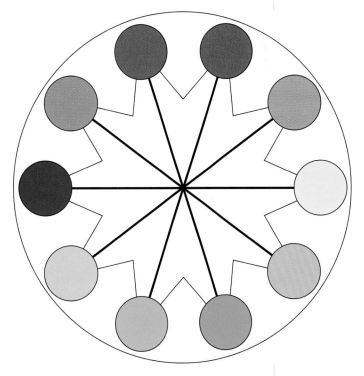

Figure 8.9

color system as well as those of the traditional, subtractive color wheel. Keep in mind that although this newer wheel is more accurate, it is still not perfect.

RGB AND CMYK

Although there are several different color systems that may be used by imaging software, most include choices of RGB, CMYK, or both. As stated previously, RGB stands for red, green, and blue and is the method used by computer monitors and other electronic equipment. For personal printing, this does not usually present a problem because many home and office color printers are set to read and print these colors. But in the case of most professional printing, CMYK is used. Like RGB, CMYK stands for the colors mixed to produce a hue: cyan, magenta, yellow, and black.

The first three colors of the CMYK system are actually the secondary colors from the additive color method and are also the true primary colors of the subtractive color method. If this seems a little confusing, simply remember that CMYK is what is needed for print. This may mean that it is necessary to convert images that you have created to CMYK if they will also be used in any print media. Be aware that although many computer imaging applications can convert the colors from RGB to CMYK easily, not all of them can. The way around this problem is to save your work as a file that is compatible with software that can perform the conversion and then import the file into that software and make the switch.

Color Properties

When designers discuss color, they often throw around a lot of different terms. Words such as **hue, tint,** and **shade** are used to refer to different colors but often are misused. Most of these terms describe specific attributes of a color's properties and are not simply another word for **color.** In this section, the main terms that refer to color and their properties are defined and explained.

Hue

The first property of a color is its *hue.* Hue refers to the major color that makes up the specific color being discussed. For example, the color pink has a red hue. Hues are generally limited to the primary and secondary colors from the color wheel. They are the same as the major colors from the visible color spectrum (red, orange, yellow, green, blue, and violet). Many people maintain that it is also acceptable to include brown in this list for purposes of discussion, even though it is actually made up of several hues. Just like pink, any variations of colors will fall under one of these main hues, although sometimes it may be difficult to decide which hue has dominance. For example, ask any person what the hue of aqua is, and some will say blue, while others will insist that it is green. Their opinion will depend mostly on the intensity (discussed later in this chapter) of the hues used in the version of aqua they are thinking about.

Value

Although an entire chapter of this book has been dedicated to the concept of *value,* a few specifics about how it affects color should be covered. As stated in Chapter 6, value can be thought of as the variation of light and dark applied to an area. When this variation involves color, a couple of different terms are used. The term *tint* is used when more white has been added to a color, and the term *shade* is used to refer to the addition of black to a color.

In Figure 8.10, there are three rows of squares. The center square in each row is the original color, and the squares to the left and to the right of that square are different values of shade and tint of the original color. The center row provides a gray scale for comparison. Notice how the addition of white or black affects the appearance of the color.

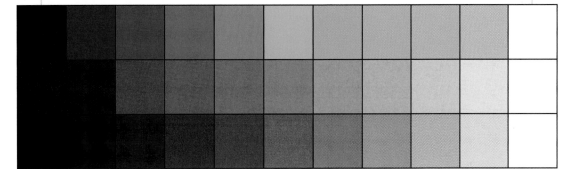

Figure 8.10

VALUE RELATIVITY AND PERCEPTION WITH COLOR

In Chapter 6, the concept of relativity was introduced. The rules of relativity apply to color in the same way they apply to an area that uses simple values of gray. If a darker color is placed next to a lighter color, the dark area will look darker, and the lighter area will appear lighter.

In addition, there is another effect that has to do with the perceived value of a specific color. For example, yellow usually appears as a much lighter color than most blues. Because blue appears darker, there may be more discernible tints (lighter values) of blue than can be made from yellow. This can have an impact on the color choices a designer makes.

In Figure 8.11, the two rows illustrate the way in which the perceived value of a color can have an effect on a design. The top row has five squares of blue, and the bottom row has five squares of yellow. Starting from the left, each square has had its tint increased by 20 percent from the square before it. The different values are clearly seen in the blue squares, but in the yellow row, even though the same differences in value have been applied, the squares are not as easily distinguished from each other.

Figure 8.11

The opposite can be true for colors that seem lighter; there may be more discernible shades (darker values) of a lighter color than a darker one. For the designer, there may be more or fewer variations of value that can be used effectively, depending on the color. This can influence the detail of an image or limit the number of color variations that can be incorporated into a piece.

Intensity

The third major property of color is **intensity** (also known as **saturation**) and refers to the level of pure color present. In Figure 8.12, there are three different flowers of the same hue and tint, but the level of intensity has been altered.

Figure 8.12

In Figure 8.12, the petals of the flower on the far left use the original color with almost full intensity. The color of the center flower has had the intensity of the main hue (red) decreased by half. The hue of the flower on the far right is still the same as the first, but the intensities of the other colors have been lowered. A colored bar at the bottom of the image shows each of the three different color intensities placed together for comparison.

About Color Names

Many people think that names like "Peacock Green" and "Aztec Gold" are universal terms that refer to specific colors. However, most color names, other than the basic hues, are pure fabrications on the part of the company that makes the pigment. Although the names are somewhat descriptive, their true purpose is to sell products. A house paint called "Golden Sunshine" will probably sell better than one named "Yellow #14." Because of this, color names are inconsistent and often change, usually depending on what sounds good to consumers. As a designer, be wary of color names and know that they are entirely transient.

SPECIAL ISSUES IN NEW MEDIA

GAMUT TROUBLE

Gamut is a term that refers to the entire spectrum of colors available for use in a specific medium; different mediums can have different gamut. As long as a designer uses only one form of presentation, there should be no serious problems. However, if a project includes several different mediums, some colors may be out of gamut for one or the other forms of presentation. To better understand this, see Figure 8.13.

Figure 8.13 is a simulated map of the different gamut that a new media artist may have to deal with. In this illustration, the larger, multicolored area represents the entire gamut of human vision. In other words, it has all the colors that a person can see. Its odd shape is due to our ability to perceive more subtle variations of

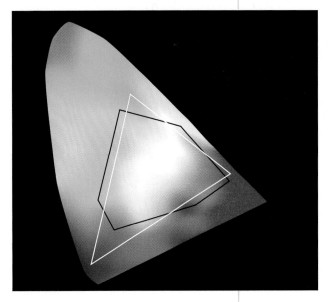

Figure 8.13

colors in some hues than in others. Earlier in this chapter, Figure 8.11 was used to illustrate this.

Inside the multicolored area is a white line that is roughly the shape of a triangle. This area is representative of all the colors that can be produced by a monitor, such as a computer screen or a television, and is the gamut used by new media artists. Note that this area does not include all the different colors that can be seen by humans, as certain colors cannot be reproduced using a monitor.

Inside the white outline is another, smaller area that is designated by a black line. This area is the gamut of color that can be produced using the CMYK color system of printing. It is even more limited than the RGB gamut used for new media. Because of this, a designer may have to take special care in choosing colors. Just because colors may have worked well on a monitor does not mean that they will when converted to print. Examples of this can be seen in any of this chapter's illustrations depicting additive color principles. Since this book uses the CMYK gamut to reproduce images, any colors found in the RGB or visual spectrum gamut cannot be accurately shown.

Colors on the Web

Another issue closely related to conflicts and limitations with different gamut arises when a designer creates work that is intended for the Web. Although computer monitors are capable of reproducing a vast number of colors and many Web browsers have High Color and True Color settings, the universal standard for the Web allows for only 216 different colors. (This number may vary, however, depending on the source. Some say that there are 256 colors available since that is what the technology allows, but the actual number depends on the browser used. For example, Internet Explorer limits the number of colors available to 212. The generally accepted number is the 216 given.)

This universal standard does not mean that there are only a few hundred colors that can be used on a Web site. (Even if this were true only a few years ago.) What it does mean is that although Web browsers can reproduce millions of colors, there are only 216 that will appear consistent from one system to the next. In other words, if you want a person viewing your Web site on a Macintosh computer, using a Netscape browser, to see the same color blue as a person running Microsoft Windows and Internet Explorer, then your chances will be much better if you stick to one of the 216 Web-safe colors.

Because of this limit in color consistency, it is important that designers developing graphics for the Web know about **Web-safe pallets.** A Web-safe pallet is a selection of colors that allows a designer to choose only those colors that are supported by Web browsers. Almost all the software that is used to create images for Web sites have a Web-safe pallet built into them. It is much better for a designer to use these colors than to have to convert them later, a process that can produce less-than-desirable results.

Dithering

The process that a browser uses when it attempts to reproduce a color outside of the Web gamut is called **dithering.** When a graphic undergoes dithering, the pixels that make up the graphic are assigned different colors that are within the Web gamut. This is done with the hope that the color of the pixels will seem to blend and create the intended color. This process is simulated in Figure 8.14.

Figure 8.14

In Figure 8.14, there are six squares. The top row of squares represent the actual colors, while the bottom row are simulations of the colors that would be produced on a Web site. In the bottom row, the squares on the left and right fall within the Web gamut, but the center square is a color that is not one of the 216 Web-safe colors. The center square illustrates how dithering uses Web-safe colors for each of the different pixels in an effort to produce the intended color. Although the appearance of dithering has been exaggerated in this illustration, the effect on Web graphics is similar.

Dithering is not always as much of a concern with images that appear photographic. In photos, there are already variations of color across the pixels, and the effect of dithering often is not as obvious. This is not true for areas of solid color. In graphics that use large areas of a single color, dithering can form a pattern of colored pixels that not only ruin the image but also come nowhere close to producing the intended color.

SUMMARY

This chapter provided information on both the additive and the subtractive method of color and introduced a few of the basic concepts that govern color. It also defined several terms that are used when referring to color and discussed a few of the issues related to color and new media.

1. Create an image that uses different values of the same hue.

2. Make an illustration using different intensities of the same hue.

3. Create a design using only *Web-safe* colors.

REVIEW QUESTIONS

1. What is the difference between the additive and the subtractive color method?

2. Which color method is used for new media?

3. What are the three primary colors of the additive color method?

4. What are the three secondary colors of the additive color method?

5. Which three colors are traditionally accepted as the primaries in the subtractive color method?

6. What is tint?

7. What is shade?

8. What is intensity?

9. What is a gamut?

10. What is a *Web-safe* pallet?

11. What is dithering?

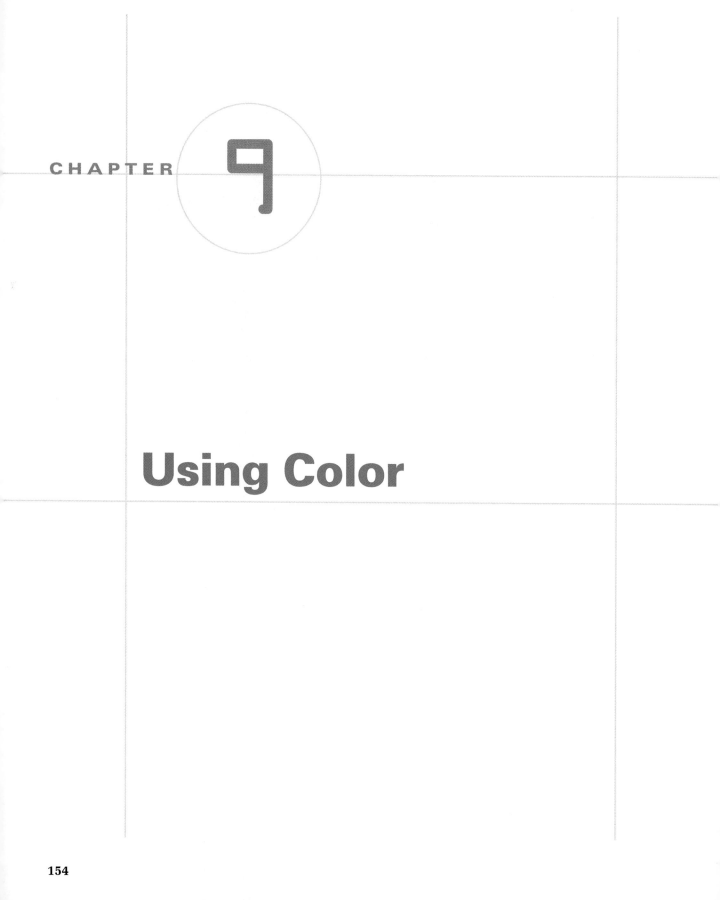

Using Color

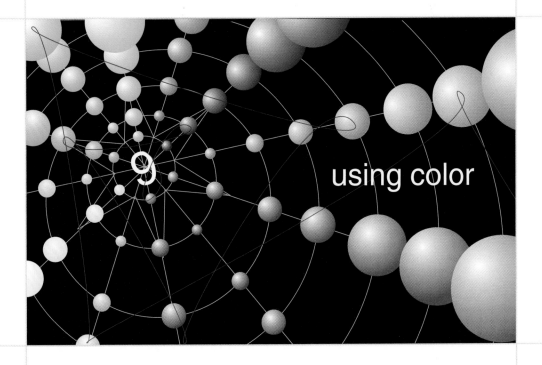

9 using color

When it comes to using color, choosing the basic hues for any design is usually the easiest part. If a designer is going to portray something accurately, it will likely be the same color as the object is in the real world. For example, if the artist is drawing a leaf from a tree, it will probably be green. Even if the drawing of the leaf needs to be blue because it is a part of a logo or because the entire design is to be done in blue, the basic hue has usually already been determined.

After the basic hue has been selected, the color choices begin to become more complex, especially when there needs to be multiple colors used together. Using the example of the leaf, if it is to be detailed enough to have several colors of green, which greens should be used? Or, if the leaf is going to be blue, which blue should be used for the stem and which blue should be used for the leaf itself? Regardless of whether a designer is using imaging software costing hundreds of dollars or a box of old paints, the choice of which colors to use beyond the basic hue can require some thought.

Making Informed Color Choices

Color combinations in design can require planning and thought because of the relative nature of color. Specific colors can appear significantly different because of the other colors around them, and different color combinations can have different effects on the entire design.

When it comes to combining colors in design, there are no hard rules. The designer is limited only by one's creativity and the intended message. Although the choices for color combinations seem to have no restrictions, there are a few principles that can guide a designer in making the most effective choices. This chapter outlines those principles.

Key Points

▸▸ **The Relativity of Color**
▸▸ **Complementary Colors**
▸▸ **Color Contrast**
▸▸ **Three-Color Combinations**
▸▸ **Color Temperatures**
▸▸ **Emotional Associations with Color**
▸▸ **Symbolic Associations with Color**

Alike but Different

Because there are so many properties that affect the way a color appears, colors of the same hue can look very different when placed next to each other.

In Figure 9.1, the same image is repeated four times. In this illustration, all the pictorial elements remain the same except for the color of the

Figure 9.1

background, the large circle, and the triangle. All three elements have either a yellow or an orange hue, but the properties of the colors used have been changed in each of the different images. Notice how the different combinations of yellow and orange dramatically change the overall look of each image. In some cases, the different elements seem to be completely different colors. What is actually a yellow may look green, or an orange may look brown when placed next to a color of the same hue that has different properties.

Color Relativity

This same effect is not limited to colors of the same hue but can also occur when different colors are used close to each other. This is illustrated in Figure 9.2.

Figure 9.2

In Figure 9.2, there are three separate images. In each, the colors of the crayon are the same, but the color of the background has been changed. In the first image, the background is yellow. Even though all the colors used for the crayon are of a yellow hue, they look green when compared to the bright yellow. In the next image, the background is blue, and here the crayon looks more yellow in color. In the final image, the background is a darker green. Here, the crayon appears to be a much lighter green. Although these perceived color shifts are subtle, they do have an influence on the appearance of the images.

In Figure 9.3, there are two images placed side by side. At first glance, the image on the left appears to be a target using the same colors of red and blue, but when the circles are moved and placed near the colors of the same hue, it is evident that there are actually four different colors used.

 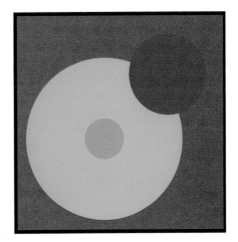

Figure 9.3

Color Unity

The principles of the relative nature of colors can be used in several different ways. One way is to use similar colors to bring unity to a design. Unity is covered in detail in Chapter 10, but for this section think of unity as making the different elements of a design appear to belong together through the use of color. An example of how color can be used to do this can be seen in Figure 9.4.

Figure 9.4

In Figure 9.4, there are a number of separate elements that have different characteristics. In this image, there are only two hues used, but because all the colors used for each of the elements are derived from one of these hues, the different elements look as if they belong together in the same image. If different hues were used for each of the elements, the illustration might not have the unity that it does.

Complementary Color

Another way to use the relative nature of color to enhance a design is to work with complementary colors. Complementary colors are those that are direct opposites on the color wheel. For example, the complementary color of blue is orange, and the complementary color of yellow is violet or purple.

When complementary colors are used next to each other, they appear brighter and livelier. In some extreme examples, complementary colors can produce an optical illusion in which the line that is formed between the two colors will seem to vibrate. By using complementary colors, a designer can make images that seem to glow or visually pop from the picture plane.

Figure 9.5

In Figure 9.5, the swimming man is made up of bright oranges, while the water and sky around him are different blues. Through the use of these complementary colors, the swimmer almost seems to glow. The contrast between the bright oranges and the blue also makes him stand out from the background. In this illustration, the bright green goggles also seem to visually pop from the surrounding area. This is because the oranges used for the swimmer contain a large amount of red, which is the complementary color of green.

The use of complementary color does not need to be as dramatic as presented in Figure 9.6. It can also be used more subtly to add a small amount of life to an image.

In Figure 9.6, there are two versions of the same drawing. The first uses colors that are based on the hue of violet for the shadows and darker areas of the image. Violet is a complementary color to yellow, which is the main hue for most of the image. This makes the crate and the area around it appear brighter. The second image is the same, but browns have been used where the violets were used in the first image. Although the second image may be more accurate in portraying the colors as they would appear, the drawing that uses complementary colors is more interesting to look at.

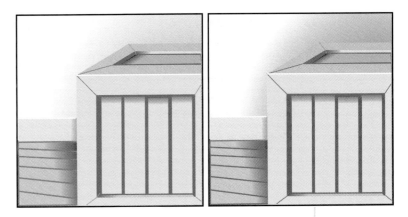

Figure 9.6

Rewriting History with Color

A few years ago, there was a huge controversy raging in the art community about the work of Michelangelo. This controversy arose when the Vatican decided to clean the ceiling of the Sistine Chapel and a few art scholars did not like the results.

The fresco on the ceiling of the Sistine Chapel is one of the most famous and most revered works of art in the world. It took Michelangelo four years to paint an area that is about 5,800 square feet, almost 70 feet above the chapel floor. The finished work was incredible, and it truly is one of the world's greatest art treasures.

For hundreds of years, generations of people have flocked to see this remarkable work. What they saw was a vast fresco painting that depicted various scenes from the Bible in a style that seemed dark and foreboding. The work contained about 300 individual human figures that looked heavy, as if they had been painted by a man who was more used to working in stone than colored pigment. Of course, this was true; Michelangelo had always insisted that he was a sculptor, not a painter. Regardless of the personal summation of his own painting skills, he had created a masterpiece.

The controversy over this magnificent work began as the cleaning started. It arose because as the huge fresco was cleaned, its appearance began to change.

The intent of the project was not only to preserve the work but also to bring back the original appearance of the painting. The technicians and experts who performed the cleaning insisted that they had taken extreme care. Before they would even touch a small area, it would be photographed, X-rayed, and documented. They studied each layer of the painting to determine what was a part of the original work and what had been added by others at a later time.

When they began, they first had to remove hundreds of years of soot from candles and torches that been used to illuminate the church long before the invention of electric light. In addition to the soot, there was at least one coat of varnish that had been applied hundreds of years earlier in an effort to preserve the work. Not only did they have to carefully remove this layer, but they also had to undo the work of several well-intentioned monks who had attempted to clean the ceiling with wine and bread a few hundred years earlier.

What was found under all the grime and bad attempts at preservation by earlier generations was a painting that was vibrant and full of color. The fresco was no longer the dark and somber ceiling that had been looked at by millions of people for all those years; it was now a work of brilliant color.

Over the years, more than a few scholars had written extensively on the way the ceiling had looked during their own lifetime. They had based much of their opinion on how the ceiling looked to them when they saw it and had followed the reasoning that, as a sculptor, Michelangelo would have naturally made his painting look heavy and dark. Many of these scholars had even staked their professional reputations on these ideas. The loud outcry from them was that the masterpiece was being ruined by the cleaning.

When it was pointed out that much of the apparent darkness had come from centuries of dirt and degradation, some even went so far as to say that the artist knew how the work would age and that he had intended for it to eventually become dark and somber. Others said that Michelangelo himself must have applied the heavy coat of varnish that was found regardless of what the records or scientific evidence said.

The debate raged on while the meticulous cleaning continued. It seemed that each issue of every art publication had at least one article or letter to the editor that took one side or the other. I found the arguments quite amusing since the public had not been admitted in to see the work and since a large number of the people who were making the most noise hadn't even seen the finished ceiling yet.

Finally, the finished work was opened for all to see, and the controversy reached its peak. That month, a prominent art magazine ran large, full-color, before and after pictures. I quickly scanned the images, and in an instant I knew the truth. What I saw were brilliantly painted images full of breathtaking color. These were completely different from the images that I had studied in my art history classes. But there was one thing that stuck out so much to my artist's eye that I had no doubts as to which side of the debate I would now be on.

In the pictures, I could clearly see that Michelangelo had used complementary colors in his painting. There was a figure wearing a yellow robe, but the folds of the cloth were rendered in its opposite color, a violet. In another place there was an orange cloth, but the area next to it was painted using a bright blue, again the complementary color. No skilled artist would use complementary colors in the same area of a painting unless they were trying to make the colors vibrant and add brilliance to them. To me, it made complete sense, especially if someone would have to look up 70 feet to view the fresco. The colors would have to be bright and would need to stand out for someone to be able to see them at that distance.

As I looked at the pictures in the magazine, I thought that the painting was even more beautiful than the version of the one I had seen before. For me, the controversy was over. It must have been over for most others, too, because the argument died out pretty quickly after people began to see the incredible work.

Contrasting Colors

The concept of contrast as it applies to design was covered in detail in Chapter 6, but what was not addressed was how contrast can affect the use of color. Even with color, the basic idea behind contrast is still the relationship between light and dark areas as design elements, but because there are so many color choices, a designer may be faced with additional decisions beyond those for an image that uses only black, white, and grays.

For example, if an artist has made an image with a bright red flower in the foreground and would like it to contrast with the background, choosing the background color could be fairly complex. Since the flower has color, the background could be either darker or lighter and still have contrast. Even after the decision to make the background lighter or darker has been made, the artist is still faced with choosing the color that will be used. If the artist wants all the colors of the image to be of a similar hue, then one could simply use a darker red. If the image needed to be bright, the designer might use a darker green since it is the complement of red. This combination could make the image of the flower vibrant. Beyond these two approaches, entirely different effects could be achieved by choosing colors such as blue or purple for the background.

The key to using contrast with color is to have a clear idea of how an image is to look. Once a designer knows what one is looking for in an image, a little experimentation can help determine the best contrasting colors to use. For a new media designer, this kind of experimentation can be used frequently since colors can be changed or adjusted fairly easily.

Combining Color

After a designer has chosen the main color to be used for an image, he or she may be faced with deciding what other colors might work well in the design. This figure gives examples of a few of the different combinations that produce color harmonies. These combinations are not written in stone but rather are a place for an artist to begin color selection.

For each example, the 12-step color wheel is shown beside a simple drawing that uses the specific color combination. To the right of each illustration is a brief explanation of the system used to select the harmonious colors.

Note that each of the 12 pie shapes includes different values for each hue. The lightest tints of a hue will be found near the center wedge while the darker shades are on the outside edge. Most of these examples deal with the major color of each part of the wheel, but the last two deal with tint and shade. The specific illustrations show this.

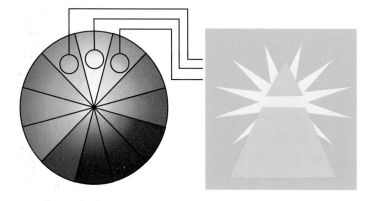

Analogous

This combination is made by choosing a specific color and using the colors that are on either side of the original hue.

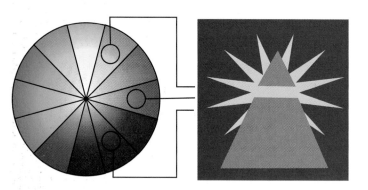

Alternate Analogous

This color selection method is similar to the first, but the second colors used are two steps of the color wheel away from the original.

Figure 9.7

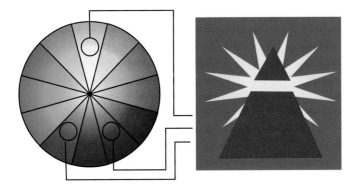

Split Complement

This combination begins by finding the the color that is opposite the original on the color wheel, then taking the colors on either side of that contrasting color.

Triad

This combination is made by selecting three colors that are equidistant around the color wheel. Each color will be four steps around the color wheel from the last one selected.

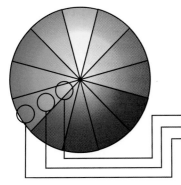

Monochromatic

This combination is made by using a tint and a shade of the original hue. This harmony only uses one hue, hence the name.

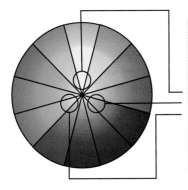

Value Variation

This combination is made by using any of the other methods, but instead of using the pure colors, the selections are made using tints or shades of the chosen colors.

Figure 9.7   *(continued)*

Looking at the Combinations

In Figure 9.8, there are several squares with different arrangements of colors that contrast. Although the background of each square is darker than the text, the color combinations produce completely different results. In some squares, the text is clear and easily readable; in others, the text almost seems to glow because of the background color used. This phenomenon can be even more pronounced when the different colors are produced by the additive light of a monitor. Because of this, new media artists must pay special attention to color contrast combinations. This is of the most concern when text is used. Text is read by clearly distinguishing the shape of the characters against a background. If the combination of background and text colors makes the outlines of the characters difficult to see, then the combination is a poor choice. As a general rule, it is good to have the most contrast possible between the two without using colors that make the text difficult to read.

Beyond the Science of Color

So far, a large amount of information has been given about the principles of colors and their properties. What has been presented is the foundation of color theory and how different hues can work together in design, but these

Figure 9.8

are not the only concepts that govern the use of color. A few other ideas that apply to the use of color have less to do with the scientific and more to do with the symbolic and with perception. The following section addresses a few of these concepts.

Temperature

One of the unique qualities of color has to do with the tendency of humans to perceive that certain hues have a temperature. Colors are often described as being either **warm** or **cool.** This is not to say that a certain hue will feel warmer than another but that they look as if they might.

Figure 9.9 is a pyramid shape made up of different-colored triangles. The triangles to the left are seen as cool colors, while the triangles to the right are considered warm colors. The triangles down the center of the pyramid have gradients of color that fade left to right. At the bottom of the illustration is a band that represents the colors of the visible spectrum of light and how the different waveforms fall into either warm or cool colors. In most cases regarding color temperature, the main hues can be divided into blues, violets, and greens as cool colors and into reds, oranges, and yellows as warm colors. A good way to remember which colors are cool and which are warm is to think of the colors that a designer might use to depict fire and the colors that might be used to portray water.

Figure 9.9

Although this way of remembering which colors are cool and which are warm usually works, it is not always true. This is because the appearance of colors can be manipulated by adjusting their properties or by placing other colors near them. In this way a color that is normally seen as cool can be made warm and vice versa. For example, a green (generally a cool color) can have enough yellow saturation added to it that it will look warm, especially if it is surrounded by other colors that will enhance the effect.

By now, it should be understood that the relative nature of colors can dramatically influence a piece. Color relativity can have an even greater impact on the use of warm and cool colors.

COLOR TEMPERATURE AND COMPLEMENTS

Earlier in this chapter, the concept of complementary colors was introduced. Notice that the complement hue of each color is one that is an opposite in regard to warm or cool. The complementary color of orange (a warm color) is blue (a cool color). This is the same for each of the different hues.

THE EFFECTS OF COLOR TEMPERATURE

What is important about warm and cool colors is the psychological effects that are associated with them. Cool colors are thought of as soothing and peaceful. It is believed that they actually have a relaxing quality. Warm colors, on the other hand, are seen as exciting and active. They grab a viewer's attention. Reds, oranges, and yellows are all used for warning signs because they stand out visually from the background and because humans tend to associate those colors with danger.

As a designer, it is easy to use these kinds of associations to solicit a particular response from a viewer. If an artist wants to attract attention, one will often use bright, warm colors. If a particular design would be better if it promoted a feeling of calmness, cool colors are usually the best choice.

Figure 9.10 uses warm colors to bring a sense of unity to the entire image as well as to make it more exciting. The warm colors also make the space seem more compact and dense. Although the woman may already appear dangerous and threatening because of her twisted posture and the fact that she is holding a pistol, the heavy use of the color red adds to this.

Figure 9.11 depicts part of an ancient battle scene using mostly cool colors. It is ironic that even though this image shows much more activity than Figure 9.10, it appears more calm through the use of cooler colors.

Figure 9.10

The right half of the image, where the chariot's horse is outlined against a black background, gives the illustration an element of mystery that is enhanced by the quietness of the colors chosen. Also, notice that the warmer colors in the image tend to seem cooler because of the other colors around them. A good example of this is found in the flesh tones. Compare the overall look of these colors with the similar colors found in Figure 9.10. Even though these colors are almost the same, their relative temperature appears different in each image because of the other colors surrounding them.

Figure 9.11

Color and Emotion

One of the more peculiar influences of color on design is its association with specific emotions or personality traits. Although these color associations are generally used as figures of speech, they are so well known that they can influence how a viewer sees a piece, whether the designer intends them to or not.

I feel sad and blue today.   *The man was a yellow coward.*
He was so angry he saw red.   *She was green with envy.*
His mood was a black one.

A few of these color associations are directly linked to something that can be observed. For example, the color white is often associated with fright. This is because someone's face may become drained of color if one is frightened. Or the color red may be associated with anger because, if a person is angry, one's face may turn red because of increased blood flow caused by emotional stress. Although these two examples may be obvious, there are other color associations that are far more obscure and their origins all but forgotten. For example, the phrase "green with envy" has its roots in a piece of Greek poetry from the seventh century B.C. In this poem, a Greek word meaning "pale" was used to describe the face of someone who is mourning a lost lover. The same Greek word has also been interpreted as "green." Because of this dual interpretation, the pale face of an envious person eventually became green with envy. The relative association with the color green and the emotion of jealousy is still taken for granted today, but the source of the association is almost 3,000 years old and originates from a

Figure 9.12

completely different language. Regardless of their origins, these kinds of color associations can cause a viewer to read an emotion into an illustration or design. Because of this, designers should be aware of the associations that can be made through colors and use them accordingly.

An example of color association with emotion can be seen in Figure 9.12. In this illustration, a figure is shown sitting alone in the lower-right corner. His head is down, and his posture is less than outgoing. Through the use of a pallet that is almost entirely blue, this image has a feeling of melancholy and depression. It is easy to imagine that the person in the image is sad and lonely.

Figure 9.13 is an illustration of nearly the same image as Figure 9.12 but with an entirely different pallet of colors. In this image, all the blues have been replaced by red hues. Because of the color choices, the narrative of this drawing seems to have changed. Now the figure looks angry. He is alone because he wants to be. He sits fuming with emotions that are hostile instead of the depression that is perceived in Figure 9.12.

Figure 9.13

Symbolic Color

Colors often have symbolic meanings or associations that can be used by a designer to communicate a message. A common example of this is the use of red, white, and blue (the colors of the American flag) to promote an association with patriotism. This use of color can be a powerful design tool, but a designer must exercise caution when using it because color symbolism is culture dependent. That is, a symbolic color association in one culture may be entirely different in another culture. For example, the color white is associated with purity and virtue in many Western societies, and it is because of this symbolism that white is the traditional color for a bridal gown. In India, however, the color white is symbolic for mourning and would not be appropriate for a wedding. In that culture, wearing white would be the same as wearing black in the West.

If there were only a few specific color associations, such as black or white, for the symbolic color of mourning, it might not be too difficult for a designer to avoid problems, but the symbolic color associations seem to change in nearly every geographic location. Sticking with the example of the symbolic color for mourning, black and white are not the only colors used. In Turkey, the color for mourning is violet, in Burma it is yellow, and in parts of Africa it is brown.

Before the popularity of the Internet, this was not a major issue, but because of increased cross-cultural communication, the associated symbolism of color can become a problem, especially if a project is intended to be viewed by people from different cultures.

Imagine that you are creating a Web site that you want to be bright and cheerful. You choose a pallet that is yellow because you think that it looks warm and friendly. But to someone from another culture, your color choices are viewed the same way as someone from the West might see a Web site with a black pallet.

The key to using symbolic color (or avoiding negative associations) is to know your audience. Who will see your design, and what are their symbolic associations with specific colors? It is also important to know that color association is not limited to cultures from different geographic locations but that colors can be symbolic to certain groups within the same culture. An example of this is the color red in the financial world. In reference to finances, "in the red" means that there is more money owed than a person or company has. Because of this, red would be a poor color choice for a new media presentation made by a bank or other financial institution. The designer might not even be aware of such associations.

SUMMARY

This chapter covered the use of color in design and built on the principles of color introduced in Chapter 8. Several different concepts were explained, such as the relativity of color and how the appearance of color can be manipulated through the use of other colors. Other topics covered were contrast with color and the use of color combinations. This chapter ended with a section that addressed a few of the mental associations made with color (temperature, emotion, and symbolism) and how they could be used by designers.

Figure 9.14

1. Create a detailed image using only colors that all share the same hue, such as all reds or all greens.

2. Make an image the uses complementary colors. For an example, see Figure 9.14.

3. Make an illustration that uses complementary colors for shadows and darker areas. For an example, see Figure 9.6.

4. Create a simple illustration that uses the three color combinations. Make the same image several times but use different combinations.

5. Make an illustration that is enhanced through color associations, such as emotion or symbolism.

6. Using only warm or cool colors, create an image that is enhanced by color temperature.

7. Make a simple image that utilizes color relativity by using colors that will appear different when placed next to each other. For example, use a yellow but make it look green through the use of other colors in the image.

REVIEW QUESTIONS

1. What are complementary colors?

2. What are contrasting colors?

3. What are the three main hues that are classified as cool colors?

4. What three hues are classified as warm colors?

5. What are contrasting colors?

6. Name several emotions that are associated with specific colors.

7. Name one symbolic color from your own culture.

8. Name a color that has a different symbolic association in two different cultures.

THREE

Previous chapters dealt with the most basic of the visual elements used in design. Topics such as line, space, and color were introduced, defined, and explained. These basic elements are the building blocks of design, but their use does not stop with simply understanding and applying them individually. Much like atoms that bond to form molecules, the elements of design can be combined to create even more complex design components with impressive results.

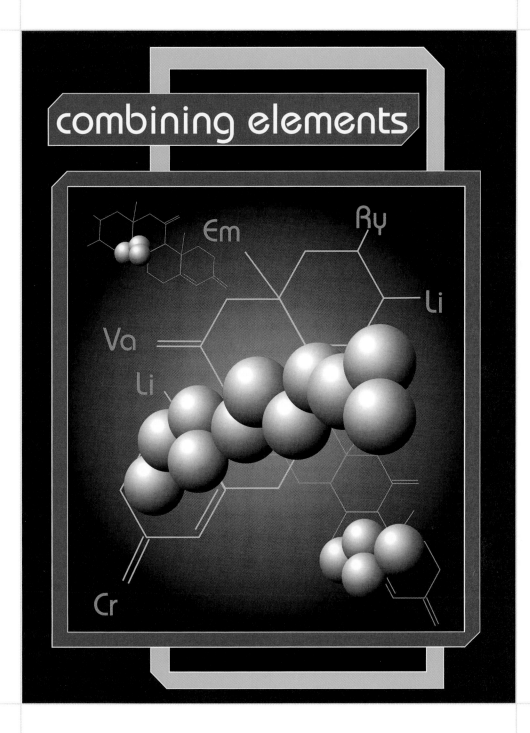

combining elements

CHAPTER **10**

Composition and Layout

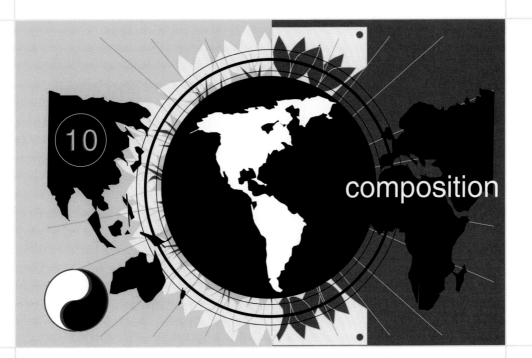

10

composition

Of all the elements of design covered in this text, *composition* is arguably the most important. In its simplest definition, composition is the use of design to make all the different elements of a piece work as a whole. In essence, it is the glue that holds all the other elements together. Without the effective use of composition, all the other parts of a project are greatly diminished and, at best, exist as little more than separate units that have been lumped together.

To a large extent, composition is developed through the use of two different concepts—unity and layout—as well as many other elements of design. In fact, it is the other elements of design that are used to create effective unity and layout. Because of this, much of what is introduced in this chapter builds on design concepts that have been covered in previous chapters. It is expected that readers will have at least a fundamental understanding of these earlier topics.

Breaking Down Composition

In order to provide a more solid explanation of a design element that is often difficult to define, this text deals with composition by breaking down the subject into two of its major components (unity and layout) and exploring those elements in detail.

Unity

In most cases, a design needs a sense of **unity** for it to work well. That is, all the different parts of the design should look as if they belong together. If this is accomplished, the entire design will be viewed as a complete whole, with all the elements working together. If a design or image does not have unity, the different elements of the design can seem out of place, the result of which can make the viewer bored, disinterested, or even confused.

CREATING UNITY

Nearly any of the visual elements that were introduced in previous chapters can aid in bringing unity to a design. One way to accomplish this is to use the different elements in a way that is consistent throughout the entire piece. For an example of this, see Figure 10.1.

Figure 10.1 has a sense of unity because the style of the drawing and the treatment of the different elements are similar throughout the entire piece. (For more on style, see Chapter 16.) For example, in this drawing the different surfaces of the face and the armor have the same mix of solid color areas and color gradients. Also, the entire piece is rendered in a consistent style (one that is commonly found in comic book illustrations), and the line quality is the same throughout the drawing.

Figure 10.1

Figure 10.2 is almost the same as Figure 10.1, except a few of the unifying qualities have been removed. For example, the color treatment and

Figure 10.2

rendering style of the man's armor is now different from his face and helmet. In this version of the drawing, the surface areas of the armor have less detail and value. Thus, these areas appear flat in comparison to the face and helmet. If someone were to pay close attention, it might even look as if the head and the body of the figure came from two different drawings. Because of the inconsistencies, the unity of the drawing suffers, and the illustration does not appear to be as well crafted.

CONCEPTUAL UNITY VERSUS VISUAL UNITY

Just because the parts of a design have some connection does not mean that a piece has visual unity. For an example of this, see Figure 10.3. This image is full of various references to the number 5. A few of the different elements are the numeral 5, a clock face that is set at five o'clock, and, in the upper-right corner, five dots that are arranged as they would be found on a die.

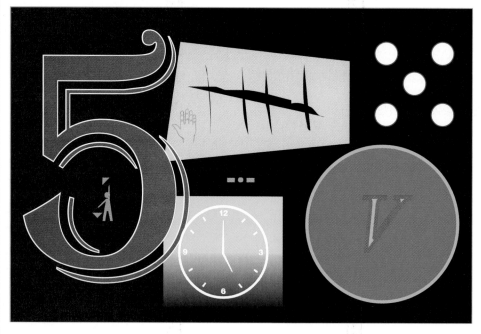

Figure 10.3

Although the references to the number 5 form a strong association between each part of the illustration, none of these connections are visual. Connection of the different elements of an image through meaning or reference is called **conceptual unity**. It is true that conceptual unity can play a large role in any design, but for a graphic to be completely effective, the different elements must work together visually.

Figure 10.4 has 16 different elements; some are letters of the alphabet, and some are simple drawings. Because all are similar in treatment, this example has a sense of visual unity. Some of the techniques that have been used to bring the different elements together are similar

Figure 10.4

size, similar color choices, and a series of uniformly arranged squares placed behind each element. The specific visual devices that have been used to promote visual unity in Figure 10.4 are space (the arrangement of the squares and the placement of each in the square), shape (each object has one of four shapes behind it that are repeated throughout the drawing), and line (all the separate elements of the piece have a similar line quality).

THE BIGGER PICTURE

So far, the examples given to define the concept of unity have been self-contained images, and any explanations have specifically addressed design elements that went into those illustrations. But where unity is really needed is in new media projects that are made up of several different components.

Part of the designer's job is to make all the different elements of a project visually work together. To accomplish this, it is often helpful to think of the entire project as a single design and to treat the separate elements as if they were all part of the same image. If a designer approaches a project in this manner, the same methods for creating unity can be used when designing the individual parts. An example of this can be seen in Figure 10.5.

In Figure 10.5, there are two illustrations of interfaces for the same game. The first image has all the necessary components, but the various parts do not have a consistent appearance. In fact, many of the parts do not look as if they belong to the same game.

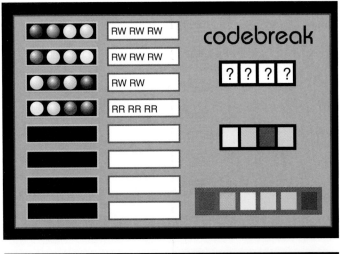

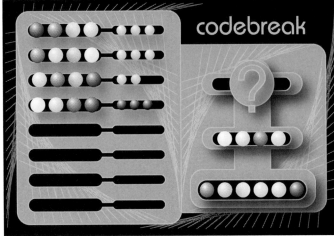

Figure 10.5

The second image in Figure 10.5 has the same components, but the treatment of the different elements is similar throughout the entire piece. Color, line, and shape have all been used to give the interface unity.

BEYOND THE SINGLE SCREEN

When it comes to new media design, unity is not something that is limited to a scene or a page; rather, it should exist throughout an entire project. Unity with the different parts of a project will make the piece seem complete, as if all the parts belong together. It can also help orient the viewer. Imagine a Web site with a large number of links where every page looked different. Visitors might not know if what they were seeing was a page on the original site or if they had followed a link to some other site.

UNITY TOOLS: USING THE ELEMENTS OF DESIGN

The following is a brief list of ways that the different elements of design can be used to create visual unity in a single piece. For more details, see the specific chapters that cover each element.

- *Space:* Unity can be created by grouping objects together in space or by arranging them in a pattern.
- *Line:* Similar line quality used on different elements can bring unity to an image. Line used as direction devices can also bring different elements together.
- *Shape:* As stated in Chapter 5, similar shapes will be visually grouped together by a viewer. One way to accomplish this is to arrange the different objects in a design so that they form groups of similar shapes. For example, an illustration that contains several objects could be arranged so that the

objects are grouped into rough triangles. The repetition of the triangle throughout the image can be used to cause the viewer to associate the objects with each other.

- *Value:* By using similar values throughout an entire image, a designer can achieve unity. Use of a consistent light source can also bring unity to the different elements in a design.
- *Texture:* Textures that appear similar can create unity in an image.
- *Color:* By choosing a pallet with similar hues, an artist can bring unity to the separate elements of a piece. The same thing can be accomplished by using the same tint, shade, or intensity of the different colors in a design.

Composition and Layout

While it can be said that visual unity brings the elements of a design together through technique, the layout of a design has even more effect on composition. An easy way to think of layout is as the arrangement of all the elements of a design in the space of the piece.

For there to be effective composition, the layout should enhance a piece by making all the separate elements work together in a way that surpasses a mere collection of different components. In other words, composition should be used to create a whole that is greater than the sum of its parts.

EVOLUTION OF A LAYOUT

To better explain composition in design, this section shows the process of layout by using an imaginary project as a step-by-step example. The project is a CD-ROM presentation of several narrative stories, but in this example we will deal with only one of the Introduction pages.

Figure 10.6 is an illustration of the content that will be included on the Introduction page. There are images of a child riding in an aircraft, a drawing of the aircraft, and a sphere that is a representation of the sun. In addition to these graphics, there is also a title and three navigation buttons. These elements already have a degree of unity through color. What remains is to arrange them in a way that is visually pleasing and makes the presentation easy to use.

Figure 10.7 shows the first step in the layout process. The designer has arranged the images in a diagonal line across the

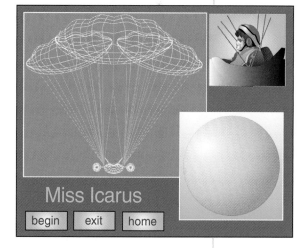

Figure 10.6

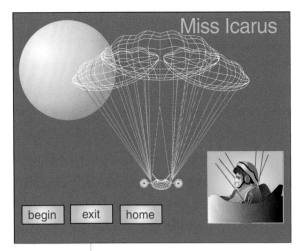

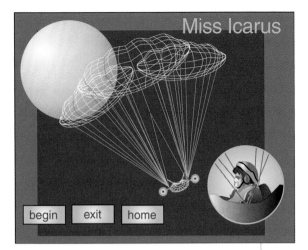

Figure 10.7   **Figure 10.8**

space in a way that makes their placement appear less random and more balanced. This line will lead the viewer's eye from the top to the lower part of the page. In addition to placing the images in a line, the designer has also removed the backgrounds and borders of two images to help make them appear less separated in the design. The title has also been moved to the top of the page.

In Figure 10.8, there are several dramatic changes. The first of these changes has been made to the drawing of the aircraft. By rotating the aircraft, the design appears to be more dynamic, as if something is happening. The new angle of the aircraft also reinforces the direction of the implied line formed by the other images.

Another change has been to the image of the child riding in the aircraft. This image has been made into a circle instead of a square. The circle echoes the shape of the sun and makes the different elements seem more uniform. In

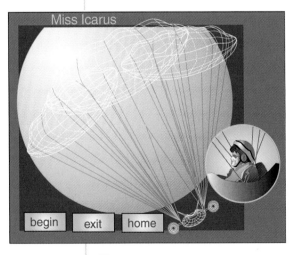

Figure 10.9

addition, a large square has been added behind the separate images. This square is an example of using a shape to group different elements together.

Figure 10.9 illustrates the next step in the layout process. In the previous arrangements, the separate images were given the same amount of importance by keeping them roughly the same size, but in this step the designer has increased the size of the aircraft and the sun. Because of space limitations, the two enlarged images were stacked. Using multiple layers of graphics makes the design appear more dense and full.

The other change in this step was to move the title from the right side to the left side, where the viewer will be likely to see it first. It was also shrunk to fit in the available space.

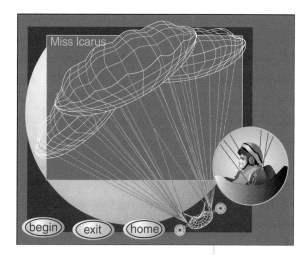

Although these modifications to the layout have made the piece more interesting, they have also created a few new problems, several of which are solved in the next step, shown in Figure 10.10.

In this step, the designer identified some problem areas brought about by the last changes made. The first was a shift in the color scheme of the entire piece.

Figure 10.10

Enlarging the drawing of the sun made the yellows and oranges dominant and overpowered the other colors. In addition, the bright yellow did not provide enough contrast to make the drawing of the aircraft clear and the placement of the aircraft looked as if it was about to crash into the sun. Yet another problem was with the title. There was little room to place it anywhere that was not over the sun, where it would be nearly invisible.

To solve these issues, the designer created another colored square in a layer between the sun and the aircraft. This cut down on the amount of area in the layout that was yellow and orange and provided the contrast that was needed to make the details of the aircraft more visible. It also separated the aircraft from the sun and opened up an area to place the title.

With these problems solved, the designer turned to the navigation buttons. These needed to stand out so that they could be easily identified as controls, but they also needed to fit in with the rest of the design. As they were, they looked like blue rectangles that were just stuck near the bottom of the page.

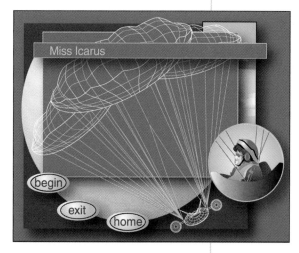

To give the navigation buttons more unity, the designer changed them to ovals that simulated the shape of the balloons on the aircraft and also fit better with the other circle shapes in the design. To make the buttons distinct from the other graphics, a wide border was added.

At this point in the layout process, all that remained was to add a few finishing touches. Figure 10.11 shows those additions.

Still unhappy with the placement of the buttons, the designer decided to place

Figure 10.11

them in a curve along the bottom edge of the sun. This accomplished several things, such as integrating the buttons with the other elements of the design and creating an implied line that brought the viewer's eye back to the main areas of the page.

In addition, a rectangle that was filled with a texture that emulated the sky was placed on the right side of the page. This rectangle gave balance to the entire layout and brought more light blue into the design. The presence of the rectangle also adds another layer of depth to the image.

The final adjustment was to the title. It was placed in a rectangular bar across the uppermost layer in the layout. This separated the title from all the other graphics, but not in a way that visually overpowered the other elements.

SPECIAL ISSUES IN NEW MEDIA

LAYOUT TRADITIONS

Many of a viewer's expectations for layout are based on the traditions of printed material. Although new media projects are not limited to these conventions, they can be useful tools to enhance the viewer's experience. This section explores a few layout traditions and how to break away from them in new media projects.

The Influence of Print on Layout

The written word and its method of presentation have greatly influenced the arrangement of visual composition. In the West, people have learned to look for certain layout standards to organize and prioritize information. The following is a list of a few of these standards, with some suggestions on how they might be used in a new media project:

- *Scanning from left to right and from top to bottom:* Because this is the pattern that is used to read, it has become a standard way for a viewer to examine any visual presentation. By arranging elements with this convention in mind, a designer can have some control over the order in which a viewer encounters a screen's content.
- *Looking for a title near the top:* Traditionally, subjects are given a title that is placed in a dominant position, near the top of the page. The exception to this rule is when the title exists on a page separated from the rest of the text. In this case, it is often placed near the center of the page. These are two very good areas for placing titles and any elements that would be used to identify the content.

- *Larger elements are more important:* Items that have more significance are often larger so that they attract the attention of the viewer. In new media projects, the more important content can be made larger than the other elements or given more space.
- *Captions will be near the images they describe:* Although this may not always be true, especially in magazine publications where layout space can be limited, it is an accepted convention. If captions are used with images in new media projects, the designer does not have the luxury of placing them on another page. Each screen should be a self-contained unit.
- *Items near the top or on upper layers will be more important:* In print, an element's placement in the layout is often used to designate significance. This convention can be used in new media projects in the same way.
- *References to additional information, such as "continue" or "more," will be at the bottom of the information:* This is used to let the reader know that the information continues beyond the current page. Thus, a new media designer can place controls at the bottom of any content that may be continued on another page.

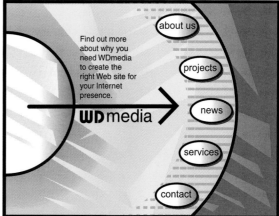

Figure 10.12 On this home page, the different bits of information have been arranged in a composition that is contrary to many of the conventions of traditional layout. The title is below the text, and even though the navigation buttons are the most important part of the page, they have been placed to the right of the content.

Viewers will already be familiar with each of these methods for organizing information in a layout, so these methods can be useful to new media designers. This does not mean that these rules cannot be broken or at least bent a little. Figure 10.12 is an example of how a design can still work while ignoring many of the traditional layout conventions.

Working with the Grid

Another print design technique that can also be useful when it comes to developing the layout of a new media project is the grid. The grid is a series of intersecting lines that are used to align the elements on a page. This approach is closely related to using implied line to create a uniform and balanced layout.

There are several ways in which grids can be used, depending on the software a designer is working with. In some applications, the software has

Figure 10.13 The first image illustrates the use of the grid to align the graphics on the page. The image shows the finished layout with the grid removed.

the ability to produce a visible grid that can be used as a guide to place the different content in the work area. When the work is saved in the final format, the grid will be automatically removed from the graphic. Figure 10.13 shows an example of this.

Another way to use the grid as a design technique is to create a series of guidelines that aid in the alignment of different elements within a layout. Some imaging software applications have guide features built in. Like the full grids in other applications, the guides will be automatically removed when the graphic is saved in its final format. If the software that a designer is working with does not have any sort of grid features, it is a simple matter to draw lines that will act as guides. The lines can be removed manually before the final version is saved. Figure 10.14 shows two images. The first is an illustration of the finished layout, and the second shows the guidelines still in place.

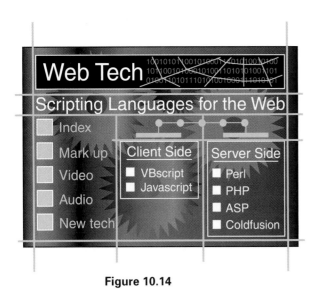

Figure 10.14

Nongrid Layouts

As mentioned earlier, the grid is a device that has been extensively used in print, but new media projects need not be limited to this layout approach. Because of interactivity, new media projects can use layouts that rely on other conventions. Figure 10.15 is an example of a design that does not use a grid for its interface layout.

Figure 10.15

Figure 10.15 shows an interface design for a children's game. In this example, the layout used is an illustration of a hall with links to other content provided through parts of the drawing; by clicking on objects or open doorways, the viewer is taken to other parts of the project. Instead of a design model that is derived from page layout, this interface simulates the exploration of a tomb.

The Metaphor

In literature, a metaphor is the use of a phrase to form an implied comparison, such as "all the world is a stage." In many cases, the nongrid design uses a visual metaphor to communicate the various functions of an interface. Examples of this are interfaces that simulate a television and a remote control to view various "channels" or an office setting that contains images of different equipment such that, for example, clicking on a filing cabinet accesses stored files. The advantage to using common metaphors is that the viewer will often already understand the function of the elements in the layout.

Composition Concepts: All for One and One for All

The goal of a designer should be to create an image that has no extra or unnecessary elements. Of the elements present, each should enhance the others as well as the overall design of the entire work.

As was illustrated in the section "Evolution of a Layout," the use of composition in design can be something that develops as a layout is created. Although many of the major decisions about composition can be made before a designer even begins to work on a piece, adjustments to the different visual elements may need to occur along the way.

There is a danger that many designers encounter when they develop an attachment to a specific element of a design, especially after it has ceased to work in the composition: the designer's fondness for some element may stand in the way of its removal. An example of this might be a certain part of an image that was originally conceived for the design but, as the work developed, didn't seem to fit anymore. If the designer likes the element so much that he or she cannot bear to change or lose it altogether, the whole image may suffer. When it comes to good composition, every element of a design should be able to pass the following test:

1. Does the element fit with the rest of the piece?

2. Does the element enhance the other parts of the design?

3. Does the element help move the viewer's eye around the entire piece?

4. Does the element make the design more interesting?

If you apply this test to any part of a design and come up with a negative answer to any of the questions, it is probable that the element should be altered to better fit the composition or maybe removed altogether.

Composition and Complex Design Elements

In the rest of this text, many of the combinations that are covered deal specifically with composition. The manner in which they are addressed will be in terms of how they affect a design, but the concept of composition will constantly be in the background. Always try to keep in mind how each of the complex combinations covered in the rest of this text apply to composition and unity.

SUMMARY

This chapter introduced the concept of composition as well as two elements of design that play a major part in composition: unity and layout. It also explained the importance of unity and presented several methods for creating unity through the use of design elements. A step-by-step example was given of a layout's development, and common layout conventions were explained. This chapter also covered how to judge if specific elements truly belong as a part of any composition.

REVIEW QUESTIONS

1. What is composition as it applies to design?

2. What is unity as it applies to design?

3. How can other elements of design be used to create unity? Give an example.

4. What is the layout of a design?

5. How can the grid be used as a layout tool?

6. How do a grid layout and a nongrid layout differ?

7. Give an example of a metaphor used in a nongrid layout.

CHAPTER 11

Balance

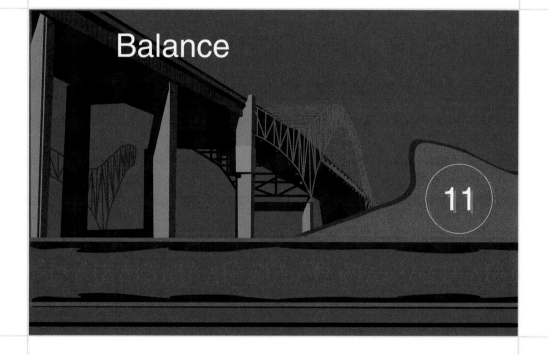

Balance

11

Visual balance is another element of design that can be used in developing composition. Balance, as it refers to design, is about the parts of an image and how they compare to the other elements of the same image. A way to think of balance is by assigning an imaginary weight to the different elements of a design and thinking of the entire piece as a set of balance scales on which each element is weighed against the others. If one part of an image overpowers the rest of a design, it can be said that the image does not have balance. An image that does not have good balance will not seem to have unity, and the design may even make the viewer uncomfortable.

All elements of design, such as size, color, and even the arrangement of objects in the space of an image, can have an influence on the balance of piece. These different properties can add or subtract imagined weight to specific parts of a design.

Balance Concepts Covered

Balance can be affected by several factors, but it mainly comes down to the location of the point of focus, the arrangement of the elements, and the visual weight that those elements have. The rest of this chapter addresses these factors individually.

Weight of Elements by Size and Groups

One of the most obvious elements that can have an effect on the balance of an image is the size of objects in that image; objects that are larger seem to have more visual weight than smaller objects. This is attributed in part to the fact that the larger objects take up more of the space in a design. Closely related to this is the visual weight attributed to objects that are grouped together. In this case, the group of objects seems to have a combined weight and again take up more space in the design layout. For several examples of these design concepts, look at Figure 11.1.

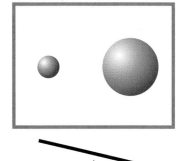
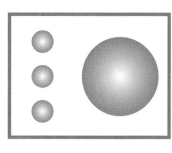
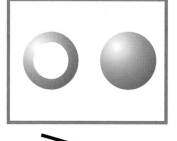

Figure 11.1

In Figure 11.1, there are three illustrations with a small image of a balance scale below each. In the image on the left, there are two spheres, one of which is much larger than the other. It is easy to see that the difference in size would make this image appear unbalanced. The scale at the bottom of the image tips toward the larger sphere to illustrate this.

In the center image, there are three smaller spheres and one very large sphere. As visual elements, the three smaller spheres grouped together seem to have the same weight as the larger sphere. This makes the image appear balanced.

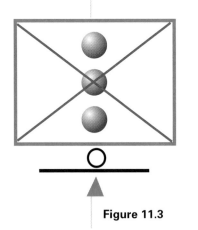

Figure 11.2 On this Web page layout, the buttons in the lower-left corner are visually grouped together. They seem to balance the drawing in the upper-right corner of the same composition.

In the image on the right, the two spheres are the same size, but the center of the one on the left contains empty space. Because of the negative space, the sphere on the right appears to be visually heavier (see also Figure 11.2).

The Point of Focus

Most images have a point of focus, or the area of a design that attracts the most attention. A good design will often have implied lines and other elements that lead the viewer's eye to the point of focus. The point of focus is also usually the place in an image around which all the other elements are balanced. If the area of a design is thought of as the scale on which the different elements are weighed, the point of focus becomes the fulcrum.

Figure 11.3 shows three illustrations of how the focal point of an image becomes the center of balance. In the image on the left, the focal point is in the center of the image space. The three spheres are arranged so that either side of the focal point is the same and appears balanced. This sort of composition is referred to as **symmetrical** and is characterized by a design that is roughly similar on both halves of an image.

In the middle illustration, the point of focus is found in the lower-right corner. Part of what makes this area the point of focus is the single larger

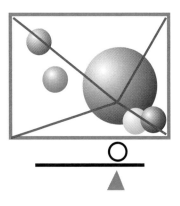
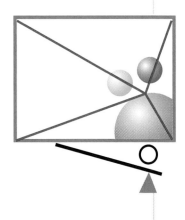

Figure 11.3

sphere placed among the smaller ones. Because the larger sphere is different from the other elements, it will attract the viewer's attention. This image also has balance, but how balance is achieved here is a little more complex than in the first image. A way to understand how the composition works in this illustration is to think of it like a beam that has been balanced on a fulcrum. If one part of the beam is longer, it will require less weight to balance a heavier object on the shorter end. In this image, the negative space that separates the smaller spheres on the right side performs the same as a longer beam would.

It is obvious that the illustration on the right does not have balance. In this image, the focal point is also in the lower-right corner, but there are no visual elements that counterbalance the left side of the design.

Using Lack of Balance to Create Tension

As previously mentioned, a lack of balance in an image can be disconcerting to the viewer, but a designer can use this to one's advantage. If your goal for a certain design is to make the viewer uncomfortable or to create a sense of tension, then making an unbalanced image might provide the exact sort of effect you are looking for.

Figure 11.4 is the opening shot of a media presentation. In this layout, the drawing of the mask is placed on the right side of the screen. The large amount of negative space on the left creates a sense of tension. It looks awkward, as if something is missing; the viewer expects something like text or another image to eventually appear in this open area. (In this presentation, the title fades into view and gives the layout balance before moving on to the next screen.) A new media designer could use this kind of tension to direct a viewer's attention to an area where something will change.

Figure 11.4

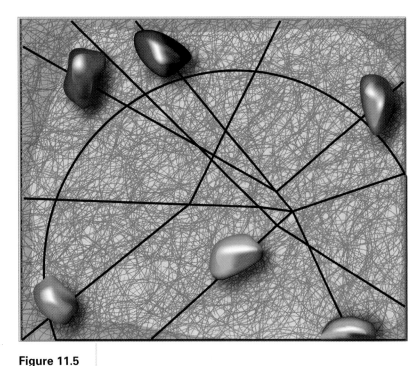

Figure 11.5

Division of Space

How the space of an image is used has a large influence on balance. In regard to balance, space refers to both the area that contains the image and the area of the different elements themselves. This section covers balance in a way that is related to the image space itself.

Arrangement in Space

In Figure 11.5, the different pictorial elements have been arranged around the design space in a way that brings balance to the entire piece. The colored stones and the dark lines work together so that no area of the illustration dominates or overpowers any other. Because of this, the viewer's gaze is kept moving around the image from element to element.

To demonstrate how the balance of space can affect composition, three smaller versions of Figure 11.5 have been reproduced in Figure 11.6. In this illustration, each of the smaller images has the same visual elements, but they have been arranged differently in the image space.

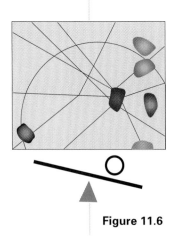 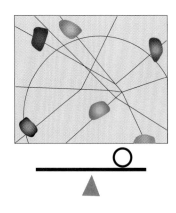 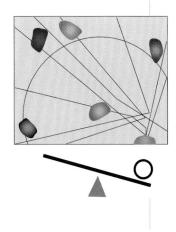

Figure 11.6

In the image on the left of Figure 11.6, the stones have been moved to the right side of the space. This dramatically shifts the visual weight of the entire piece and throws off the balance.

In the center illustration, the elements have been left in their original positions. In this image, a center of focus is created by the converging lines. This center of focus becomes the area around which all the other elements should balance. Because of the distribution of stones around this point, there appears to be fairly even weight in all parts of the image.

In the illustration on the right, the lines converge in an area near the lower-right corner of the image. Since the focal point has been shifted, the left side of the drawing seems empty, and the entire piece is out of balance even though the stones are in the same arrangement as in the original image. Because of this, the left side of the image looks as if it is wasted space.

Balancing Irregular Elements

It is easy to see how the arrangement of similar elements around the point of focus can achieve balance, but not all designs use elements that are the same size. If an image contains a variety of shapes, balancing the design can be rather complex. Figure 11.7 is an example of a complex image that has balance.

In the image in Figure 11.7, the artist has used several different techniques to achieve balance. He has used the arrangement of objects of different sizes and the negative space to balance an illustration that has a

Figure 11.7

point of focus far to one side. In Figure 11.8, the different elements of the piece have been simplified in order to present a clearer example.

The key to understanding the balance that exists in Figure 11.8 is to locate the point of focus. Although the gas masks attract the viewer's attention, they are not the point of focus. In this image, the artist has used several actual lines as well as many implied lines to direct the viewer's eye to a place to the right of the larger figure. In this illustration, a few of these lines have been emphasized in red, but others that are obvious have been left as they are. A red circle has been drawn over the image to indicate the point of focus.

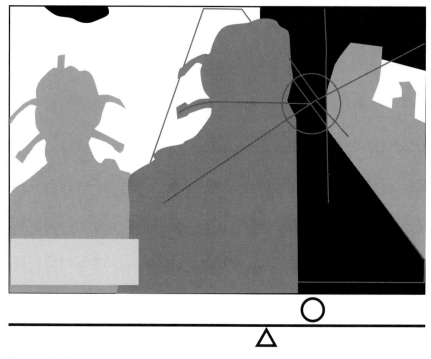

Figure 11.8

Now that the point of focus has been determined, the next element to find is where the elements seem to balance. Usually, this is near the point of focus, but in this case it is to the left, where the larger figure ends and the heavier black area to the right of the figure dominates the layout.

On either side of this place in the image, the area of the objects is large and seems to have a lot of mass. However, because of the negative space to the left of the larger figure, it does not have the same weight as the right-hand third of the image. This is not the only element that throws the balance of the image to the right. Because it is not the same as the point of balance, the point of focus also counts as an element that has visual weight.

The combined weight of the point of focus and the heaviest area of the image are enough to throw the balance of the piece far to the right. To compensate for this, the artist has included another smaller figure to the far left, but this alone does not add enough visual weight to balance the piece. A small dark area above the smaller figure is added, as is some text. These additional elements are enough to bring balance to the layout.

Other Spatial Arrangements and Balance

In design, there are a few compositional arrangements that seem to automatically bring balance to an image. These have been recognized by artists for hundreds if not thousands of years and have been used frequently. Most of these are formulas that rely on the principles that have already been introduced in this chapter. But instead of spending a great deal of time working out the location of each element, a designer can use them as a template for a balanced image.

THE RULE OF THIRDS

The first of these formulas is often called the *rule of thirds.* This approach is used by dividing the space of an image into three equal parts and making each of the sections relatively the same visual weight. An example of this can be seen in Figure 11.9.

Figure 11.9

In Figure 11.9, the image space has been divided into three equal parts, each having an equal amount of weight. Even if one of these parts did not have the same visual weight as the other two, our perception of the rule of thirds would tend to make us see them as equal.

Small World News

The World	Sports	Weather
World Summit Opens	The New Yankees?	☀ By Region
Rethinking the E.U.	Draft Upsets!	
	Between the Seasons	Weekly Forecast
Middle East News		Almanac
Asian News		
European News		
North American News	Sports Site of the Day	Today in History
South American News	www.djackzone.com	
Australian News		

Figure 11.10 In this layout for a Web news portal, the content has been divided into three equal sections. Even though each rectangle contains a different amount of information, the design of the Web page appears to have balance.

The rule of thirds is commonly used in advertising and new media where there is a large amount of content that needs to be included in a layout. The division of the space into three parts can be either vertically or horizontally and is a good way to include several elements without making a design too busy (see also Figure 11.10).

THE GOLDEN SPIRAL

The *golden spiral* is a form of composition that has its root in the rule of thirds, but in this case each third is divided again by three. This creates a series of nesting rectangles. If a curved line were drawn connecting all these rectangles, it would form a spiral. The golden spiral is based on mathematical principles and is associated with mysticism in some cultures. Figure 11.11 is an example of how it can be used to bring balance to a composition.

In Figure 11.11, there are two images. The first is a drawing that illustrates how a golden spiral is created by redividing each space into thirds. The second image is a drawing that demonstrates how the composition of a golden spiral can be used. In this drawing, the spiral forms an implied line that balances the image. Even though the elements of the image are not actually a part of the line implied by the spiral, if they follow the general direction, the viewer will tend to see them as if they were.

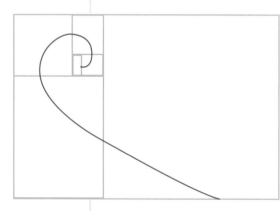

Figure 11.11

RADIAL AND CRYSTALLOGRAPHIC BALANCE

Radial and crystallographic are two kinds of balance related to symmetrical balance in composition, but they are special enough to have their own terms.

In Figure 11.12, there are two images. The image on the left is an example of radial balance. In this illustration, the visual elements radiate from a central point of focus. The image on the right is an example of crystallographic balance and has been created by using a uniform pattern to form a balanced composition.

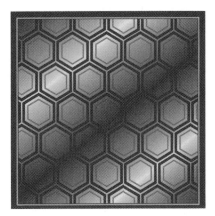

Figure 11.12

Balance and Value

Another way to achieve balance in a design is through the use of value. Much like size or area, the value of an element can influence its visual weight. A general rule is that the darker the object is, the more weight it will have in a design. This may seem simple enough, but because of the relative nature of value, the rule may not always seem to hold true. The value of the background or of other objects in an image can nullify or even reverse the effect. In a design where there is a range of values, the contrast of the different elements will become important to the balance of the image. In cases like this, it will be the difference in value when compared to the other parts of an image that will have the most influence on the visual weight of the specific parts of the design.

In Figure 11.13, there are three drawings that illustrate how value can affect balance in an image. Each of these images is explained separately.

In the image on the left of Figure 11.13, there are two spheres that have the same size and are arranged symmetrically in the space. Ordinarily, this image would appear to have balance, but the sphere on the right is significantly darker in value than the sphere on the left. The darker sphere seems to have more visual weight than the lighter one. Because of this, the image appears unbalanced.

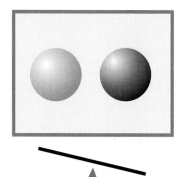 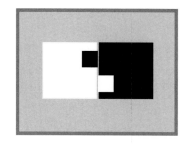 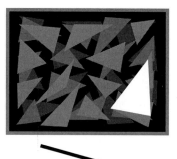

Figure 11.13

In the center illustration, the rule that the darker part of an image will seem heavier has been nullified by using a background that has a middle value. In this image, the white area seems to have nearly the same weight as the black area. This is due to the relative nature of value. Because the white and black areas have the same amount of contrast against the background, they appear to have the same visual weight, and the image is balanced.

The illustration on the right uses the relative nature of value to reverse the general rule. In this image, most of the elements have a darker value. Because of this, the white triangle is in dramatic contrast with the other parts of the image. The extreme contrast between the white and the darker values gives the triangle the appearance of having more visual weight.

Balance and Color

By now, a pattern concerning the visual weight of design elements should be apparent. In many instances, the difference between one part of a composition and the other elements brings a viewer's interest to that part. This interest gives weight to a particular element. In the case of color, the same holds true: the difference between the color of one element and the colors used in the other parts of the image gives that element its weight.

For an example of how color can affect the balance of an image, look at Figure 11.14. In this figure, there are two images. The image on the left is the same as the image on the right, but it is in black and white. In this illustration, the balance of the piece seems slightly off because any visual weight that the different parts of the image have is based on the contrast of values. In the right-hand drawing, the same image is displayed in full color, but this drawing seems to have more balance. The sense of balance is achieved because the color red stands out in the composition. The red star in the upper-right corner adds visual weight to that part of the image, but in the

Figure 11.14

black-and-white image, since it has the same value as the background, it completely disappears and makes that part of the composition appear empty.

Figure 11.15 is a series of drawings that illustrate how using color differences can influence the visual weight of design elements. An explanation is given for each of the three images.

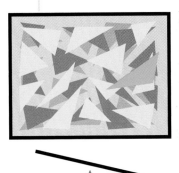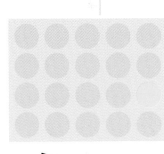

Figure 11.15

The first of the three drawings in Figure 11.15 is an image that uses warm colors for most of the illustration. Only one triangle is a light blue. The difference between the warm and the cool colors makes the single triangle stand out from the image and gives it more weight.

In the middle image, various colors are used, but the majority are shades of their original hue. The exceptions to this are the black and the red triangles. These two parts of the composition stand out from the rest of the image because of the difference in their color values.

In the image on the right, all the colors are of the same hue, but because one circle has a greater intensity of yellow than the other elements of the illustration, the viewer's attention is attracted to it. This throws the balance of the entire image to the right, even though the elements are arranged in a way that is very symmetrical.

Balance Using Other Elements

One of the keys to achieving balance in a design is an even distribution of visual weight. In addition to the methods of manipulating visual weight that have already been covered, there are a few more elements of design that can be utilized. What is unique about these elements is that they do not always fit the rules of balance that have been discussed thus far.

Texture and Visual Weight

The use of texture is one of the elements where exceptions to the rules that govern visual weight can be found. Much like value, texture used for the purpose of balance can be dependent on the other elements around it.

In Figure 11.16, there are three images used to illustrate the effect that texture can have on balance. In the image on the left, there are two rectangles. In this drawing, the rectangle on the right appears to have more weight because of the texture on its surface.

In the middle drawing, the exact opposite is true. Here, both the background of the image and the rectangle on the right have texture. This makes the solid rectangle on the left appear to have more visual weight.

The image on the right has textures applied to both rectangles. Even though it might seem that the rectangle on the left should have more weight because of the larger area of the pattern, it is actually the rectangle on the

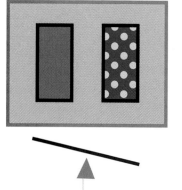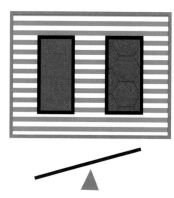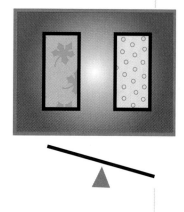

Figure 11.16

right that seems to have more weight. This is because the smaller pattern makes the object appear more dense and therefore, heavier.

COLOR AND VALUE IN TEXTURE

Two other elements that can affect the visual weight of images that have texture are color and value. In many instances, the rules that govern balance as they apply to color and value can dominate an image. For an example of this, look again at the three illustrations in Figure 11.16, but this time concentrate on their visual weights based on color and value. If the images are looked at with this in mind, the balance can seem reversed in each case.

Implied Motion and Balance

In Figure 11.17, the basic rules of balance do not seem to hold up. In this illustration, there is a kangaroo on the right side of the image, while the left side remains empty. Under normal circumstances, this image would appear unbalanced, but because of the implied motion of the kangaroo, there is an imagined weight added to the area that the animal is jumping into.

Figure 11.17

In this example, the viewer recognizes the potential for the space to become filled and imagines that the kangaroo continues its jump into the empty space. Because of this, in the mind of the viewer, the kangaroo almost exists in two places at once and balances the image.

SUMMARY

This chapter introduced the visual element of balance as it applies to composition. The first topics covered were the concepts of visual weight and the point of focus and how both influence the perceived balance of a design. To better explain the use of these elements, a thorough analysis of balance in a complex image was given. This chapter also covered using the lack of balance to create tension in a layout. In addition, several traditional systems for achieving balance were covered. These included design conventions such as the rule of thirds and the golden spiral. The remainder of the chapter presented methods for manipulating visual weight through the use of different design elements. Specific elements that were addressed were size, position, value, and color.

EXERCISES

1. Make a design that is balanced by using two or more elements to achieve this (such as color and arrangement, value and size, and so on).

2. Create an image that uses the lack of balance to bring tension to the piece.

3. Make a design that is weighted toward one side of the image using one element but is weighted toward the other side using a different element. For example, the colors used in the image make it appear heavier on the right side, but the values used make it appear heavier on the left. Together, the two bring balance to the image.

4. Create an image using the rule of thirds.

REVIEW QUESTIONS

1. What is balance as it is applied to design?

2. What is the point of focus?

3. What is the rule of thirds?

4. What is the golden spiral?

5. Describe radial balance.

6. Describe crystallographic balance.

7. When using color, how can an element be given more visual weight?

8. Generally, is a darker value seen as lighter or heavier for the purposes of visual weight?

9. What other elements can overpower the effects of texture on balance?

10. How can implied motion affect balance?

NOTES

CHAPTER **12**

Perspective

n its most general definition, perspective is the way that something looks from a certain point of view. In design, the term *perspective* is often used to refer to the appearance of three-dimensional objects portrayed in illusionary space. A more accurate term for this element of design would be *linear perspective.*

The basic approach to linear perspective is to arrange the different parts of an image in a way that enhances the illusion of a third dimension. This is illustrated in Figure 12.1.

In Figure 12.1, there are two drawings of a table. In the image on the left, the different parts of the table have been drawn in an arrangement that roughly represents how the table might appear to a viewer, but there has been little attention to how the table would realistically appear in space. In the image on the right, the different parts of the table have been drawn using linear perspective. The use of this technique makes the image on the right look more accurate and increases the illusion of three-dimensional space in the drawing.

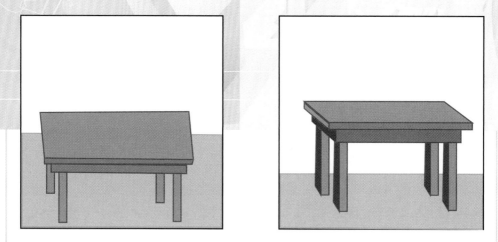

Figure 12.1

Strict Rules of Perspective

Unlike many of the other elements of design, if an image is to look accurate, linear perspective has a large number of specific rules that must be followed. In fact, the rules that govern linear perspective are so many that a separate book could be written on the subject. Thus, only the most basic topics are covered in this chapter. These principles will be enough to serve as a foundation for the use of linear perspective in design.

Key Points

▸▸ **The Vanishing Point**
▸▸ **One-Point Perspective**
▸▸ **Two-Point Perspective**
▸▸ **Additional Rules of Linear Perspective**
▸▸ **Isometric Perspective**
▸▸ **Twisted Perspective**

The Vanishing Point

In Chapter 3, the concept of illusionary space was covered, and several rules of design were introduced. One of these rules stated that an object will tend to look smaller if it is farther away from a viewer. A more detailed explanation of this rule includes the definition of the vanishing point and how it can be used to accurately depict the size of an object in illusionary space.

The vanishing point is a place in an image where the implied lines of linear perspective converge. The vanishing point can be thought of as the farthest point in an image that can be seen by the viewer. An example of this can be seen in Figure 12.2.

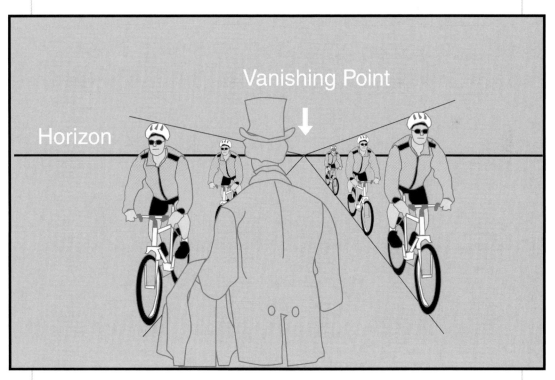

Figure 12.2

Figure 12.2 is an illustration of a man watching several bicyclists approaching. From the point of view of the man, there are a series of implied lines (indicated by actual red lines) directed toward a vanishing point on the horizon. These lines represent the top and bottom of each of the bicycle riders (assuming they are all the same height).

True to the rules of linear perspective, the size and position of each bicycle rider are determined by these lines. If the vanishing point were placed in some other spot in the image, the implied lines would be altered to converge at the new point. To remain consistent, the size of each bicycle rider would then need to be adjusted to fit inside the new lines.

One-Point Perspective

Figure 12.3 is an illustration that has two parts. The first part is a linear perspective drawing of a set of railroad tracks, while the second is an inset image that provides an aerial view of the same scene. In the linear perspective drawing, one of the most obvious visual properties is that all the lines that move away from the viewer converge at the single vanishing point near the horizon. It is from this single vanishing point that this type of drawing gets its name. This kind of linear perspective is referred to as **one-point perspective**.

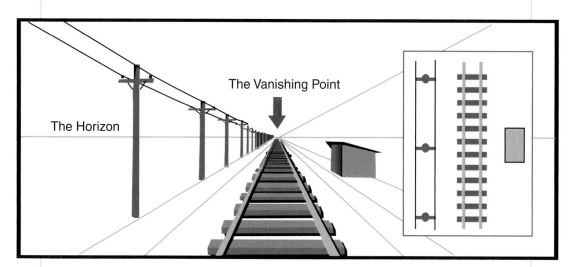

Figure 12.3

There are two basic rules that govern one-point perspective. The first is that all the vertical and horizontal lines in the drawing remain parallel. For example, in Figure 12.3, the telephone poles form vertical lines that are drawn in the same direction and remain parallel with each other. The same rule applies to the horizontal lines. This can be seen in the railroad ties, which are drawn in the same direction across the picture plane and remain parallel to the other horizontal lines.

The only lines that do not remain parallel are those that move away from the viewer in space. In one-point perspective, the second basic rule is that all the lines that show the third dimension (depth) converge at the vanishing point.

Linear Perspective and the Organic

This system of accurately portraying objects in space seems straightforward enough when used to depict objects that are made up of straight lines, but linear perspective can also be applied to objects that are more organic. One of the best ways to do this is to mentally convert the organic form to one that is more linear and then fill in the details.

In Figure 12.4, a running figure is shown using linear perspective. The second image illustrates how the conventions of one-point perspective have been used to help determine the size and position of the different parts of the figure.

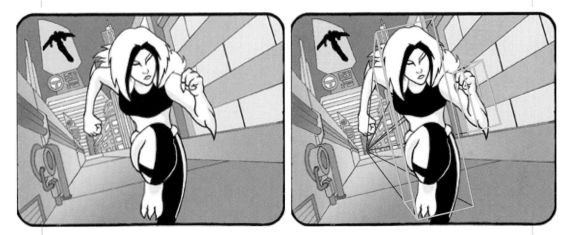

Figure 12.4 *Strissa Runs,* by Robb Epps.

Two-Point Perspective

Figure 12.5 is an example of two-point perspective. As in the case of one-point perspective, this kind of linear perspective gets its name from the number of vanishing points used. Figure 12.5 differs from the typical one-point perspective drawing in that the only lines that remain parallel are those that are vertical. All the other lines converge at one of the two vanishing points.

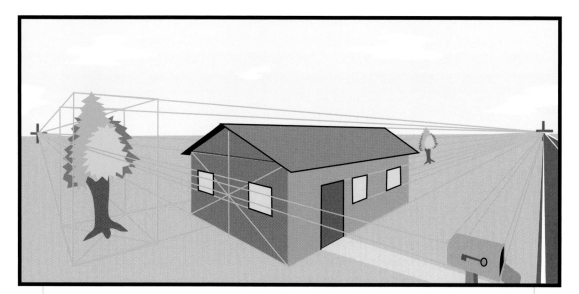

Figure 12.5

Rules for Two-Point Perspective

When making a two-point perspective drawing, it is important to draw all the lines that would normally be parallel to the same vanishing point. In the illustration in Figure 12.5, all the horizontal lines on the front of the house angle toward the vanishing point on the right, while all the horizontal lines on the side of the house angle toward the vanishing point on the left. This method is also applied to all the objects in the image.

A Few Methods for Using Two-Point Perspective

There are a few methods that can make the use of two-point perspective more affective. The first is to place the objects in the image at an angle instead of directly facing the viewer. In Figure 12.5, if the house were seen from the front only, it would be difficult to show the lines that moved toward the second vanishing point. Because the house is angled so that one corner appears closer, the lines that move in the direction of either vanishing point can be clearly seen.

The second method is to keep the vanishing points as far from each other as possible. If the points can be actually placed outside the picture, the effect is even better. By placing the two vanishing points as far apart as possible, the illusionary space will look more realistic.

Although this works well in drawings where realism is important, a designer can also bend these rules to make an illustration more interesting.

In Figure 12.6, the vanishing points have been moved relatively close together. Using these vanishing points to dictate the size and position of the different elements gives the drawing of the castle a distorted perspective. In this image, the closest tower appears very large compared to the others, and the angles of the structure are exaggerated. This technique can be used to create images that appear quirky and stylized.

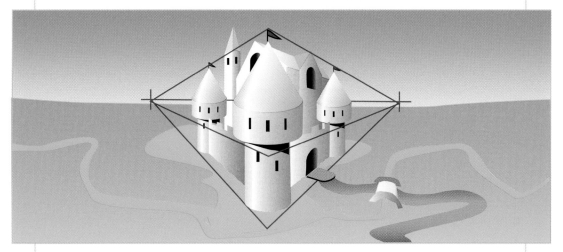

Figure 12.6

Trusting Your Eye

In some cases, no matter how accurate a designer's use of perspective methods, certain elements of a drawing may not look correct; an object in the distance may appear too large or the space between objects will seem awkward. This comes from trying to portray three-dimensional elements on a two-dimensional picture plane. When this occurs the designer may have to ignore a few of the mathematical rules of perspective and redraw elements so that they look right. Do not worry too much over this if the image looks better with a little modification. In design it is usually more important that the image looks good than for the image to be perfectly accurate.

Expanding on Perspective Techniques

What follows are several illustrations that show a few more perspective techniques. These can be very helpful for determining the distance of objects in illusionary space as well as how objects will appear from a certain point of view.

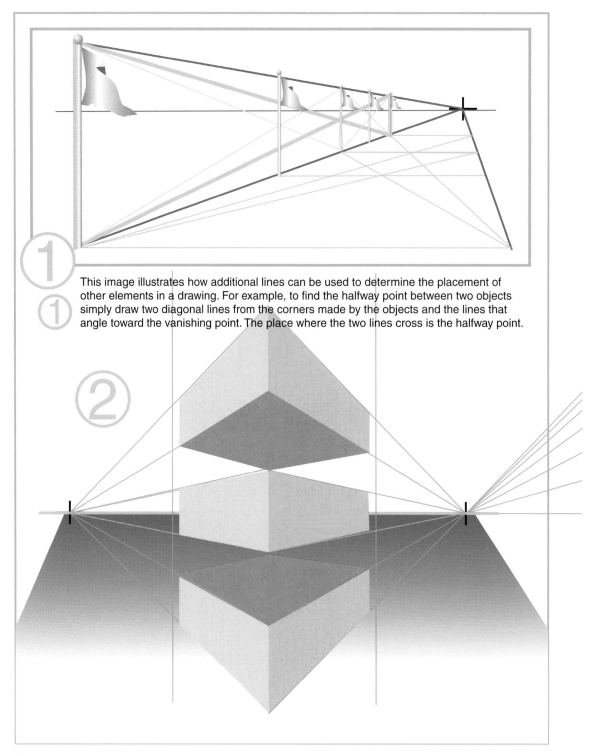

This image illustrates how additional lines can be used to determine the placement of other elements in a drawing. For example, to find the halfway point between two objects simply draw two diagonal lines from the corners made by the objects and the lines that angle toward the vanishing point. The place where the two lines cross is the halfway point.

Figure 12.7

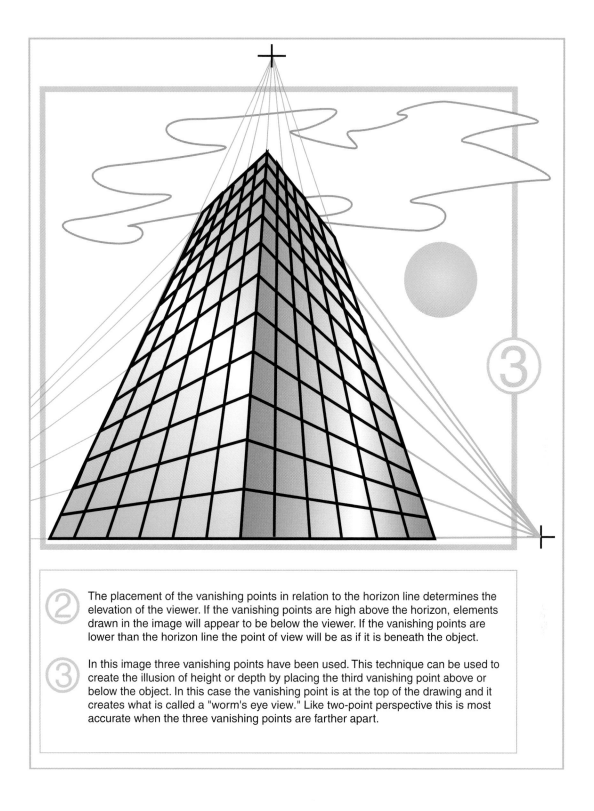

The placement of the vanishing points in relation to the horizon line determines the elevation of the viewer. If the vanishing points are high above the horizon, elements drawn in the image will appear to be below the viewer. If the vanishing points are lower than the horizon line the point of view will be as if it is beneath the object.

In this image three vanishing points have been used. This technique can be used to create the illusion of height or depth by placing the third vanishing point above or below the object. In this case the vanishing point is at the top of the drawing and it creates what is called a "worm's eye view." Like two-point perspective this is most accurate when the three vanishing points are farther apart.

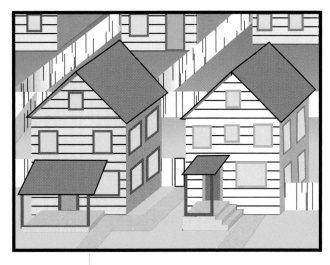

Figure 12.8

Isometric Perspective

There is another kind of linear perspective that does not use vanishing points but instead keeps all lines, regardless of direction, parallel. This is called **isometric perspective** and is often found in Eastern art and the work of Western artists before the Renaissance. Figure 12.8 is an example of isometric perspective.

In Figure 12.8, the horizontal and vertical lines are no different from those that might be found in a typical one-point perspective drawing. What is different are the lines that are directed away from the viewer. In isometric perspective, these lines remain parallel and are drawn at an angle instead of converging on a vanishing point. This kind of perspective can be used when accuracy in illusionary space is not as important to the design as is showing more of the object being portrayed.

Figure 12.9

Twisted Perspective

So far, the types of perspective that have been covered in this chapter have been concerned with creating accurate illusionary space. There is another kind of perspective that does not fall into this category but should be mentioned: **twisted perspective.**

One of the main attributes of twisted perspective is that it ignores the rules of linear perspective in order to convey more visual information about an object. Some of the best examples of twisted perspective can be found in cave drawings. In these images, it is evident that it was more important to the artist that all the different parts of an animal be seen by a viewer (four legs, two horns, and so on) than to accurately portray an animal in space. Figure 12.9 shows a contemporary example of twisted perspective in an illustration.

Figure 12.10

PERSPECTIVE AND NEW MEDIA

Using perspective in new media applications can be both easier and more difficult, depending on the specific software that is being used. If a designer is using an application that is made to create three-dimensional images, problems of perspective are handled by the software. Usually, the artist need only choose the point of view, and the perspective is taken care of. An example of this is seen in Figure 12.10.

In Figure 12.10, there are three spheres that were created using three-dimensional software. The spheres were then arranged in the space, and the application made the perspective calculations. Each of the spheres was then rendered appropriate to the point of view.

Three-dimensional software can make the use of perspective easy for an artist, but other kinds of software can make perspective more difficult than if the drawing were done by hand.

If a linear perspective drawing is done by hand, the designer can simply mark the vanishing points and then use a ruler to ensure that all the lines have the correct angles. The artist does this by placing the ruler along the line from the vanishing point and then using the ruler as a guide. Designers who use computer software to create images do not have this luxury.

An effective way around this handicap is to draw a series of lines that will serve as visual guides for any objects in the drawing. Figure 12.11 is an illustration of this technique.

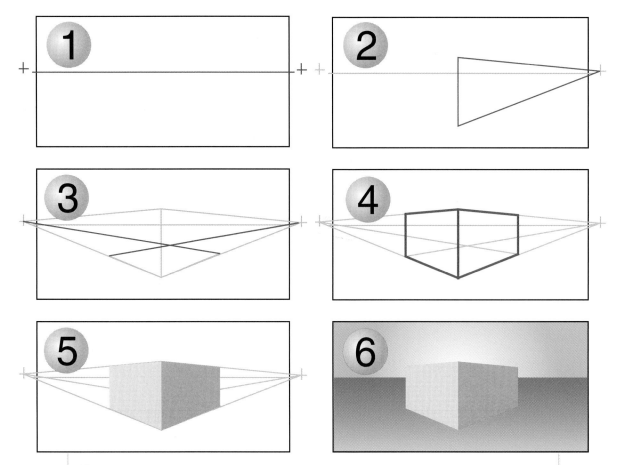

Figure 12.11

Figure 12.11 is made up of a series of drawings that shows the steps in creating guides for a perspective drawing:

1. The first step is to establish the two vanishing points and the horizon.

2. The next step is to draw the first guidelines. In this image, the corner of the box and the two lines that converge at one of the vanishing points are drawn.

3. Step 2 is repeated for the lines that meet at the second vanishing point. Lines are then drawn where the backside of the box will be.

4. The intersections of the various lines indicate where the edges of the box will be placed. The outline of the box is then drawn using the guidelines.

5. The area of the box is filled in.

6. The guidelines are removed, and the rest of the image is completed.

This chapter presented the basic conventions found in perspective drawing. One of these conventions was the vanishing point and its use in several different methods for producing linear perspective. Through the use of illustrations, guides for the use of these methods were shown. This chapter also introduced isometric and twisted perspectives as design elements. Finally, this chapter addressed creating perspective through the use of imaging software and provided a step-by-step example of using guidelines as an aid in perspective drawing.

EXERCISES

1. Create a drawing using one-point perspective. An interior view of a room would work well for this exercise.

2. Make a drawing using two-point perspective. Landscapes with buildings are a good choice of subject.

3. Make a drawing of a sitting person using either one- or two-point perspective.

4. Make a drawing that uses three vanishing points. The third point will be either above or below the object.

5. Draw an object using isometric perspective.

6. Create a drawing that uses distorted perspective by keeping the vanishing points relatively close.

REVIEW QUESTIONS

1. What is linear perspective?

2. In one-point perspective, which lines converge at the vanishing point?

3. In two-point perspective, which lines converge on which vanishing point?

4. How does isometric perspective differ from other types of linear perspective?

5. What is twisted perspective?

Repetition and Rhythm

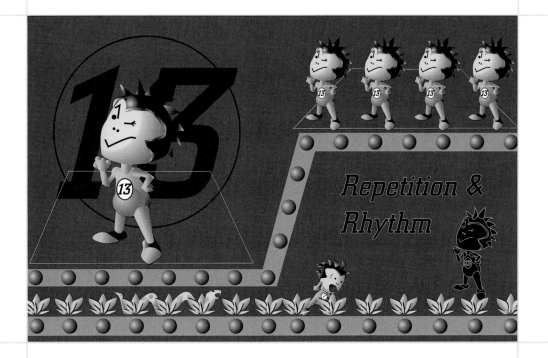

t is commonly understood that people are comfortable with what is familiar to them. What this means for a designer is that people are often quick to recognize and accept words, sounds, and other forms of communication that include elements they have experienced before. Because of this tendency, design techniques such as repetition and rhythm can be used to introduce familiarity and promote understanding in projects.

Defining Repetition and Rhythm

Key Points

▸▸ **Creating Repetition**
▸▸ **Visual Vocabulary**
▸▸ **Using Repetition**
▸▸ **Visual Rhythm**

In design, the term **repetition** refers to a visual element that has been repeated within the same work. The simplest way to create repetition is to use a similar visual element several times within the same piece. In general, the elements do not need to look exactly alike, but the more the elements have in common, the stronger the effect will be.

Rhythm can be thought of as the use of repetition in a way that also brings the element of space into play. This is very much like rhythm found in music; a song can have a repeated beat that creates a rhythm over time. In design, the same thing can be accomplished by repeating a series of elements, but instead of repetition over time, the element is repeated across the space of an image or layout. Just like a piece of music, this works best if the elements have some similarities and are arranged so that they are at regular intervals.

Figure 13.1 illustrates a few of the different ways that repetition can be created in design. In this image, several different elements of the drawing have been repeated and arranged so that they create a visual balance. Some of the elements that have been repeated are nearly the same, while others share only a few similarities. An example of similar elements would be the two blue arrows near the middle of the image. Even though the arrows point in opposite directions and their colors are slightly different, they are enough alike that a repetition of the form has been made.

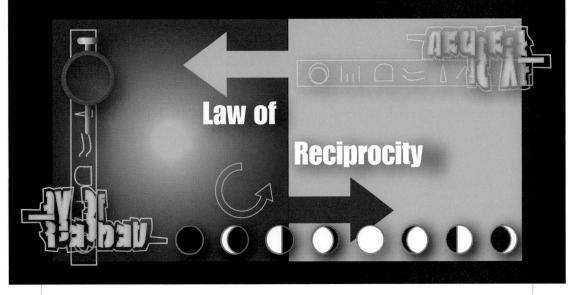

Figure 13.1

For an example of entirely different elements used to create repetition and rhythm, look at the red circle in the left side of the image. A little lower and to the right of the red circle is a rounded area formed by a gradient of colors. Next to this area is the outline of an arrow that also makes a partial circle. These three elements create a repetition in the drawing because of their similarity of shape. Their placement near each other at relatively regular intervals in the space of the drawing also creates a rhythm.

In this same drawing, the clearest example of rhythm is the smaller black and white circles that emulate the phases of the moon. A visual rhythm is created by these elements because they are arranged in an implied line and are placed at equal intervals in space (see also Figure 13.2).

Figure 13.2 Interactive projects lend themselves well to the use of repetition and rhythm. This is because it is often necessary to repeat many of the elements, such as controls or content areas, in the same layout or across several screens of a project.

Creating a Visual Vocabulary with Repetition

As mentioned in the opening of this chapter, the use of repetition can be a strong design technique because of the visual appeal of familiar forms. In fact, it is our ability to recognize familiar forms that allows us to see an image as a representation of some object. For example, we can comprehend a picture of a face because the shape of a face is familiar to us. Understanding this concept is important when it comes to creating and using a visual vocabulary in design.

Vocabulary Analogy

To better understand the idea of a visual vocabulary, think about the process that takes place when someone hears a word for the first time. Usually, the person can guess at the meaning of the word from how it was used in a sentence. From then on, any time that the word is encountered, the understanding is reinforced. After the word has been learned, not only will it be understood, but the familiarity of the word can even help the person comprehend more of a conversation that uses the same word.

This same thing can occur in design. By repeating some element in a work, the designer can teach the viewer a new piece of a visual vocabulary and then use it again. The similar objects become somewhat familiar to the viewer; even elements that are not exactly alike. For an example of this, see Figure 13.3.

Figure 13.3

On the left side of Figure 13.3, there is a drawing of a white tree. Next to the tree are three other forms that have some visual similarities with the original tree. The basic form of the tree is repeated, but each of these other elements does not stand out as much from the background as the original. Because the viewer was introduced to the original tree, one will understand that these three additional forms are also trees. Without the introduction of the first tree, the simplified forms might not be as clear.

Repetition of Basic Shape or Form

In many cases, the elements that are repeated do not have to be exactly alike. A few general similarities between the elements are often enough to make the use of repetition successful. For an example of this, look at Figure 13.4.

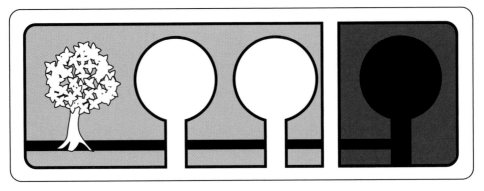

Figure 13.4

In Figure 13.4, the same white tree from Figure 13.3 has been used, but the series of tree forms have been replaced with cutout shapes. In this image, the same sort of repetition has been used as in Figure 13.3, but with completely different elements. The basic shape of the tree and the other elements are similar enough that a viewer will recognize the repetition.

This image illustrates that a designer is not limited to repeating the same element over and over to create repetition but can use other elements with similar attributes. By making use of other design elements, such as shapes, shadows, or similar forms, a designer can repeat a basic element throughout an image without being blatant.

SPECIAL ISSUES IN NEW MEDIA

USING A VISUAL VOCABULARY

The use of repetition and the concept of teaching a "visual vocabulary" to a viewer is important to designers who work with new media; especially for those who create Web sites or other interactive pieces.

In an interactive project, the viewer needs to be able to quickly learn the visual vocabulary of the work so that one can interact with the piece. If the design is confusing, the work may have less-than-desired results. For example, if all the buttons on a Web site look completely different or are scattered around the page, a visitor might become frustrated while trying to figure out how to navigate the site. But if all the buttons look similar, the visitor has to learn only one new visual element and will then understand how to use the others.

The main idea to keep in mind is that controls should be consistent. One of the best ways to do this is through repetition (see Figure 13.5).

Figure 13.5 This illustration shows two versions of the same interface. The first version uses graphics and icons that are inconsistent, while all the buttons in the second version are similar.

Avoiding Confusion

Often, many designers succumb to the temptation of creating unity in a project by making all the elements too similar. For composition, using elements that look alike is a good idea, but if those elements include interactive controls, the result can be confusing for the viewer. For an example of this, see Figure 13.6. In this Web site, the designer is showing visitors that they should click on a certain kind of graphic to navigate the site, but the title bar above the text looks too similar to the navigation buttons. The title bar could easily be mistaken for a control element. In this example, no matter how many times the viewer clicks on the title bar, nothing will happen.

The easiest way to avoid this kind of confusion is to keep the navigation elements of a project distinct. This does not mean that similarity and unity should be ignored altogether; rather, there should be some

Figure 13.6 The navigation buttons and the title bar in this image are too similar to promote clear understanding. It is likely that a viewer would become confused about which elements are for navigation and which are for information.

Figure 13.7

attribute that sets the controls apart from the other elements. In Figure 13.7, the interface from Figure 13.6 has been remade in a way that is less confusing for the viewer. Here, the color of the background and text on the title bar has been altered. Although the shape and palette are similar enough to the other elements to give unity to the piece, there is an obvious difference between the title bar and the navigation buttons.

Rhythm

Another way that repetition can be used in design is to set up a visual rhythm. The concept of rhythm was introduced in the beginning of this chapter, but this section provides a few more details about how it can be used in an image. As mentioned before, rhythm is a very effective way to bring unity to an image. An example of this can be seen in Figure 13.8.

Figure 13.8 is a drawing of two zebras. The stripes of the zebras create a visual rhythm of black and white shapes across the entire image. If this were

Figure 13.8

an illustration of two horses, the basic shapes and forms would be the same, but because of the repetition and rhythm created by the stripes, the drawing is made more interesting. In fact, the rhythm formed by the stripes becomes the main focus of the image.

Altering Rhythm

One of the most effective ways to use rhythm in design is to alter it. This is done by first establishing a rhythm and then changing it in some way. When a designer uses this technique, the change in rhythm becomes a point of interest to the viewer. Figure 13.9 shows several examples this.

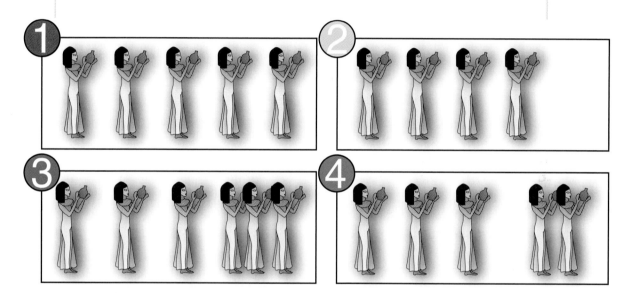

Figure 13.9

In Figure 13.9, there are four different illustrations, each of which demonstrates a different way of altering rhythm. In the first image, the figures of Egyptian women have been equally spaced. The spacing of the repeated image creates a visual rhythm. Because the repetition is unchanged, no area of the drawing seems more important or more interesting than any other.

In the second image, the same rhythm is established, but the pattern does not continue across the space of the entire image; instead, an area on the far right is left empty. The absence of any figures in this space creates a break in the rhythm and becomes a point of interest in the illustration. The viewer naturally focuses on this area because it is different from the others.

In the third image, the figures begin on the left with the same rhythm found in the other illustrations, but the figures on the right side of the drawing are placed closer together. The change in rhythm attracts the viewer's attention and makes this area of the image seems more important, as if something is happening here.

The fourth image combines several of the techniques from the other images. As in the other illustrations, a rhythm has been established by the repetition of the figures. This is followed by an empty area and two more figures that are placed very close together. This makes the two figures stand out from the others and become the focal point of the image.

Nonlinear Rhythm

Figure 13.10

Nearly all the examples of rhythm given so far have been created by using elements arranged along a single path. Although this way of creating rhythm is the easiest to recognize, it is not the only way that it can be used in design. Rhythm can also be created by arranging elements in different areas of an image in a way that creates balance. This approach is closely related to our tendency to mentally group similar shapes, but it is not limited to objects of the same shape. By repeating some visual element throughout an image, a nonlinear rhythm can be made. For an example of this, look at Figure 13.10.

Figure 13.10 has been made by repeating several elements in the same image. The most obvious rhythm in this drawing is the series of L-shaped areas that repeat from the top of the image to the bottom. These elements form a linear rhythm that leads the viewer's eye from the top to the bottom of the image.

Another rhythm is created by the areas of small octagons. Because of the similarity of the pattern, all the different shapes that are made up of the octagons are mentally grouped together. The most notable of these are the red octagons near the middle of the image. Even though these areas are different shapes, they have enough visual attributes in common that a viewer will see these as a repetition of the same element. In several other places around the image, the same patterns of octagons appear in solid black or gray. Although these do not stand out as much as the others, they will also be grouped with the red octagons and help establish a balance as well as create a sense of unity throughout the image. Their placement forms a rhythm throughout the drawing, and the negative space created by their absence becomes areas of focus.

Placement and Rhythm

It has been shown that one way to create rhythm is through the repetition of visual elements that have similarities, but this is not the only way to establish rhythm in an image. Another approach is through the arrangement of the elements used. An example of this can be seen in Figure 13.11.

In Figure 13.11, three completely different objects have been drawn so that they are equally spaced within an image area. Because each element is roughly the same size and is given the same amount of visual importance, their arrangement forms a rhythm. This rhythm could be expanded to a larger image by simply adding more objects in the same pattern. In this image, the placement of objects in a repeated pattern, rather than the repetition of a similar element, establishes the rhythm (see also Figure 13.12).

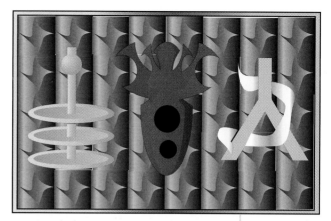

Figure 13.11

Figure 13.12 This illustration uses rhythm to create a series of implied lines that radiate from a point of focus.

SUMMARY

This chapter introduced repetition and rhythm as elements of design. After providing a general definition, the two concepts were covered in detail in separate sections. The first section dealt with the creation of repetition and explained the concept of creating a visual vocabulary. This was followed by examples of how to use repetition in design. The second section addressed the use of repetition to create visual rhythm and used examples to demonstrate its use.

EXERCISES

1. Design an interactive interface that uses repetition and rhythm in the layout.

2. Create rhythm in an image with several different elements.

3. Create an image that uses nonlinear rhythm.

REVIEW QUESTIONS

1. What is repetition? Give an example of how repetition could be used in a new media project.

2. Do repetitive elements need to be exactly the same?

3. Explain the concept of teaching a "visual vocabulary" to a viewer.

4. What is visual rhythm as it applies to design?

5. What is nonlinear rhythm? Give an example.

_____
_____
_____
_____
_____
_____
_____
_____
_____
_____
_____
_____
_____
_____
_____
_____
_____
_____
_____
_____
_____
_____
_____
_____
_____
_____
_____
_____
_____
_____
_____
_____

CHAPTER 14

Association

14

ICON
INDEX
SYMBOL

ASSOCIATION

O ne of the ways that humans interpret the world is through associations. We associate objects with words (both spoken and written) and assign meanings to specific symbols. In fact, it is only by associating ideas with symbols that we are able to communicate with each other. An example of this is the word *dog.* When someone reads the word, they have a general concept of what is being communicated, even though the three letters of the word do not look anything like a dog, nor do they have any other attributes that would remind someone of a dog (see Figure 14.1).

Even if a designer drew a picture of a dog, the image would still not be a dog. The drawing is only a representation of an animal that a viewer would be able to recognize. The viewer associates the image of the dog with the real thing and with what one knows about dogs (how they look, how they behave, and so on).

Semiotics

Communication through association falls under the study of **semiotics.** One of the basic premises of semiotics is that all things can be classified in one of two categories: the signifier or the signified. The signifier is the something that the signified is associated with. In Figure 14.1, the signifiers are the silhouette of the dog and the word *dog.* In this case, the signified would be an actual dog.

At its foundation, the association of some meaning or idea is how visual communication works. The designer creates an image, and the viewer is able to interpret enough from it to understand the general concept of what the image is about. Without the power of association, there would be no communication—and no designers.

Key Points

▸▸ The Symbolic
▸▸ Sensory Association
▸▸ Association with the Viewer

Figure 14.1

From Visual to Conceptual

Now that the basics have been covered, we move beyond the simple representation of an object to more specific and complex uses of association in design. As an element of design, association relies on the viewer's past experiences. Its use depends on the ability of the viewer to understand a mental concept beyond what can be seen in an image. What the designer tries to accomplish is to make an image that transcends what can be described through vision alone.

The rest of this chapter focuses on a few approaches to using association in design.

Symbolic Association

Symbolic association can be broken down into two different kinds. The first kind is an image that uses some symbol to communicate an idea. The addition

Figure 14.2

of the symbol adds meaning that might not otherwise be known without it. Figure 14.2 is an example of this.

Figure 14.2 is a drawing of mouse that is obviously love struck. The viewer knows this because of the little hearts floating around its head. If the hearts were not present in the image, the viewer might not receive enough information from the pictorial elements to understand the emotional state of the mouse.

The second kind of symbolic association does not necessarily use an actual symbol but relies more on pictorial elements to provoke an emotional response from a viewer. Nearly everyone has seen images that have made them feel sad or other pictures that have made them laugh. The association that is taking place is with an emotion. It is practically impossible for a designer to create an image of some emotion. Rather, the designer must either portray a figure that exhibits the emotion or cause viewers to feel the emotion themselves.

Some of the best examples of this kind of association in design can be seen in propaganda-style posters. These images are made to evoke emotions, such as patriotism, a sense of duty, or even an adversarial attitude toward an enemy.

Figure 14.3 was created to provoke an emotional association. Because of the imagery used, the viewer will imagine a sense of danger and feel some of the emotions associated with it.

Sensory Association

Another approach that can be used by designers is the association of visual imagery with information from the other senses. Chapter 7 addressed how the use of texture in design relies on an association with the sense of touch, but

Figure 14.3

this is not the only sense that can be triggered through an illustration.

Visual association with the other senses is so strong that huge amounts of money are spent each year on advertising that uses this approach. Think of the typical restaurant commercial. Many of these include mouthwatering images of great-looking food that are associated with taste. Five minutes before seeing the commercial, you were not even hungry, but now all you can think about is how good that food would be.

Figure 14.4 uses the association with another sensation to convey a message. The image of the hypodermic is automatically associated with the sting of the needle.

It has been held as fact for some time that taste and smell, as well as the other senses, are closely keyed into the parts of the brain that carry out memory functions. By using sensory associations, a designer can communicate with the more rudimentary parts of the mind in an effective way.

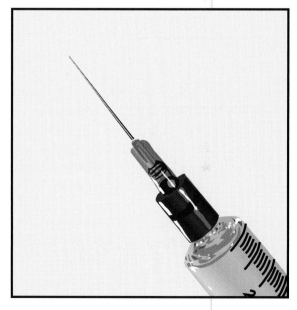

Figure 14.4

Comparative Association

Another kind of association that is rarely addressed yet plays a large role in design has to do with the comparison of different elements within an image or, in some cases, the absence of anything to compare. Many designers use this kind of association in their work without ever giving it much thought, but it can be a very useful tool when consciously used. An example of this can be seen in Figure 14.5.

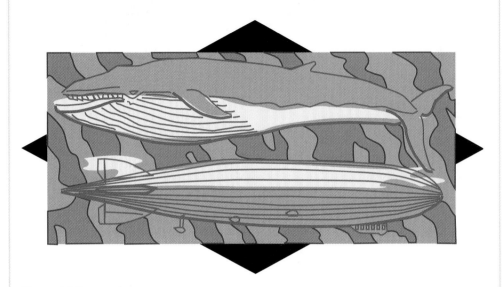

Figure 14.5

In Figure 14.5, there are two main visual elements. These elements are stylized drawings of a whale and a zeppelin. Because everything else in the drawing seems less important, the focus of the image becomes the two main elements. As a result, the viewer will automatically begin to compare the forms of the zeppelin and the whale as well as the relationship between the two. They will look for similarities and differences between the two objects and may even go so far as to think about the objects beyond what is presented in the image. For example, the viewer may think about how a zeppelin moves through the air compared to how a whale moves through the ocean.

What occurs is that the viewer begins to develop new associations between the elements of the drawing. Generally, a viewer will compare the different elements of any image in an effort to gain understanding about the content, associating each component with the others.

When There Is Nothing to Compare

When an image does not have more than one object with which to form any associations, something peculiar happens. In images with a single object of focus, the viewer will associate the image with oneself. In other words, the

Figure 14.6

Figure 14.7

comparison that takes place is between the object and the viewer. For an example of this, look at Figure 14.6.

Figure 14.6 is a drawing that confronts the viewer. There is little else to look at in the illustration except for the face that stares out of the image. In this drawing, the viewer is forced to personalize the image. It is almost as if one becomes a part of the image because there is nothing else to associate the main object with. By default, the viewer places oneself in an imagined relationship with the solitary object. For a defining comparison, look at Figure 14.7.

Figure 14.7 is almost the same as Figure 14.6, but it contains one exception. In this image, a second element of focus has been added. Because of the addition of the bee, the entire illustration has changed. The viewer is no longer confronted by a solitary element but becomes a witness to the scene taking place. The viewer falls back on comparing the face with the bee and the relationship between the two.

SUMMARY

This chapter began by explaining the relationship between association and communication. The next section introduced two different approaches that are commonly referred to as symbolism. This section also addressed the evoking of emotion through the use of association. The third major topic covered in this chapter was the use of association with other senses in design. This chapter ended with a section that explained the association of objects in an image with each other and the association with the viewer.

EXERCISES

1. Create an image that evokes an emotion.

2. Make an image that a viewer will associate with a sense other than vision such as taste or smell.

1. Give a general definition of *association* as it applies to design.

2. What two concepts are covered by the term *symbol?*

3. In semiotics, what is generally meant by the *signifier?* What is the *signified?*

4. Give an example of a sensory association.

NOTES

CHAPTER 15

Abstraction

Abstraction is probably one of the most misunderstood techniques that can be used in design. This may be due to the common misconception that the word abstract means anything strange or weird. Although an image that uses abstraction may appear odd, it is not the strangeness that defines it as abstract. Others may believe that abstraction is not an element of design at all but actually a kind of style. (See Chapter 16 for more on style.) It is true that there are some styles that rely on abstraction to achieve a specific look, but it is how this element is used that gives the style its distinctive appearance, not the other way around.

The first thing a designer should understand about abstraction is what the word really means in regard to design. In its simplest definition, abstraction can be thought of as a departure from representational accuracy. That is, abstraction can be thought of as a trade-off of realism for elements that will make the image more interesting or bring more unity to a piece. An example of this is a drawing that, instead of the usual and expected flesh tones, uses bright blues to depict a person. In this example, the bright colors make the illustration of the person more interesting but less realistic. Although this example is simple, it is a clear illustration that abstraction is a purposeful alteration of realism to enhance a design.

Why Use Abstraction?

There are several different reasons a designer might choose to use abstraction in an image. The first reason has already been mentioned: to make the image more visually interesting. What follows are a few other reasons for using abstraction as an element of design.

Key Points

▸▸ Reasons for Using Abstraction

▸▸ Methods for Abstracting Images

▸▸ Nonrepresentational Abstraction

A Way of Seeing

Another reason that a designer may use abstraction is to call attention to some specific element of an image. In such cases, the designer is helping the viewer see something in the same way the designer sees it. For an example of this, look at Figure 15.1.

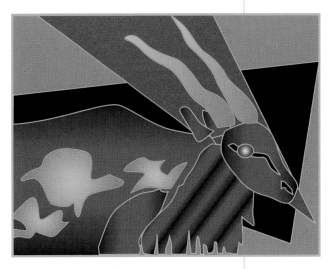

Figure 15.1

The designer's intent for Figure 15.1 was to share how he or she saw the antelope as a series of connected shapes. If the artist had drawn the antelope as accurately as possible, the viewer might become focused on the image of the animal instead of paying attention to how the different shapes formed the figure. By abstracting the general form and removing the unnecessary elements, the designer has left nothing to look at except for the parts that he or she wants the viewer to concentrate on.

This approach to abstraction can be especially useful when it comes to creating associations with different elements within a design. Figure 15.2 shows an example using abstraction to bring unity to an interface.

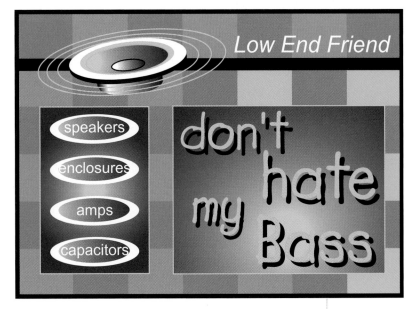

Figure 15.2

The speaker in Figure 15.2 has been drawn in an abstract manner. A photograph of a bass speaker could have been used, but the designer chose to make the speaker appear similar in shape to the navigation buttons. This kind of abstraction is also based on sharing a way of seeing with the viewer. In this case, the designer is showing how much a speaker (with a little help from abstraction) looks like a typical interface button.

A Detective Story

Yet another reason a designer might choose to use abstraction is to create a sense of mystery. If the source of the image is not immediately recognizable, a viewer will study the image and try to figure out what the piece is about. If this approach is used, the image becomes a visual puzzle for the viewer to solve. Using abstraction in this way can generate more interest in the image, but it can also have a few negative results. If the abstraction is too extreme, the viewer may become frustrated and not bother to attempt to figure out the source of the image or may come up with one's own ideas that have nothing to do with the intent of the artist.

AN ARTIST'S TALE

Everyone Sees Something Different

During a certain period of my career as an artist, I had begun working with different techniques of abstraction. In my work, I continually pushed the use of abstraction until I was making images that were not really about anything; they were simply large paintings that were made up of shapes and colors as the only elements. There was really nothing that these images were "about" except pure design.

While I was working on the images, I never really thought about what a person looking at the paintings would read into them. I assumed that they would see them for what they were: abstraction taken to its furthest end. But, while exhibiting one of these pieces, I learned that I was greatly mistaken.

I learned of my error by listening to the opinions of two different people who were looking at the same painting. The first man insisted that the painting was a scene from a science fiction novel. He gave a lengthy explanation about his theory and even went so far as to point out a spaceship and several other elements to his companion. The second man argued that the painting was not about a spaceship at all but rather was about "the restrictive nature of organized religion." I was completely amazed at both of these interpretations since I saw the painting as nothing more than colors arranged in a composition. As far as I was concerned, there was no spaceship and nothing about religion anywhere in the painting.

In the end, the man who saw the spaceship purchased the painting, and I was happy to let him see all the stars and galaxies that he wanted since he had paid me a pretty decent amount of money. Little did I know that the saga (and my lesson about abstraction) was far from over.

Almost a year had gone by, and I had all but forgotten about the painting until I came home from my studio one afternoon and found the piece in my living room. As it turned out, my wife had really liked the painting, and although she didn't say anything, she was disappointed when it had sold. Without bothering to mention anything to me about it, she had purchased the piece back from the spaceship man.

Later, during a phone conversation with my sister, I was relaying the incident to her and attempting to describe the piece. When she finally understood which painting I was talking about, she said, "Oh, you mean *The Grinning Bad Man*!" She didn't see anything about spaceships or religion either, but she did go on to tell me that she had always thought the painting was about a bad man who could be seen smirking in the middle of the piece.

The painting now hangs near the front door of my house, and it seems that every guest who comes inside has some detailed story about what he or she sees in the piece. I gave up a long time ago trying to explain that the piece is only an abstract design and isn't about anything; now I just listen to each person's interpretation and accept the lesson that people will tend to read their own thoughts into abstracted images.

Approaches to Abstraction

Altering the Original

One of the ways to use abstraction is to begin with an accurate depiction of what will be drawn, choose those parts of the object that you want to accentuate, and work from there. This technique is especially well suited for creating images with a computer because the alterations can be made in gradual increments. Better yet, if a mistake is made or the abstraction is pushed too far, the alteration can be easily undone. Figure 15.3 is an example of this process.

Figure 15.3 is comprised of a series of images. The first image is the original illustration of a ballet dancer, and every image after that is a step-by-step snapshot of the alterations made. The final image is the finished work.

The intent of the designer was to create an abstracted image that captured the basic form of the dancer but that represented it in a way that looked as if it was a completely different object. At each step in the alteration process, certain parts of the image are accentuated and unnecessary details removed. Near the completion of the image, details are reinserted to give the shapes dimension.

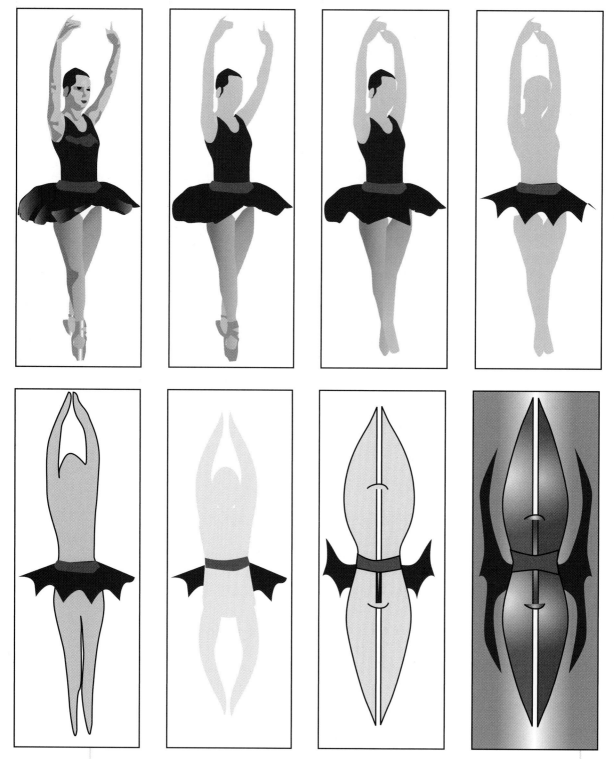

Figure 15.3

When working this way, it is often advantageous to have a general idea of what you would like the finished image to look like, but it is not always necessary. Experimentation with the image along the way can bring about some very good results.

Changing the View

Another way to introduce abstraction to an image is to change the view of some object so that it is not immediately recognizable. By presenting something in a way that is uncommon, a viewer will tend to see the image as a collection of forms and shapes instead of as a portrayal of an actual object. This can be seen in Figure 15.4.

Figure 15.4 is an image that has used abstraction by dramatically changing the view of the object depicted. In this illustration, a drawing of a zipper was made extremely close-up, and many of the details were accentuated. Because of the unfamiliar viewpoint, the image looks like a collection of shapes and colors—until the zipper is recognized.

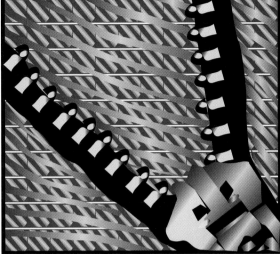

Figure 15.4

Using Style to Create Abstraction

As mentioned in the introduction to this chapter, many artistic styles are actually the abstraction of an image in a specific manner. For this method of abstraction, a designer may use a consistent technique to create an image. An example of such a technique can be seen in Figure 15.5.

Figure 15.5 is an image that uses a style called **pointillism** to portray a moth. The method of this style is to depict objects using only small dots of color. Because only dots are used to draw the moth, many of the details are lost, and an abstracted image is created. This approach is less about making a realistic image than about creating viewer interest through the use of style.

Figure 15.5

Mixing Metaphors

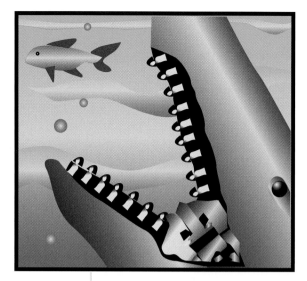

There is another kind of abstraction that is more conceptual because it relies on the mixing of visual information in an unexpected way. This is done to generate interest or to convey an idea. An example of this might be an illustration of a hotdog. The designer makes the hotdog appear as if it was made of some unexpected material, such as marble, instead of looking like the typical picnic food. This sort of abstraction is often referred to as a **visual pun.**

Figure 15.6 is another example of a visual pun. In this image, the abstracted zipper from Figure 15.4 has been used in place of the shark's mouth. The use of the zipper illustrates a metaphor for the teeth and makes the image humorous or ironic.

Figure 15.6

Nonrepresentational Abstraction

So far, all the approaches to abstraction that have been covered have begun with a specific object and the altering of its appearance, but there is another kind of abstraction that does not use this method. This kind of abstraction, called **nonrepresentational abstraction,** uses the elements of design without attempting to portray any object at all. Figure 15.7 is an example of this.

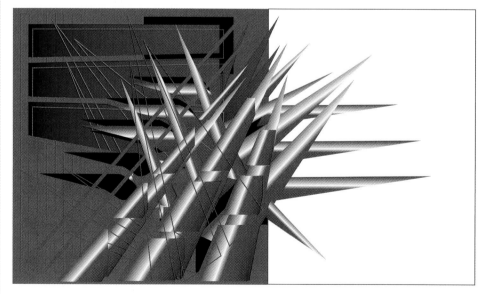

Figure 15.7

Figure 15.7 does not illustrate any specific object. Instead, it uses visual elements alone to lead the viewer's eye, promote unity, and create a composition. This kind of abstraction is design in its purest form. A way to think of this approach is by comparing it to music without lyrics. A song's lyrics usually tell something like a story, and the music is used as a background to support the story. But if the piece is strictly instrumental, without lyrics, the music alone conveys any concepts the piece may contain. This is also true for nonrepresentational design. In this ultimate kind of abstraction, it is color and form that make the image, without the "lyrics" of actual objects to rely on.

SUMMARY

This chapter introduced the concept of using abstraction as an element of design. Several reasons for using abstraction were given, as was how it could be used. The chapter went on to explain a few general techniques for abstracting images. The last section explained nonrepresentational abstraction and how it approaches "pure design."

EXERCISES

1. Create an abstracted image by beginning with a realistic illustration and altering it until the basic form remains but the object becomes something different.

2. Make an image by depicting an object in extreme close-up or at an odd angle so that it is not immediately recognizable and appears abstracted.

3. Make a visual pun by combining two different objects in a way that is unexpected but that makes some sense in the image. (See Figure 15.6 as an example.)

4. Create an image using nonrepresentational abstraction.

REVIEW QUESTIONS

1. Define the term *abstraction*.

2. How can abstraction create a sense of mystery in an image?

3. How does the use of style promote abstraction?

4. What is a visual pun?

5. What is nonrepresentational abstraction?

CHAPTER 16

Style

In design, the term style is often used in more than one way. It can either refer to the overall appearance of the design (often made by a certain approach or technique applied to it) or be used to mean a specific recognized historical style. To prevent confusion, a detailed definition for both of these uses of the word is given.

Style as technique. The word *style* can be used to refer to the treatment of the visual elements in a design. For example, if an image is made to look torn, scratched, and faded, it can be said that it has a worn or rough style. In this example, the word *style* refers to the overall look and the techniques used to create the piece. This is very similar to drawing a line in a certain way to convey an emotion. The definition for this use of the word is a technique used to convey information beyond plain representation (e.g., the designer drew the logo in a style that made it look cold and metallic).

Style as an artistic movement. The word *style* can also be used to identify a design in reference to a recognized historical period of art (e.g., the designer created a logo that captured the look of art deco).

In this context, style will usually reflect when and where it was made. For example, an image from an interior wall of an Egyptian pyramid will look different in many ways from a Renaissance painting. Much of this has to do with the different ideas held in each culture as well as how those ideas were used in the art of the period. This is not to say that a contemporary designer could not emulate a style from the past, only that the original version of that style was a product of that culture and time period.

Using Style as Technique

Style as a technique can have very strong associative qualities for the viewer. This association is usually why a particular style is used. An illustration of association and style can be seen in Figure 16.1.

Figure 16.1 is made up of four illustrations. The first image is the original; the other three have been altered using different styles. Notice how the approach to each of the other images affects the meaning of the work through association. Each illustration is basically the same in content and composition, but the style causes the viewer to make assumptions about the author of the message. These associations add meaning to the image.

Key Points

►► **Use of Style as Technique**
►► **Use of Style as an Artistic Movement**
►► **Visual Glossary of Different Artistic Styles**
►► **Creating and Applying Style**

Style as Context

A powerful way that style can be used is as a **context.** Style used as context creates a world for the information to exist in. For example, the style of a Web

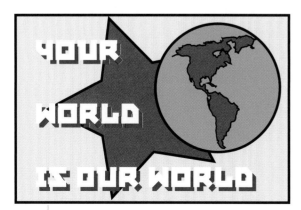

Figure 16.1

site may make it look trendy and fashionable, high tech, or even very business-like. In new media design, this use of style is often called a **theme** (e.g., an interactive project that makes use of circus imagery could be said to have a circus theme).

Using style as context can be a useful vehicle for giving the viewer additional information; especially if the goal and the intended audience of a project is taken into consideration. For clients, this use of style should reflect the impression they want to give the viewer about the project and about themselves.

Creative Context

Figure 16.2

Using style to create context need not be limited to creating stuffy and dry interfaces for business projects. Depending on the purpose of the piece, you may be able to really use your creativity and come up with some interesting designs. An example of this can be seen in Figure 16.2.

Figure 16.2 uses a style associated with a certain period of history. Although this may seem closely related to the second definition of the word *style* (referring to a particular movement in art history), here it is treated as a technique for creating a design.

In the illustration, there is a play on the word *revolutionary* and the style of the image. There would be no association if the style that is used did not appear similar to engravings from the late 1700s. Because of the viewer's ability to recognize a historical period through the style, a pun is made.

Another interesting thing about style is that it need not always rely on the familiar; it can also be used to create an entirely new context. An example of this can be seen in Figure 16.3.

Figure 16.3 uses a style that makes the imagery look strange and alien. This approach adds a sense of mystery because the style is not easily identifiable.

Style as an Artistic Movement

The second definition of *style* given in the introduction of this chapter referred to the identification of a specific movement in art history. These

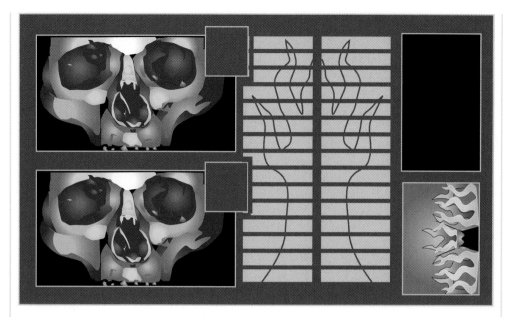

Figure 16.3

movements can be considered closely related to the concept of style as technique. Many of them began as experiments in style as technique. The difference is that the specific technique or look has become established in history as a certain style.

Style and Philosophy

Few people outside of art and design circles are aware that most of the styles that have been developed in the twentieth century are actually visual examples of ideas on aesthetics and critical thinking. In many cases, the artists are using style to illustrate specific concepts in philosophy.

A classic example of this would be surrealism, which is a style that is known for its dreamlike images. The ideas behind surrealism are based on Freudian psychology, and artists who work in this style will often use concepts from the writings of Freud to influence their images.

Visual Glossary of Style

Although all styles usually have some concept behind the way they appear, it is often easier to understand the nature of different styles by seeing examples. Figure 16.4 depicts several common styles with a brief description and a list of a few artists who are known for that particular kind of work. Designers should familiarize themselves with these styles and the concepts behind them through additional sources.

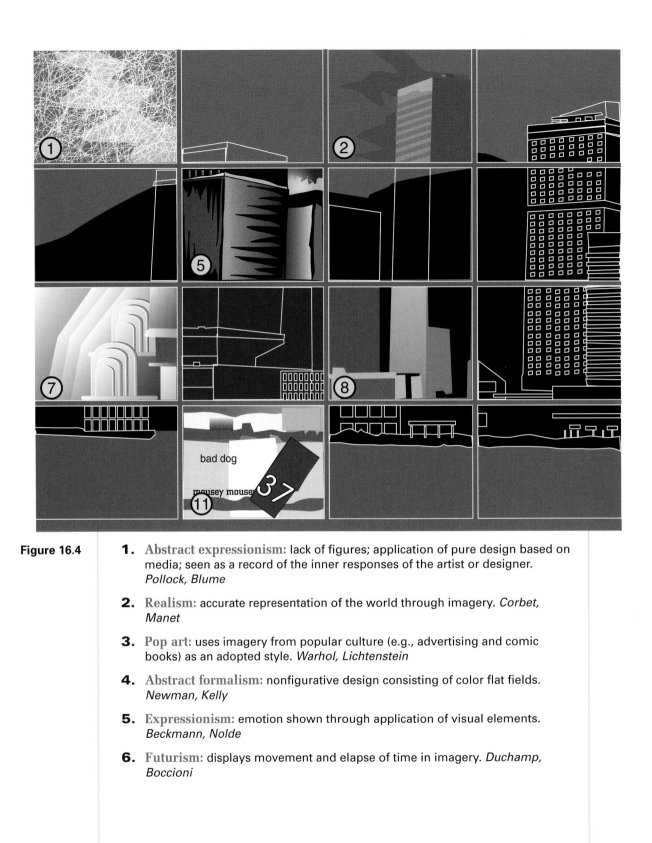

Figure 16.4

1. **Abstract expressionism:** lack of figures; application of pure design based on media; seen as a record of the inner responses of the artist or designer. *Pollock, Blume*

2. **Realism:** accurate representation of the world through imagery. *Corbet, Manet*

3. **Pop art:** uses imagery from popular culture (e.g., advertising and comic books) as an adopted style. *Warhol, Lichtenstein*

4. **Abstract formalism:** nonfigurative design consisting of color flat fields. *Newman, Kelly*

5. **Expressionism:** emotion shown through application of visual elements. *Beckmann, Nolde*

6. **Futurism:** displays movement and elapse of time in imagery. *Duchamp, Boccioni*

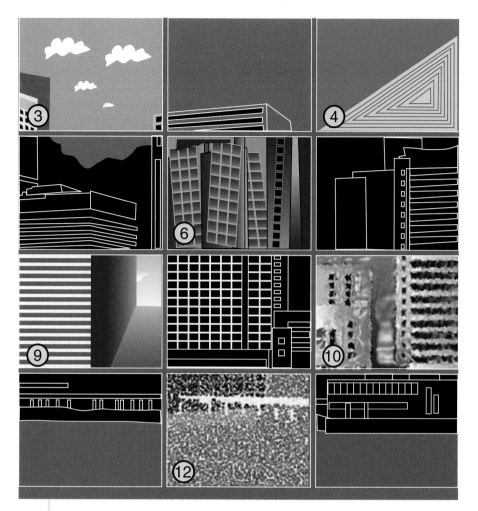

7. **Art deco:** usually applied to the design of objects; geometric and rectilinear approach to breaking up the image plane. *Leger, Mondrian*

8. **Cubism:** flattening of objects or showing more than one perspective at the same time. *Picasso, Braque*

9. **Surrealism:** portrays imagery as dreamlike; based on Freudian psychology. *DeChirico, Dali*

10. **Impressionism:** objects viewed through the effects of light and atmosphere. *Monet, Renoir*

11. **Dadaism:** nihilistic and strives to overturn all conventions of design; anything goes. *Duchamp, Schwitters*

12. **Pointillism:** systematic distribution of colored dots on a white background.

Creating Style

The tools used to make an image can have a large amount of influence on the appearance of style. That is, how the image was made can affect how it looks as much as the ideas behind it. This may seem like an overly simple concept, but designers should be aware of how much the tools they use can influence the outcome of an image.

A good example of how the media that is used can dictate the look of a style can be found in the works of the impressionists from the late 1800s. This style looks the way it does partly because the artists created the works using paint on canvas. One of the recognizable features of this style is that the paint was often applied in heavy daubs that were raised off the surface of the canvas in a way that became textural.

This method of painting has become so associated with impressionism that many people often mistake other styles that use this technique as being impressionistic as well. On the other hand, it would be difficult to make an impressionistic painting by using some other medium such as charcoal. The attributes that give the painting an impressionistic style cannot be created as well without the heavy globs of paint. As a designer, it is important to keep in mind the influence of the tools that are used on the finished product.

AN ARTIST'S TALE

Style in New Media and the Influence on Fashion

Some time ago, a family member came to visit me while wearing a shirt made by one of the trendy new designers. The shirt was covered with some pretty interesting graphic images that attracted my attention, but what made the shirt's design even more intriguing to me was that, because of the style, I was able to recognize which imaging software the designer had used to create the graphics. An example of the style can be seen in Figure 16.5.

I didn't think much of this at the time, but later I saw a television show in which an interior designer was using the same sort of graphics on the walls of a room. Again, the same style was obvious, and it was easy to guess what software had been used because of it. After seeing the program, I became curious about the origins of that particular style, and I turned to the best resource for information of that sort: the Internet.

What I learned was that the style itself wasn't very old; it had been around only a few years, and it had been born out of the introduction of vector graphics in new media. I did a little research on some of the designers who had begun developing the style first and found that they were using the software that I suspected. I also learned that one of the reasons that this style

Figure 16.5 The style of this image is derived from vector-based drawing.

had a certain look was because of the way the software rendered the vector images.

As the software became more commonly used, a number of designers began to adopt the specific style. Eventually, they began using it in other areas, such as print and clothing graphics.

The thing that I found most interesting was that newer versions of the same software no longer limited the look of vector graphics to flat areas of color. Even though designers could now add detailed modeling to their images, they were still creating images that looked as if they were made with software that was several versions older.

What had occurred was that technology had evolved quicker than style. The old look was still considered "hot," and even though the software tools had become more sophisticated, designers were still producing images in a style that had come about partially because of earlier limitations. In essence, the nature of the tool had produced the style, but the style had remained popular long after the limitations were gone.

Issues in New Media

As the previous story illustrates, the abilities of the tools available to new media designers can have a large impact on the style of their work in terms of both the way in which software creates images (e.g., vector versus raster) and the way in which style can be influenced by the particular brand of software used. Some software applications can do some things better than others.

This does not mean that one brand of software is better than any other; it simply means that one kind of software might be more useful for a specific design than another. As a new media artist, it is important to familiarize yourself with the tools and to use the best one for what you are trying to accomplish. A mechanic would not do very well tightening a bolt by using a hammer. The same rule can be applied to design: the right tool for the right job.

Good designers do not allow the tools to hinder their creativity. If you have a certain idea for a design, it is a bad practice to accept second best because your favorite software doesn't do exactly what you need. It is much better to either figure out a way to create the piece you have envisioned by trying new methods or get your hands on some software that will allow you to do it right. Somewhere out there is a tool that will perform in the way you need it to.

SUMMARY

This chapter covered the visual element of style. In the introduction, two different uses for the term *style* were introduced and explained. The first was as a look or as the techniques applied to the elements used in a design. The second was as a reference to a movement in art history. This chapter covered both concepts in detail. For style as techniques, it presented several uses of style, such as association and as context. For style concerned with movements in art, a background on the use of philosophy was given and a visual glossary that included several major styles provided. The chapter ended with commentary on the influence of tools and style.

EXERCISES

1. Create an image that uses a specific style to give more information about an image.

2. Choose an artist from the past and make an image that emulates the same sort of style.

3. Divide an image into several sections and use a different style in each section. For an example, see Figure 16.4.

4. Mix techniques from two different styles to create a new style.

5. Use style in an image to make it look as if it was created in a different historical period.

1. Define the term *style.*

2. What are several ideas that can be conveyed using style?

3. How can style be used to create a context?

4. How can the tools a designer uses affect style?

5. Pick a specific style from art history and list several visual characteristics of that style. What are the ideas behind that style that influence the way the style looks?

CHAPTER 17

Emphasis

emphasis

17

In any form of communication, some parts of the information may be more important than the others. What is most important can depend on the context of the communication and what information is needed by the person receiving it. This can be better explained using the following sentence: Mary walked home.

If it is already understood that someone walked home but it is not known who, the important part of the sentence is the name of the person. If the information that is needed is how Mary arrived home (e.g., by taxi or by bicycle) then the important part of the sentence is the word *walked*. Finally, if we know that Mary walked somewhere but don't know where she went, the word *home* becomes the vital bit of information.

As with other forms of communication, the same concept can be applied to design; that is, some parts of an image or layout may be more important than others. In spoken communication, emphasis can be put on a certain part of a sentence through an inflection of the voice, but in design, emphasis can be given only through the use of other visual elements.

Making a Difference

To add emphasis to some part of a graphic, you use design techniques to focus the viewer's attention to the specific part. This is usually done by somehow making the specific part of the image different from the other areas of the image. A simple illustration of this can be seen in Figure 17.1.

In Figure 17.1, there are two versions of the same image. The first image has no emphasis placed on any part. Because of this, the entire image is seen as a collection of equal parts.

In the second image, one of the faces is a different color. The change in color gives emphasis to the face, and it receives more of the viewer's attention.

Key Points

▸▸ **Making a Difference**
▸▸ **Emphasis through Various Elements**
▸▸ **Keeping Balance and Unity in Mind**
▸▸ **Emphasis in New Media**

Figure 17.1

Emphasis through Various Elements

As was stated in the beginning of this chapter, emphasis given to some part of a design is achieved through the use of the other elements of design. In every case, it is an element of design that has been used to make the part visually stand out from the rest of the design.

In Figure 17.2, there are a series of repeated images that illustrate this. The image in the upper-left corner is the original, and there has been no emphasis placed on any of the three chess pieces. In each of the other images, emphasis has been given to the one of the three chess pieces using a different design element.

As an exercise, examine each of the images and identify the element of design used to emphasize one of the pieces. (e.g., line, shape, or value).

Figure 17.2

Keeping Balance and Unity in Mind

The major way to add emphasis to some part of an image is to make it stand out from the rest of the image, but this can often run contrary to the desire of maintaining balance and unity in the piece.

For example, when emphasis is placed on some part of a design, it is given more visual weight. This may shift the visual balance of the work, and it may be necessary to adjust the other parts to bring balance back to the piece. An example of this can be seen in Figure 17.3.

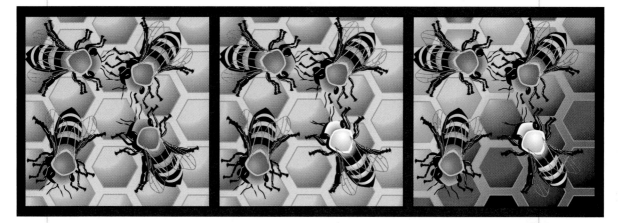

Figure 17.3

In Figure 17.3, there are three versions of the same image. The first is the original, unaltered image, and it consists of four bees scattered on a honeycomb. Because the objects, colors, and values are evenly distributed, the image has balance.

In the second image, emphasis has been added by changing the color of the bee in the lower-right corner to white. The white bee is in stark contrast to the other colors of the image and becomes the point of focus. By moving the point of focus to the lower corner, the balance of the image is thrown off.

In the third image, the background colors around the white bee have been given a darker value. This balances out the values between the background and the white bee and divides the image space into two equal parts. These adjustments compensate for the emphasis added to the single bee, and balance is restored to the layout.

Much like the way in which balance can be thrown off, adding emphasis to some part of a design can disrupt the unity of a piece. It is important to make certain that the element used to create emphasis does not go too far. If the added emphasis makes the part look as if it no longer fits with the design, some adjustment may be necessary. This is illustrated in Figure 17.4.

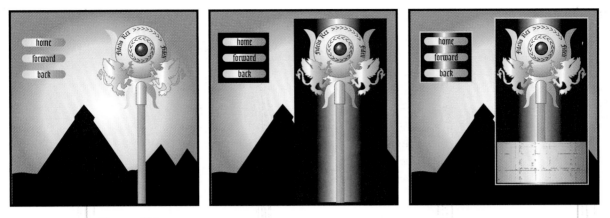

Figure 17.4

The first image in Figure 17.4 shows a layout that includes an interface of three buttons, a background image, and a drawing of a staff. Because of the background color, parts of the staff and the buttons become lost. It is obvious that these areas could benefit from the use of emphasis.

The second image shows the staff and buttons emphasized by the placement of a black rectangle behind each of them. A white glow is also added to the staff. Although these changes do make the buttons and staff stand out from the rest of the layout, the image now looks awkward and unfinished.

In the third image, the problems with unity have been solved by a few additions. A gold edge has been added to further separate each of the black rectangles, and a white glow has been added behind the buttons. These design similarities create unity between the two rectangles. Because there was still a problem with the black of the staff's rectangle blending into the black pyramid, a small wall section was added, and the staff was shortened so that it fit entirely inside the rectangle. The image now looks as if it has three parts (the background, the interface, and the staff) that are held together with the unity of the design.

Emphasis in New Media

Because the new media designer must often give the viewer hints about how to use a project or call attention to a specific bit of information, emphasis can be a useful tool. An example of this is the navigation controls on a Web site. If the goal of a Web site were to lead viewers to a specific page, it would be helpful to give those links some sort of emphasis. You could include a large flashing arrow that said, Click Here Now! but it might be better to use a more subtle approach.

Emphasis through Layout

Although you could use any of the various design elements to draw the attention of a viewer to some bit of information, one of the more effective ways to guide a viewer to content is through the use of layout. For an example of this, see Figure 17.5.

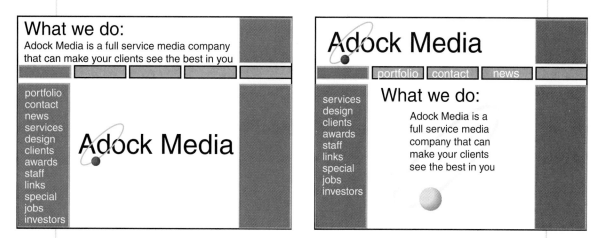

Figure 17.5

Figure 17.5 is made up of two similar Web pages. The main difference between these versions is the placement of content within the same layout. In the first image, the company logo is placed in the center of the design, while a small amount of text about the company is found at the top of the page. By arranging the content this way, the logo is given emphasis and seems to be the most important part of the design.

In the second image, the content has been reversed, and now the small amount of copy has become the focus. In addition to this, three important links have been removed from the long navigation list on the left and placed on the gray bar below the logo. Separating these links from the others has given the links emphasis.

Layout and Emphasis Rules

Books and articles on new media design promote their own theories about where the most prominent areas of a layout are. You will often be given rules that tell you where to place navigation elements (e.g., on the top or on the left side) or where to place the logo (again on the top or to the left). This well-intentioned advice does not seem to take into consideration the infinite number of creative possibilities; instead, it is locked in a design tradition rooted in print. Figure 17.6 is an example of a design that breaks a few of these rules but still remains effective.

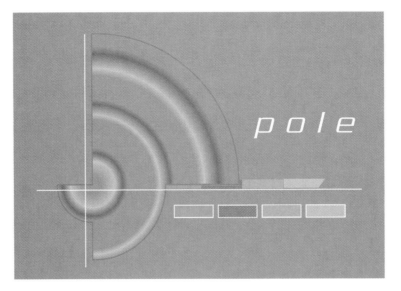

Figure 17.6

According to some of the conventions of new media design, Figure 17.6 has a few problems. The navigation is toward the bottom of the page, and the logo is far to the right. A part of what makes this layout work despite a disregard for the rules is that it is not crammed with content. There is not a lot of clutter to distract the viewer, and a little emphasis (e.g., the subdued colors of the navigation buttons) is enough to attract attention to the right places.

In this example, the rules were broken not simply for the sake of breaking them but rather as a result of careful design. In your own work, it is important to keep in mind that it is okay to bend and break the rules when using layout to give emphasis, but this should be well thought out and intentional.

SUMMARY

This chapter focused on the use of emphasis to draw a viewer's attention to certain parts of a design. Several examples were given on how the different elements of design could be used to create emphasis. This chapter also discussed the effects of emphasis on balance and unity, and it closed with a section on the use of emphasis in new media projects, especially the use of layout.

EXERCISES

1. Create a series of repeating objects in an image. Experiment with various ways of adding emphasis to one of the objects using the different elements of design.

2. Begin with an image or a design that you made for one of the earlier exercises from this text. Add emphasis to some part of it. Afterward, adjust the design so that it still has unity and balance.

REVIEW QUESTIONS

1. Define the term *emphasis* as it applies to design.

2. Identify three ways to add emphasis to a navigation button on an interactive project.

3. How can the use of emphasis change the balance of a design?

4. How can unity be affected through the use of emphasis?

5. How can the arrangement of content in a layout use emphasis?

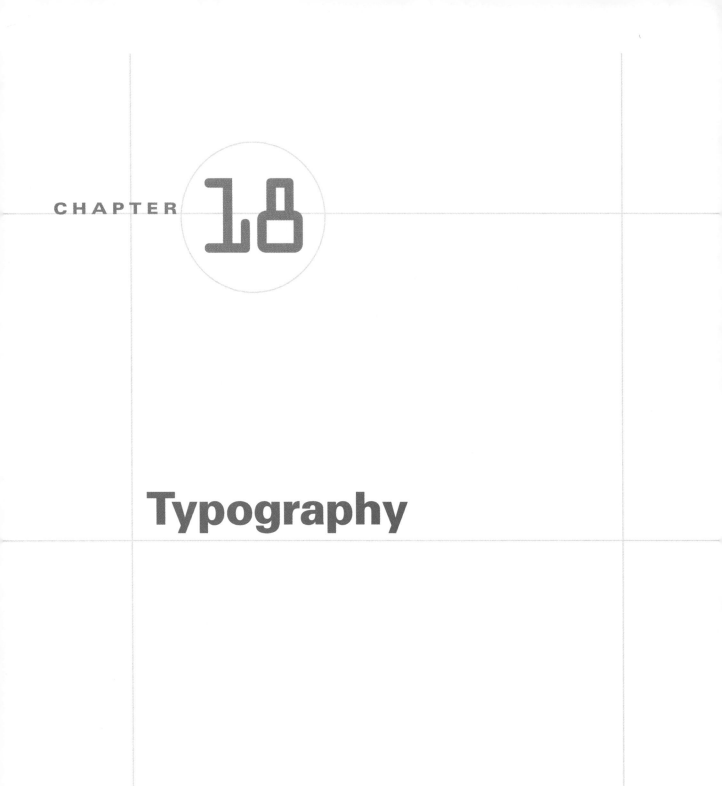

CHAPTER **18**

Typography

281

Typography is sort of a catch-all word that includes the arrangement, style, and appearance of text. For example, the font used for the words that you are presently reading, the spacing, and whether the words are italicized all fall under typography.

In design, type is just as important as any other visual element. Some will even argue that type is the most important element in effective communications.

Unfortunately, type is often one of the most overlooked and underutilized elements of design. This is especially true in new media projects. It is not uncommon for an inexperienced designer to put a great deal of effort into the creation of a graphic or a layout, only to almost arbitrarily choose a font to be used in the project. This sort of approach to design could be compared to dressing in the finest clothing for a formal occasion but then reaching into a dark closet and pulling out two random shoes. (With a little luck, they might at least match each other.)

Using type in an effective way requires an understanding of its basic principles. After learning the fundamentals of typography, the designer can make educated choices and increase the effectiveness of one's design.

Terminology: Font versus Type

Key Points

▸▸ **Type Terminology**
▸▸ **Anatomy of Type**
▸▸ **Type Families**
▸▸ **Type as a Visual Element**
▸▸ **Type in New Media**

It is not uncommon to hear the terms **type** and **font** used interchangeably. Technically, a font is a complete set of a specific type in one size and style. In other words, *Arial* would be an example of a certain type, while *Arial, 12pt.* (12 point is a measurement of type size) would be a font.

In general conversation, this might not matter much since the topic will usually be in reference to a specific section of text, but when discussing typography, it is useful to make a distinction between the two terms.

Anatomy of Type

The place to begin a detailed study of type is with the parts that make up a character. For most people, the shape of a character has been taken for granted since they first began to read. (The letter "A" looks like it does, and there is nothing more to it.) Few people care to know that all the parts of the letters and numbers that have been familiar since childhood have a specific name and purpose. For the designer, it is important to understand the differences in type families and other concepts covered in this chapter. The key to this lies in knowing the different parts that make up each character. Figure 18.1 defines a few of the most basic parts of type anatomy.

Figure 18.1

Type Families

It is the treatment of these different parts of type anatomy that defines **type families.** In the next section, several of the basic families are shown and their differences pointed out.

Old Style

By far the earliest example of printed type, **old style type** has its origins in Roman inscriptions and the writing style of Renaissance manuscripts. In fact, one of the distinguishing features of old style type are serifs that maintain shapes similar to cuts made by the chisels of Roman stonemasons (see Figure 18.2). Other prominent attributes of this type are larger x-heights, a diagonal stress, and an abrupt transition from thick to thin strokes.

Galliard Roman

Times Roman

Figure 18.2

Transitional

Transitional type began to appear around the late 1600s and early 1700s, and its features create a sort of half step between the characteristics of old style and modern type. A few of the changes from old style are smoother transitions from thick to thin strokes, a vertical stress, and serifs that are less angular (see Figure 18.3).

Century Schoolbook

Baskerville

Figure 18.3

Modern

Modern type was developed during the 1700s and had a more mechanical appearance than the earlier kinds of type. Its distinguishing attributes are severe transitions from thick to thin strokes and serifs that are thin and horizontal (see Figure 18.4). Modern type also maintains the vertical stress found in transitional type.

Bodini

Madrone

Slab Serif

Slab serif type is also referred to as Egyptian and developed as a result of a popular fascination with the history of that culture. The two most prominent features of this type are the thick, squared serifs and a subtle difference between thick and thin strokes (see Figure 18.5).

Playbill

Berthold City

Sans Serif

Sans serif type first appeared in the early 1800s. It has been speculated that the first sans serif types were developed by removing the serifs from slab serif type. The most obvious distinction of sans serif is the absence of serifs from the characters (see Figure 18.6). Another common attribute that marks sans serif type is a nearly uniform stroke.

Helvetica
Century Gothic
Gill Sans

Script

Although not always classified as traditional type, **script type** is common enough to warrant inclusion. Script type is by far the easiest to identify. Because its purpose is to emulate cursive handwriting, there are few universal features. The major attribute that many script types have is a look of continuity from one character to the next, as if a word was written without lifting the pen (see Figure 18.7). This effect is created with beginning and ending strokes that meet the same strokes of other characters. Although this feature is common, it is not present in all script type.

Figure 18.7

Decorative

Decorative, or **novelty, type** is reserved in its own category because it is difficult to classify. A specific decorative type could have many attributes in common with other types, or it could be more illustrative (Imagine a type called *Kitty* with each character made from the shape of a cat.) (See Figure 18.8).

DIGITAL ICG   Comic Sans

Bauhaus

Figure 18.8

Working with Type

Working with type can be an art form all its own, and as with any other designing art, a few guidelines can serve to make the inclusion of type more effective.

The first rule of type is that it must be legible. If some bit of type is not readable, then it probably does not belong in the design. The designer should keep in mind that the main purpose of type is to communicate. A viewer will need to be able to read the words conveyed with the type in order for communication to take place.

More Is Not Always Better

Part of what makes type readable is the viewer's familiarity with the shape of each character. The more a type departs from the traditional recognized shape, the more difficult it becomes to read. Figure 18.9 shows an example of how this can affect a design.

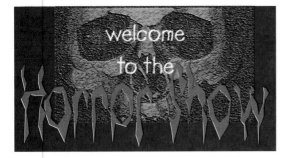
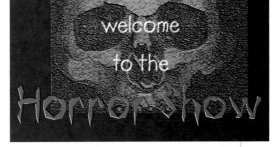

Figure 18.9

Figure 18.9 is made up of two different versions of the same graphic. In the first image, the shapes of the characters have been exaggerated to better fit with the subject of the graphic. Because of the extreme distortion, the type is nearly unreadable.

Although the type in the second image has the same stylistic approach, the characters still maintain much of their traditional shape. These letters are much more readable.

Making It Easy for the Reader

Even though the letters in the second image of Figure 18.9 are distorted, they can still be read. This is partly because the legibility of the words is increased by the large size of the letters and the relatively short length of what needs to be read. If the letters used were smaller or if there were many more words, the text would become difficult to read.

If the type is awkward to read, viewers can become tired or even lose their place in the text. Because of this, it is better to restrict any smaller characters or a longer line to type that is more traditional. Several examples of this can be seen in Figure 18.10.

The back of the box said that the cereal was fortified with eight essential vitamins and iron.

𝕿𝖍𝖊 𝖇𝖆𝖈𝖐 𝖔𝖋 𝖙𝖍𝖊 𝖇𝖔𝖝 𝖘𝖆𝖎𝖉 𝖙𝖍𝖆𝖙 𝖙𝖍𝖊 𝖈𝖊𝖗𝖊𝖆𝖑 𝖜𝖆𝖘 𝖋𝖔𝖗𝖙𝖎𝖋𝖎𝖊𝖉 𝖜𝖎𝖙𝖍 𝖊𝖎𝖌𝖍𝖙 𝖊𝖘𝖘𝖊𝖓𝖙𝖎𝖆𝖑 𝖛𝖎𝖙𝖆𝖒𝖎𝖓𝖘 𝖆𝖓𝖉 𝖎𝖗𝖔𝖓.

THE BACK OF THE BOX SAID THAT THE CEREAL WAS FORTIFIED WITH EIGHT ESSENTIAL VITAMINS AND IRON.

The back of the box said that the cereal was fortified with eight essential vitamins and iron.

Figure 18.10

Figure 18.10 shows the same text repeated several times, each using different type. The first section is in a conservative, sans serif type and is relatively easy to read. The next two sections use a type that is more decorative. As a result, they are more difficult to read. In fact, the reader must pause or reread some combinations of characters in order to determine the word. The last section uses a uniform type with serifs. Many designers maintain that simple serifs make characters easily and quickly recognizable.

Combining Different Type

As discussed in earlier chapters, it is important for an entire project to have unity. However, when it comes to using type, unity can cause a few problems. Different units of text may need to be differentiated from others. For example, a title will need to stand out from a body of text. If there is no difference between the two, the reader may become confused. This problem can be avoided by adding variety to the type used in a piece.

The easiest way to accomplish this is to use different sizes of the same font. By making titles and important units of text larger, the different areas of content will be clearly separated.

In projects where there are size constraints or when a designer wants to take a more creative approach, different types can be used to bring variety to a piece. Using different type in the same project adds emphasis to certain parts, such as titles and quotes, and information can be broken down into smaller units. An example of this can be seen in Figure 18.11.

In Figure 18.11, there are two units of text that are set a part by using different type. This approach clearly separates the two and adds variety to the overall piece.

Choosing which types to use in the same piece can often be a difficult process. Many designers will often hold to strict rules and never break them, such as never using more than two different types in the same piece or always using one type with serifs and one with sans serif. Figure 18.12 illustrates what can occur if one of the major *don'ts* is broken.

In Figure 18.12, the use of too many different types makes the text difficult to read and destroys any hope of unity for the rest of the design.

Figure 18.11

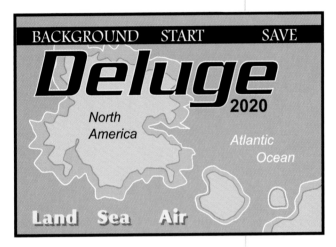

Figure 18.12

Although many of the rules have some validity, they will not always apply to every circumstance. Instead of strictly adhering to a dictated formula for using type, there are two tests that can be used to help determine what types will work together. First, can they be read without too much effort? Second, do they look good together and fit with the rest of the piece? In other words, trust your designer's eye while keeping in mind that when it comes to type, legibility is often more important than style.

Adjusting Type for Design

A designer is not strictly limited to the predetermined attributes of a particular type. By adjusting a type's properties, the contribution of type to any design can be dramatically increased. Two examples of how adjusting type can enhance a design are seen in Figure 18.13.

Figure 18.13

Figure 18.13 shows two examples of type adjustment used to improve the contribution of type to a design. In the first example, the type has been presented in its default format, but in the second version, the height of the letters has been increased to make the characters more imposing when compared to the smaller figure.

In the second example, the type has been presented in its default format and in a second version with increased tracking (discussed in the next section). The second version appears elegant in comparison to the original.

Standard Type Adjustments

Figure 18.14 shows several examples of the different kinds of adjustments that can be used for type. The figure is made up of three illustrations that demonstrate the standard type adjustments. Each of the alterations is indicated by a red line:

1. *Kerning:* **Kerning** is the adjustment of the space between individual characters so that they will appear more evenly spaced. Because of

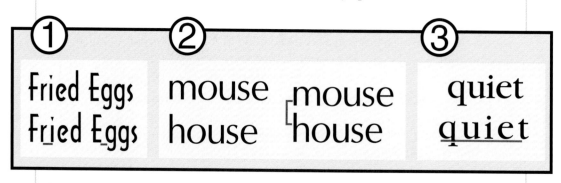

Figure 18.14

different type shapes and character sizes, the space between two letters may seem irregular. This technique is generally used to improve the appearance of words and to make them easier to read.

2. *Leading:* **Leading** refers to the line space between rows of type. By adjusting the space between rows, sections of type can appear to have more unity (as in this illustration), or complex characters can be more legible.

3. *Tracking:* **Tracking** is the overall spacing between all the characters in a section of type. Adjustments to the tracking can be used to improve legibility, add emphasis, or influence the reading of the type. (Wider tracking slows the reader.)

The ability to alter type is not limited to these standard adjustments alone. Some software applications also allow the designer to adjust specific dimensions, such as the height and width of characters.

When manipulating the attributes of type, it is good for a designer to exercise a little caution. The overadjustment of type can quickly make a mess of any design. The best rule for adjusting type is much the same as the two-part test used when selecting type for a design, namely, is it legible, and does it look good in the design? By using this simple guide, the designer can avoid most problems associated with any adjustments that might be made.

Type as an Element of Design

The best approach for using type in design is to treat it the same way as any other element. The type chosen should work with the rest of the piece both stylistically and compositionally. An example of this can be seen in Figure 18.15.

In Figure 18.15, the type, like the other elements, is simple and minimal. The serifs are relatively thin and echo the other thin lines used in this design. The tracking of the page title is wide and helps balance the entire composition as well as set up a rhythm that flows from left to right. The choice of type and the tracking adjustment blend well with the other elements, and everything looks as if it belongs in this piece.

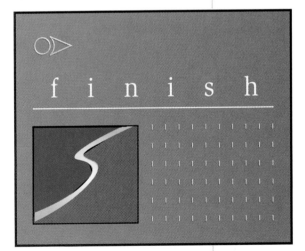

Figure 18.15

Type Is Not an Appendage

The use of type should not be an afterthought or something added to a design. It should receive as much attention in design as any line or shape. Type can even become the main element of any design. Figure 18.16 shows three illustrations in which the use of type is the most important part of each piece.

Figure 18.16

In each of the three illustrations in Figure 18.16, the use of type is the design. The other elements are there to enhance and emphasize what the type has already accomplished.

Communicating with More Than Words

Type is not limited to the words used for communication. Different characters can be used to convey an emotional quality in much the same way that line can. In addition to emotion, type can be used to convey associations. Several examples of this can be seen in Figure 18.17.

Figure 18.17   Through shape and form, the type chosen for each word communicates the same concept as the word used.

Using type this way can communicate additional information in a design. This can be seen in Figure 18.18.

Figure 18.18

Figure 18.18 shows a screen title for an interactive piece that tells a story about time travel. The futuristic-looking type used for the word *chrononauts* adds an association with technology and time travel to the image.

HISTORICAL REFERENCE

In addition to these sorts of association, type can also be used to create a historical reference through the use of style. Because certain types are associated with specific periods of history, their use can enhance a design that relies on historical reference. For an example of this, see Figure 18.19.

The fonts used in Figure 18.19 help convey an association with a specific period of history because it is a type that was commonly used during that time for posters and other printed materials.

Figure 18.19

THE TROUBLE WITH TYPE

Almost all the design issues concerned with type and new media fall into one of two categories: legibility or compatibility. These two areas are addressed next.

Legibility

The question of **legibility** truly comes down to the system used to display the type, specifically, the monitor. Most of the issues that can occur with type in a new media project have been addressed in regard to other elements in other chapters. The difference with type is that the problem is usually magnified. What follows in the next section are a few of the most serious issues.

PIXELATION

Figure 18.20

This condition has been addressed in several other parts of this book, but where it is most evident is in the use of type. Because type depends heavily on the accurate representation of characters, the reproduction of a font on a screen may not have the desired results. An example of the effect that pixelization can have on characters can be seen in Figure 18.20.

Figure 18.20 is an image that illustrates the differences between characters that have undergone pixelation and those that appear normal. In each example, the pixelated characters appear distorted and jagged.

As screen resolutions improve, this will become less of a problem. Until that time, there are a few techniques that can be used to minimize the unwanted effects of pixelization.

Figure 18.21

The first approach to minimizing the negative effects of pixelization is to use straight-back type that is sans serif or that has flat serifs. Fonts that fall into these categories have fewer parts that cross over the pixel grid of a monitor. A comparative example can be seen in Figure 18.21.

In Figure 18.21, the same method to produce pixelization was used on the second set of characters as in Figure 18.20, but in this case there was very little effect.

Another way to improve legibility despite pixelization is through the use of size. The smaller the text, the more pixelization will appear to distort the characters. By using larger characters, pixelization will not affect the readability as much.

CONTRAST

Figure 18.22

Another element of design that plays heavily into the use of type is the contrast between the characters and the background. A strong contrast is needed for the type to be legible. This is especially important when the piece will be viewed on a monitor. An example of this can be seen in Figure 18.22.

In Figure 18.22, the word *welcome!* spans across two different background areas. The last part of the word is easy to read, but because of a lack in contrast between the type and the background, the beginning of the word is almost invisible.

Compatibility

The other major issue that comes with the use of type for any new media project is that of font **compatibility.** An example of this is a project, such as a Web site, that uses a specific font. If the visitors to the site do not have the same font installed on their own computers, they will be unable to see the design as it was intended. This does not mean that no type will be displayed but rather that their computers will select a default font to replace the missing one.

There are two ways to avoid this problem that when used together can overcome this issue. The first is to use common fonts that are found on most systems. A few of the more common fonts are Arial, Courier, and Times New Roman, but there are many more.

The second method of dealing with font compatibility is to convert any type into an image. This ensures that the type will be displayed correctly regardless of what fonts are installed on a viewer's system.

The key to these two methods is to know when to use them. One of the best guidelines to follow has to do with the amount of text. If there is a large amount of type, then it would be better to use a common font. The first reason for this is that a large amount of text would create a very large image that might be difficult to manage in a project. The second reason has to do with legibility; that is, common fonts are common because they are easier to read than others. Readability is especially important when a large amount of type is used.

In contrast, if the type is for a short title or a headline and the design would suffer from the use of a common font, then converting it to an image might be the best approach.

SUMMARY

This chapter introduced the fundamentals of typography and the use of type in design. Visual examples of each concept were presented, and attention was given to specific issues with type in new media projects.

Figure 18.23

EXERCISES

1. Create a design using a single word. The type chosen and the graphics used should illustrate the meaning of the word. For an example, see Figure 18.23.

2. Make an image that evokes an association or that references a historical period through the use of type.

3. Design a single screen or page from an imaginary new media project that uses at least two different fonts.

REVIEW QUESTIONS

1. Name two type families (e.g., slab serif) and explain the major differences.

2. What is decorative, or novelty, type?

3. What is a serif?

4. What is meant by the term *sans serif?*

5. What is kerning?

6. What is leading?

7. Explain how pixelization can affect type.

NOTES

SECTION FOUR

One of the best things about new media is that it is not limited to static images and text. New media projects can make use of elements such as interaction, sound, and motion in ways that can push communication into the realm of experience. For a designer, this can be a two-edged sword. Not only must one wear the hat of an artist, but the new media designer will often have to throw a little bit of sound engineer, storyteller, and movie director into his or her job description.

This section touches on a few additional elements that designers may use in projects. In most cases, the subjects covered deal mainly with the conceptual aspects of each element. As with many of the other topics presented in this text, the guidelines given are not hard rules that must be strictly adhered to. Instead, they are simply defined boundaries. It is up to the designer to decide which boundaries will be crossed and how that will be done.

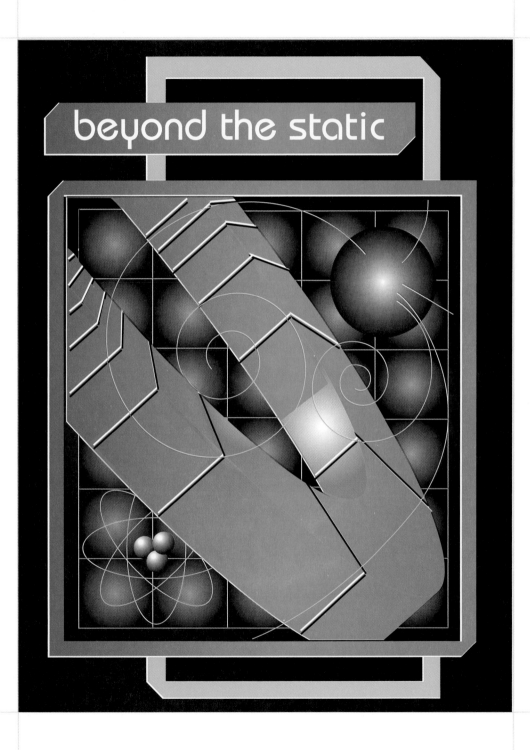

beyond the static

The Element of Time

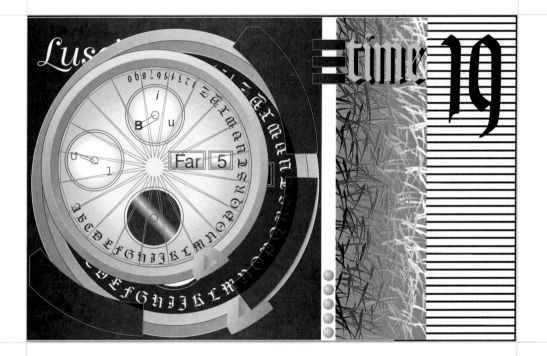

O utside of the music or motion picture industry, few design-ers think of time as an element of design. This powerful communication tool is also available to designers who work with new media.

As an element of design, time usually incorporates change. This change can be in the form of an animation, an event, or an action taken by the viewer. In one moment, the part of a design that makes use of time exists in a certain state; in the next moment, the state is somehow different. An example of this can be seen in Figure 19.1.

Figure 19.1 is an illustration of the same interface in two different states. The first image shows the original before there has been any change. The second image shows that the speedometer needle moves when the viewer places the cursor over one of the controls. This is an example of a change over time, between two states of an image.

Evolution

Evolution, as it applies to design, is the process of change as it takes place over time. Evolution can be abrupt, instantly changing from one state to the next, or it can be gradual, with several steps occurring through the entire change. In a new media project, evolution can be used to transform the display of content into an experience for the viewer. A simple example of this can be seen in Figure 19.2.

Key Points

▸▸ Evolution
▸▸ Transitions
▸▸ Pace
▸▸ Motion

Figure 19.2 is made up of a series of cells that show the evolution of an image over time. In this example, the presentation begins with a relatively sparse composition but changes as a small sprout grows into a large tree.

In the first frame, the viewer will have a sense of anticipation and expect the empty area to become filled with something. The growing tree fulfills this expectation but then surprises the viewer by growing beyond the boundaries of the picture frame.

A part of what makes evolution successful in design is the use of anticipation and the unexpected. There is a tension that is then relieved

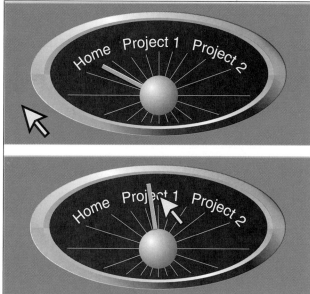

Figure 19.1

through surprise. If the anticipation is fulfilled with nothing more than the expected, the presentation can become boring.

Figure 19.2

Transitions

One of the more important parts of any evolutionary sequence is the **transition** that occurs between the different states. An abrupt jump from one state to another can be disconcerting or disorienting. By using transition effects, a designer can use time to introduce new elements and can build on the expectation of the viewer.

Figure 19.3

Good examples of transitions can be seen in motion pictures when the harshness of scene changes is softened with a dissolve or a fade. These same sorts of effects can be used in new media presentations. This can be used for the entire screen or be limited to a single element. An example of this can be seen in Figure 19.3.

Figure 19.3 is made up of four frames from the title of a new media project. In this example, separate elements slowly fade into the image. Again, the concepts of expectation and surprise are used to enhance the viewer's experience.

Evolution and Pace

The term *pace* refers to the speed of change and transitions during an evolution. Rapid-fire change can be used to promote excitement, while slow change will be seen as peaceful or ominous.

Again, the best examples of this can be found in motion pictures. Action films will often quickly flash from scene to scene, with no single shot lasting more than 3 seconds. Dramas will set a different pace by switching from scene to scene at a much slower rate. A slower pace allows tension to build.

SPECIAL ISSUES IN NEW MEDIA

EVOLUTION AS FEEDBACK

One of the most effective ways to provide feedback to a person using a new media project is through the use of evolution. By changing some element that is intended as a control device, a viewer will understand that the element can be activated in some way.

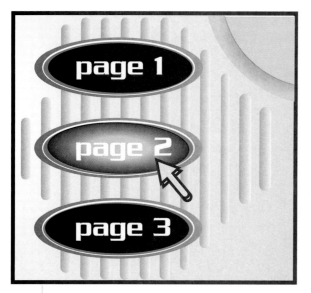

Figure 19.4

Figure 19.4 shows several buttons from a control interface. Here, an effect that emulates a glowing light has been added to the activated button. This feedback lets the viewer know that the control is operational.

Motion

Motion can be thought of as the combination of time and space. When something moves, it not only changes over time (evolution) but also changes position in space (see Figure 19.5).

In new media design, motion can be divided into two different categories, depending on what is moving. The first type of motion relates to an object or element that moves in space. The movement can be broad, like a butterfly that flaps its wings as it flutters across the entire screen, or it can be subtle, like a globe that slowly revolves.

The second type of motion has to do with a change in the point of view. In **point-of-view motion,** it is as if the viewer is moving through space while the objects and elements remain in place. An example of this kind of motion is an animation that shows the point of view of a person riding a roller coaster. In such an animation, it is the scene that changes, but it gives the illusion that the viewer is moving.

Figure 19.5   The motion of a pinball is simulated in this illustration.

This kind of motion can be a little difficult to produce because it requires the accurate use of perspective. If objects in view do not change

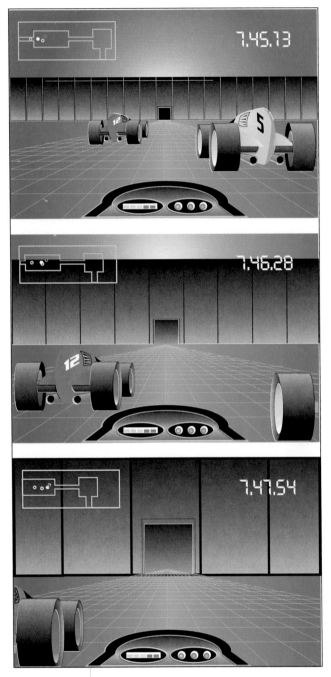

Figure 19.6

position as they would in the real world, it will appear as if the objects themselves are moving instead of the viewer.

Figure 19.6 uses three frames to illustrate point-of-view motion. In each image, the positions of the other objects change in relation to the viewer. This simulation makes use of three elements to help make the illusion more convincing.

The first element is accurate perspective. This is enhanced for the viewer by the grid markings on the racetrack.

The second element is the presence of a ground plane. In the real world, we visually determine our vertical position by looking at the horizon. These images use a well-marked horizon to help the viewer understand one's orientation in the simulation.

The third element consists of the objects that remain fixed with the point of view. In these images, these objects are the dashboard at the bottom of the screen and the information displays in the upper corners. No matter what happens in the simulation, these elements will remain in the same position. Because they are always constant, they provide a visual reference to the other objects.

SPECIAL ISSUES IN NEW MEDIA

MOTION AND DISTRACTION

It can be tempting to overuse motion and animation in new media projects. The effects that are created seem appealing, but, as with any other visual element, the enhancement test should be applied: Does the animation enhance the design, or is it really a distraction from the main parts of the piece? If the motion helps convey information or enhances the experience, then it is beneficial to the piece, but if it is little more than superficial decoration, it probably does not belong in the project.

Too often, an inexperienced designer will add motion effects because it is the kind of thing that seems impressive. But for the viewer, the spinning, fire-breathing logo in the corner is only a visual nuisance that distracts one from the content.

SUMMARY

This chapter presented the use of time as an element of design in new media projects. The first section of the chapter covered the concept of evolution and defined it as change over time. Additional chapter topics addressed other ways to manipulate the use of time. These included transitions (as a way to move from one state to another), pace (as a conscious control of the flow of evolution over time), and motion (as the combination of movement in space over time). This chapter also discussed several issues concerned with time in new media projects.

EXERCISES

1. Through a series of drawings, illustrate the evolution of an original graphic. There should be at least four different drawings in the series. For this exercise, keep in mind viewer expectation and surprise.

2. Find two examples of different transitions used in either a new media project or a movie. Compare and contrast the transitions (e.g., what the viewer sees and the effectiveness) in a few paragraphs. Feel free to use diagrams and illustrations as supporting information.

REVIEW QUESTIONS

1. Define the term **evolution** as it applies to an element.

2. How can evolution be used to give a viewer feedback?

3. How can pace be used to influence the viewer's experience?

4. Give an example of a transition.

5. Give an example of how pace could be used in a new media project.

6. What is point-of-view motion?

CHAPTER **20**

Interactivity

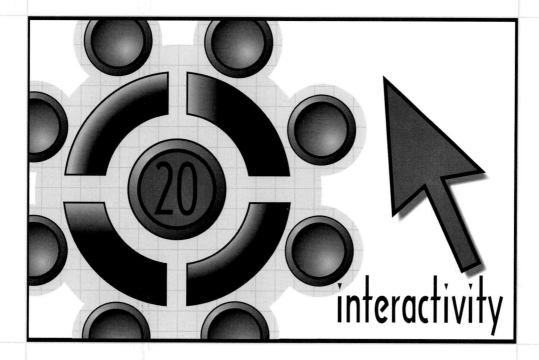

interactivity

Chapter two of this book introduced the concept of interactivity as a part of the design process for an entire project. This chapter looks at interactivity as an element of design.

In its broadest sense, interactivity can be thought of as the viewer's influence and participation in the presentation. This, of course, is participation beyond simply viewing the project. (If a new media piece is displayed in the woods and there is no one there to see it, does it still show content?) The amount of participation can be as limited as allowing control of the time spent on each part of the presentation to as complex as altering the content of the piece.

An example of the simplest form of interactivity is a presentation much like a slide show. When the viewer is ready to see the next part of the presentation, one clicks a button to load the next screen.

A more complex form of interactivity would allow the viewer to input information that altered the piece. A simple example of this is a computer-generated mad-lib application. The viewer would supply a list of requested words, and the project would assemble the words into a story. An extreme example of this same kind of interactivity is an adventure game that can have completely different outcomes, depending on the decisions made during play.

Giving Up Control

Key Points

▸▸ **Giving Up Control**
▸▸ **Navigation**

For the designer intent on effective communication, the inclusion of interactivity can be more than a little scary. Imagine allowing visitors to a Web site to choose which images will be used to help explain the text, or even giving them the ability to add their own thoughts to the content of the site. This would be sort of like giving all the passengers of an airliner access to the flight controls while the pilot sat back, crossed his fingers, and hoped for the best.

Although this analogy may seem far-fetched, there are plenty of Web sites that use this exact approach. The classic example is the unmoderated Internet bulletin board. In this kind of forum, nearly all the content is generated by the viewers, and the results are often disastrous. Floods of arguments, abuse, and offensive material often choke off any serious attempts at communication. This may not be a bad thing if it fits with the project's goal, but for this kind of project, the expertise of a designer is hardly needed.

There is another kind of interactive project where the role of the designer is crucial. These projects allow the viewer a certain amount of freedom over what content is seen and possibly the order in which it is viewed. In these kind of projects, it is the designer's job to give viewers useful information about their choices and occasionally guide them in a specific direction.

Navigation: Narrative and Sequence

Any navigation that is available to the viewer is a form of interactivity. By controlling the navigation of a piece, the viewer can manipulate the order in which the information is seen. This can have an effect on any perception that a viewer might have about the information presented. To minimize the chance that the viewer's perception does not fit with the project's goal, there may need to be some influence over the interactive choices that can be made.

An effective way to do this is through the navigation structure of the project. This does not necessarily include the presentation of the controls, even though this can also greatly influence the choices a viewer makes. Instead, the navigation structure is about the flow from one bit of content to another.

Navigation as a Narrative

One way to think of the navigation is as a story or narrative told by the designer. Some parts of the narrative may be vital to the goal of the project, while others might be important only to specific viewers. The designer helps determine how the story is told and tries to ensure that the important parts get included in the correct order.

TYPES OF NAVIGATION

What follows are three examples of different navigation structures. Each is presented in an idealized form to provide a clear definition. It is rare that a large project will use only one of these structures without any variations. Instead, a project will often be a mix that employs different structures for different parts.

Linear Navigation

The simplest form of navigation is **linear navigation.** This is the presentation of information in a predetermined order. Figure 20.1 provides an illustration of this kind of navigation.

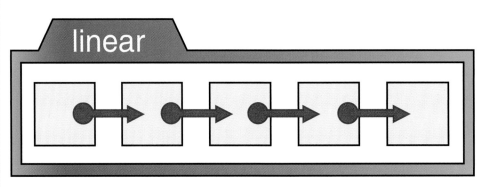

Figure 20.1

In Figure 20.1, there are a series of squares that represent parts of a new media presentation. The arrows indicate the navigational direction allowed from each part. In this example, the viewer can move to the next part of the presentation only in the order that was set by the designer.

Modular Navigation

The second example of navigation structure is called **modular navigation.** This name is derived from the grouping of content into separate modules. An illustration depicting modular navigation can be seen in Figure 20.2.

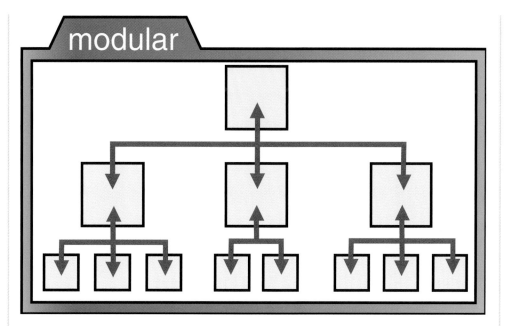

Figure 20.2

In Figure 20.2, there are several squares, each of which represents separate parts of a new media presentation. There are also red arrows that show the direction a viewer may move from one section to the next. In this example, the viewer begins the presentation in the topmost square. From this page, the viewer is free to navigate to three different sections. Each section has new sections that become available after the viewer has entered a specific module. In a case such as this, the content of the different sections within each module is related in some way. To enter a different module, the viewer needs to return to an upper-level section.

Open Navigation

The last navigation structure presented here is referred to as **open navigation.** An illustration of open navigation is provided in Figure 20.3.

In Figure 20.3, the viewer is free to navigate to any section of the presentation in any order chosen. This kind of navigation is used when the presentation requires no specific sequence. In other words, information from one section is not needed for a better understanding of the information presented in any other.

Because of this, when using an open navigation structure, it is important to keep any content in self-contained units. A good rule is to place all of the relevant material on a single page or screen of a project (e.g., each product in an online catalog has its own page or all similar products are grouped together on a page). This will prevent the need to search through the project for additional information on a specific topic.

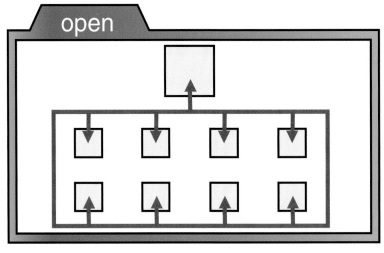

Figure 20.3

By combining these kinds of structures, a design can produce an effective new media project. An example of this can be seen in Figure 20.4. This figure uses a hypothetical case study in which several presentations and additional content are provided in a Human Resources Intranet.

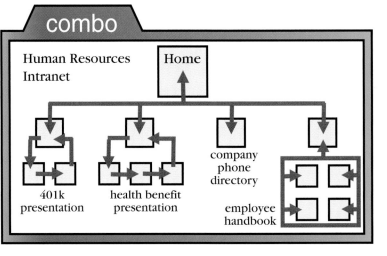

Figure 20.4

SPECIAL ISSUES IN NEW MEDIA

NAVIGATION PARADIGMS

One of the most popular paradigms concerned with navigation uses the terms deep and shallow to represent two ends of a navigation spectrum (see

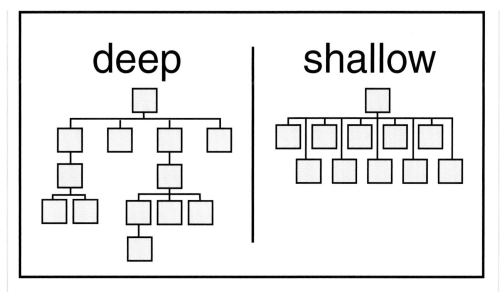

Figure 20.5

Figure 20.5). *Deep* refers to a navigation structure that is rooted in a modular navigation model. In a **deep navigation,** viewers drill down through layers of information; there would be little if any ability to navigate across modules at any but the highest levels.

In a **shallow navigation** structure, the concept of an open navigation system is allowed with access to all parts of the presentation from any other part.

In the past, a deep navigation was thought the best way to provide a large amount of material because it seemed logical to organize information in related units. This navigation structure also gave the designer a certain amount of control over the order in which the viewer accessed the information. Later, the idea was somewhat overthrown by some theorists in favor of a shallow navigation. It was thought that by keeping the information in smaller units (a single page) and allowing the viewer access to any part from anywhere, the presentation would automatically provide a customized experience. Viewers could quickly get to the specific information they needed in the order they determined.

The truth is that each kind of navigation structure has its advantages and its disadvantages. For example, although well ordered, a deep structure will often require a viewer to pass through areas already visited in order to navigate to another section. Viewers can easily become lost when they do not understand the structure of the navigation.

By using a shallow structure, the designer is required to provide the viewer with a large number of choices in navigation. This can create a confusing situation for the viewer who is faced with a large number of controls and no clear direction. In addition to this drawback, a shallow navigation structure requires that all the related content be limited to a single page or screen. This has its own problems when it comes to layout.

The goal of the designer should not be to strictly follow one structure or another but rather to develop the most useful navigation for the particular project. In reality, the best structure will usually lie somewhere in between the two extremes and will make use of the best of both concepts.

SUMMARY

This chapter reintroduced interactivity as an element of design for new media projects. Specific topics addressed were the nature of interactivity and a few of its extremes. This chapter also focused on navigation. Several examples of different navigation structures were given, including a section on current navigation theories for interactive projects.

EXERCISES

1. Explore two Web sites and draw a diagram representing the navigation structure of each.

2. Determine and explain the type of navigation model (e.g., linear, modular, or open) used for the Web sites from the previous exercise.

3. Find a Web site with a poorly designed navigation and redesign it. Explain how the changes will be an improvement from the original.

REVIEW QUESTIONS

1. Give two examples of interactivity in new media projects.

2. Define the term **navigation** as it applies to a new media project.

3. What is a linear navigation structure?

4. What is a modular navigation structure?

5. What is an open navigation structure?

6. Describe the difference between deep and shallow navigation.

Incorporating
Additional Media

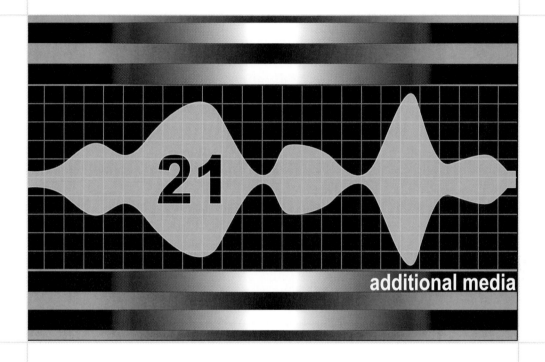

Chapter one listed the ability to include additional media as one of the main attributes that defined new media. Web sites that incorporate music, kiosk presentations with video demonstrations, and CD-ROMs that automatically connect with the Internet are only a few examples of this.

By including other forms of media in an interactive presentation, the viewer can be given a richer experience, and complex concepts can often be explained in a clearer way. (If a picture paints a thousand words, how many words does a 2-minute video account for?)

Exactly what could be considered additional media is open to a great deal of interpretation. For practical purposes, we will use a specific definition that depends on two qualities. The first is that the additional media must be something that might stand on its own as a complete unit. Examples of this are a video clip included in a CD-ROM presentation and a Java applet game on a Web site. Both the video and the game could be self-contained media pieces, but since they are used as a part of another new media project, they are considered additional media.

If this characteristic was the only basis for our definition, a case could be made that static images or text could be considered additional media since either could stand on its own. Because of this, we will also add to our working definition that additional media usually incorporates an evolutionary element. That is, the added element will change over time. (An audio file or an animation will evolve while playing; a static graphic will not.)

For the purist, the definition that we will use can get into some "chicken or the egg" type debates. (If a small animation created in Macromedia's Flash were incorporated as a part of a standard Web site, the animation would be considered additional media. But what if the smaller Flash animation is incorporated in a Flash-based Web site? Is it still added media?) The best approach is to simply avoid the headaches of a paradox and concentrate on good design. Use the definition when it works; use something else when it does not.

Key Points

▸▸ **Reasons to Use Additional Media**
▸▸ **General Cautions**
▸▸ **Presentation**
▸▸ **Audio in New Media Projects**
▸▸ **Additional Media over the Internet**

Reasons for Using Additional Media

It can be tempting to use all the available bells and whistles in a presentation. This is especially true when it comes to incorporating additional media because, as designers, we like to show off a little. As with any other element of design, "just because you can" is not usually a very good reason to include something.

The best reason to use additional media is because it will communicate the content better than some other form of presentation. In some cases it might be more effective to show viewers how to perform a task through an animation than it is to tell them how to do so with long lines of text.

Before jumping to incorporate additional media, it is a good idea to do some research into how it might change the project. Occasionally, unexpected issues arise that can ruin an otherwise effective presentation. A good example of this is the popular use of voice narration in interactive projects. In such presentations, the viewer listens to the content in the same way one would a lecture. The use of an audio presentation can make a project impressive, but it also has a few major drawbacks, one of which is the time that the presentation will take.

On the average, most people speak English at 180 to 200 words per minute. Although this rate works well for face-to-face conversation, effective verbal communication through media is much slower. How much slower is evident in the rate used during televised speeches. Over the past two decades, the typical speech by any U.S. president has been between 99 and 112 words per minute.

These numbers alone do not mean very much, but when compared to the reading rate of the average adult of 200 to 250 words per minute, they tell a story that should alarm any new media designer. The same presentation that would take a reader about 20 minutes to complete would be over 40 minutes long if it used verbal narration. If the amount of time that a presentation lasts is an issue, the addition of the audio narration might be a poor choice.

The simplest way to make a decision about the inclusion of additional media is to use the same test that you would use for any content: Does it help the presentation? Do the benefits from adding the media outweigh any issues that arise from its inclusion? If the honest answer to either of these questions is no, then the additional media probably does not belong as a part of the project. This does not mean that there are not exceptions, as illustrated in the following story.

But What if the Goal Is to Impress?

Recently, I was hired for a project that would be a dream of most new media designers: to design the official Web site of a well-known professional athlete. What made this project so great from a designer's point of view was not that it was going to be for someone famous. (That was just the icing on the cake.) The real appeal of this project was its goal: to entertain and impress visitors. The client needed a Web site that would make viewers want to return again and again and that they would be excited about and share with their friends. The solution to this was to fill the site with plenty of media effects and features that visitors could play with. For a new media designer, this kind of project is like being a kid in a toy store.

The mere thought of cramming a Web site full of effects would probably make many communication purists cringe in a corner while muttering, "But, content is king . . . content is king." Technically, they would be correct, but in this case the entertainment quality of the site was the content. In other words, "Wow! That's cool!" was the message that needed to be communicated.

I have to admit that in the beginning design stages, we planned for this site to have it all: dazzling effects, video, and an on-line auction for charity. We even considered including an interactive football game where the viewer played the part of the quarterback.

Then reality reared its ugly head.

As my design team and I struggled with many of the issues associated with including so much additional media, a lot of what originally seemed like great ideas ended up being nearly impossible. Necessity forced us to approach our use of media in a much more practical way. Our goal was still to impress and entertain the viewer, but we had to concentrate our efforts on features that

A DESIGNER'S TALE

would still be effective and not take several hours to download over a 56k modem. Finally, we had a finished project, and we published the site.

In the first three days, the Web site received over 67,000 visits and plenty of chatter on fan sites—all before the site was even registered in the search engines. That told us that the news was getting out and that it was being spread by word of mouth (or at least by e-mail). By checking the server statistics, it was also easy to see that the visitors were not all coming back to check out players' game scores. They were viewing the added media content, and in many cases they were coming back to view it again and again.

Despite the fact that no one ever saw the on-line football game, the site was still successful because of the additional media. In the end, we had a well-balanced project that achieved its goal.

Exercising Caution

As mentioned, the issues associated with the use of additional media can often outweigh the benefits. These issues might arise because of technical, design, or even legal concerns. What follows are some of the typical problems and a few ways to avoid them.

Technical Issues with Additional Media

Much of what is considered technical issues with additional media should be determined during the target audience phase of the design process. This is because a large number of such issues have to do with the software and hardware available to the viewer. For example, if a presentation includes a video clip, the viewer must have the appropriate software installed in order to see it. If sound is used, the viewer will need speakers and a sound card. If the presentation has been created in the latest version of a media-authoring software such as Macromedia's Flash, the viewer needs to have the newest software plug-ins installed. This sort of issue can be a huge problem. (Do you really want someone to have to go to a different site and download software before being able to see your work?)

The easiest way to avoid these issues is to create presentations that can be viewed on the most common systems. Although this is not a very popular choice, it does ensure the least amount of problems. Do not despair; today's latest and greatest media will be tomorrow's standard. It usually does not take the viewer very long to catch up with the latest technology.

Another technical problem with additional media has to do with the amount of data that it requires. For example, video files can be huge compared to the other parts of a project. Not only does this present a problem with storage (Is there enough room on a single CD for the presentation and all the video?), but it can also bog down a computer processor.

As technology improves, this becomes less an issue. Unfortunately, the trend seems to be that the more data can be handled, the more designers add to their projects. Because of this, technology never seems to catch up to what can be presented.

The solution to this problem is to keep an eye on file sizes. By using file compression methods and editing out unnecessary parts, you can keep media files down to a manageable size.

Legal Trouble

One of the most overlooked issues with the inclusion of media has to do with ownership and the law. In many cases, unless the additional media was produced specifically for a project, it is probably someone else's property. By incorporating it in a project, the designer may be breaking copyright law. An example of this is using a popular song as the background music for a media presentation. Although the music may be the perfect addition to the project, the legal ramifications of unauthorized use can be far reaching.

Two of the best ways to avoid this often costly mistake is to make certain that you either have permission to use a piece of media or use only original media produced for the project. Getting permission may also include paying a fee for use or purchasing the material from the owner. Even then, it is best to check with a good copyright attorney. In fact, you should always consult with a copyright attorney in regard to the use of any additional media that you did not produce yourself or that your client does not own.

Presentation: Design Issues with Additional Media

Another problem that can occur with the addition of other media has to do with the overall design and unity of the entire project. Too often, some form of media is added to a presentation without any consideration for the design of the project. The additional media is simply stuck in as is and left to fend for itself. An example of this can be seen in Figure 21.1.

In Figure 21.1, two versions of the same presentation are shown. In the first, a video is shown with the player visible. It is obvious that the appearance of the player does not fit with the design of the rest of the layout.

In the second version, the player is no longer visible, and the video has been masked so that the background appears consistent with the rest of the design. In addition to these changes, the controls of the video player have

Figure 21.1

been replaced with an interface that uses the same style as the other controls found in the project. Finally, the size of the figure has been adjusted to help balance the rest of the layout. The result is that the video has more unity with the design of the project.

The manipulation of additional media in ways such as this can be a little tricky and are very dependent on the type of software used and the technical knowledge of the designer. For the new media designer who incorporates additional media in projects, this is an area where learning a little technical know-how can pay off.

Audio in New Media Projects

There are several established uses for **audio** as a part of a new media project. Each use has a clear purpose. Using audio in a way that strays too far from its purpose can have a negative effect on the entire project. Without a doubt, poorly incorporated audio can be one of the most irritating elements of any new media piece.

The following section defines the main uses for audio in a project and covers a few of the concerns with each.

Audio as Feedback

One of the best ways to use audio in an interactive project is to provide feedback. By associating sounds with the controls, viewers can be given information about how they are influencing the interaction of a piece. An example of this is an audible "click" that is heard whenever a button is activated. By giving viewers feedback through sound, they will understand that their interaction was received and that they have brought about some change, even before the change takes place. This is especially effective for portions of a project that may take a little longer to load.

There are a few things to keep in mind when using audio for control feedback. First, the sound used should fit with the visual design of the piece. (The noise of a bleating sheep will probably not be appropriate for the activation of a button, unless the designer's intent is humor.) In addition, the different sounds used should also have unity with each other and should be consistent (e.g., using similar musical tones for various functions). As with visual unity, the project will benefit from a unity of audio elements. Unity will help the viewer learn an audio vocabulary for the controls along with a visual one.

The second concern when using audio as a feedback source has to do with file size and the length of the audio played. It is important to keep the file small so that the response will be immediate. If a control is activated and the file takes too long to load and play, the effect is worthless. When viewers click on a control and several seconds later an associated sound plays, they are not really being given any feedback.

In regard to the length of the audio played, it is best to keep it short and simple. Imagine a project where all of Beethoven's Fifth Symphony played every time a viewer moved the cursor over a control. The result would be bothersome at best. (Imagine what would happen if the viewer activated a second control before the feedback from the first had finished playing.)

Audio as Environment Enhancement

Using audio to enhance the environment of a project is often referred to as **background sound.** If used effectively, background sound can be an excellent addition to any new media piece and gives the viewer a much richer experience. But if it is used inappropriately, it can ruin an otherwise outstanding project.

One of the primary things to keep in mind is that the background sound should be as much a part of the piece as any other element. It should work with the project and not overpower the rest of the presentation. It is *background,* not content. (See the next section for more on audio as content.) The key to keeping background sound in its place is to make certain that there is stylistic unity, such as using slower, rich-sounding music for a dramatic presentation or rhythmic percussion for a fast-paced, stimulating project.

Some of the best examples of how to use background audio can be found in the music scores of movies. In film, music is often used to build moods and evoke emotions. In many cases, the viewer is even given clues about what will happen next by the background music. Studying how background music is used in movies is an excellent resource for the new media designer.

Using Repetition with Caution

A designer can often avoid problems with audio file sizes by looping a smaller file. Most new media applications include a feature that will allow a sound file to repeat. This can be an effective way to deal with background sound, but it can also produce disastrous results. For example, a designer uses a small file of five notes as the background audio and sets the loop to play continuously. In a short time, those same five notes repeated over and over can become irritating to anyone viewing the piece. A way to avoid this is to use an audio file that is long enough to include some variety in the soundtrack.

Another potential problem with looping audio comes from a poor match between the beginning and the end of the sound file. If an audio file is looped, the first part of the soundtrack will begin playing again as soon as the track has ended. If there is a severe difference between the beginning of the soundtrack and the end, the change may seem abrupt and awkward.

A worse scenario occurs when there is a delay or a change in the rhythm between the beginning and end of the sound file. When the background soundtrack starts over, any rhythm pattern that was established is thrown off, and the continuity of the loop sounds broken. As a designer using background sound, it is important to pay special attention to this issue.

One last area of caution in regard to using background soundtracks has to do with file size. It is important to be as certain as possible that the system used for the presentation will be able to handle all the project's requirements and the sound. If the processing is a little slow or if a system's resources are low, the background soundtrack will be where any trouble first appears. If the controls react a little slow or it takes a little longer to download the next page, the viewer might not even realize that there is a problem, but if the background music keeps cutting in and out, the viewer will definitely notice. In a project where the behavior of the background sound is erratic, it is better if there is no sound at all.

Audio as Content

Another common use for audio in a new media project is as content. Two examples of this are a Web site where visitors can listen to a live broadcast from a radio station and a presentation that uses a voice narration to convey information. In both examples, it is the audio that provides a portion of the content.

As a designer, it is important to weigh the benefits and drawbacks of using audio as content before committing to incorporating it into a project. In some cases, there is no choice. Both a musician's Web site that gives samples of recently released song titles and a presentation intended for people who are visually impaired definitely require audio content. But these are rare when compared to the vast majority of new media projects.

As with nearly any other element in a new media project, the key to the method of presentation is found in the goal and the intended audience of the piece. To better explain how these can influence the use of audio as content, we will examine two hypothetical projects. Both of these projects are tutorial presentations on CD-ROM and are intended to teach the user how to use a particular piece of software.

The first project is a series of tutorials that explains how to use a complex piece of new software. The second project shows how to play a game intended for prekindergarten children.

In the first project, it might initially seem a good idea to use voice narration to help convey detailed information in the various tutorials. For the person attempting to learn the material, an audio-only presentation could quickly become a new media nightmare. If the narration proceeds before a topic is fully understood or the viewer needs more information, the viewer must constantly pause or replay the audio.

Although not as stimulating, this kind of content would be better in text form. With text, the user can reread a section to gain better understanding or stop and return after looking up additional information. In addition to this, text enables the user to leave the tutorial and then pick up where one left off. An audio narration forces the user to either listen to everything over again or make one hunt with the fast-forward and reverse controls (assuming that these controls were included) for the place where one last stopped listening to the presentation.

These issues are contrary to the goal of the project since it makes learning how to use the software more difficult. In addition, the use of audio to present the content does not take into consideration the needs of the intended audience to take a break or to try each step in a set of complicated instructions.

These problems do not exist in the second project. In this case, a small amount of information is given on how to play the game. If some part of the instructional material were missed, it would not be as frustrating to replay the brief presentation. More important is the fact that text-based instructions would be a poor choice for this project since most of the users will have not yet learned to read.

General Issues with Audio

In the previous section, three ways to use audio and a few of the specific problems associated with each were addressed. What follows are two more general issues that can occur with audio and how a designer can deal with them.

CONTROL

The first issue is one of viewer control. As a designer, it is important to anticipate what sort of controls a viewer may need for any audio in a project. For example, volume is usually a matter of personal taste, and what is too loud for one person may not be loud enough for another. The required volume can even change for the same person under different circumstances. For instance, if there is a lot of background noise in the room, a viewer may need to adjust the volume in order to hear the audio.

It is often assumed that a viewer can adjust the volume through whatever system one is using to view the project. Although this is true, it may require the viewer to leave the presentation and open another window to access the controls. This can have impact on the project and can even cause the viewer to miss a portion of the presentation.

The solution to this potential problem is to design well-located volume controls as a part of the project. By using this approach, the viewer will be able to quickly adjust the audio level to one's own preference.

Another control option that the designer may consider is giving the viewer the ability to completely turn off the audio; especially if the audio is only background sound for the project.

Choosing the Right Audio

From a designer's perspective, choosing the right audio for a new media project can be intimidating, especially considering how much personal taste and association can affect the impression that a viewer might have. The key is to know the target audience and make informed decisions based on the goal of the project.

By keeping these things in mind, a designer can avoid mistakes, such as including heavy-metal background music for a Web site that reviews books on meditation and reducing stress. Music and sound in general can give impressions and emotional associations much like images can. If audio is to be included in a project, it is important that it have unity with the rest of the project, just as there should be unity between different visual elements. When in doubt, play it safe.

Additional Media over the Web

The World Wide Web is often jokingly referred to as the "World Wide Wait." Unfortunately, the use of additional media can turn this joke into a frustrating fact for the viewer. This section addresses two topics related to this issue.

Loading Screens: A Necessary Evil

The use of a loading screen is not limited to Web sites, even though this is where such a screen is most commonly found. In its simplest form, a loading screen is a bit of text that informs the viewer that some element is loading for use. This may not seem like it is worthy of being included as additional media, but some loading screens can be very complex and include animation or games to play while the viewer waits. (They also fit our definition of a stand-alone unit that evolves over time.)

For a new media designer, a loading screen can be a tool that is useful for staving off viewer frustration. In any interactive piece, it is important to let the viewer know that something is happening. If the viewer clicks on a button and the screen goes blank for a period of time, one might assume that there is something wrong or that the project doesn't work at all; even if everything is fine and the delay is nothing more than the next part being loaded. The loading screen is a handy way to keep the viewer informed and to avoid any negative assumptions about the quality of your work.

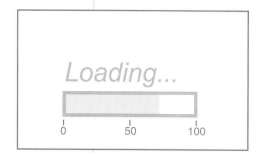

Figure 21.2

It would be nice if all that was required was a line of text that read "Note to Viewer: Please be patient. The presentation is not broken but merely loading the next part." But even if there is a nice loading screen that lingers a little too long, the viewer may assume that there is a problem. The way to avoid this situation is to create a loading screen that does something while the viewer waits. An example of this can be seen in Figure 21.2.

Figure 21.2 shows a commonly used animation that is effective for keeping a viewer informed about the state of the piece. In this illustration, the word *Loading* appears above a small bar that fills with color as time goes by.

The filling of the bar supposedly indicates how much of the file has loaded and how much time remains. For this to be an accurate reading, there needs to be a continual assessment between the size of the file, how much data has transferred, and what the current rate of transfer is. Although some applications do attempt to give a reasonably close estimate, viewers might be surprised to learn that many loading screens are little more than a simple animation roughly timed to last the length of a typical download. This might seem like a bit of underhanded dealing, but it illustrates that for the viewer what is important is only to know that something is happening. By including a loading indicator for parts of a project that may be delayed, the viewer will know that everything is working as it should.

Video over the Internet

It is far beyond the scope of this book to cover all the technical issues associated with including video as a part of a Web site, but it is important to at least understand the different options of delivery for this additional media.

Currently, there are only two main ways to deliver video as a part of a Web site. The first is to download the entire file onto the viewer's computer before it can be viewed. With the large file sizes found in typical videos, this can require a longer wait than many viewers will tolerate.

The other video delivery method is referred to as **streaming,** and it requires special software on the Web server and the viewer's computer. With streaming video, the viewer does not have to wait until the entire file downloads. Instead, the video is sent to the viewer in small pieces, and it is hoped that the transfer rate will keep up with the large amount of data being sent. This, of course, assumes that the connection is maintained throughout the transfer process.

The real trouble with either of these methods has to do with the large video files and the amount of data that can be sent. A past solution to this issue has been to decrease the video file size, but this makes for only a tiny viewing area or poor-quality images. As more Internet users become connected with broadband technologies, the standard of videos has increased, but there can still be problems. When using video as a part of a Web site, the designer should keep informed on the current state of Internet technology and know the resources of one's target audience. This is one area where things are changing rapidly.

SUMMARY

This chapter focused on the use of additional media as a part of new media projects. General topics covered were reasons for adding media and its uses. Attention was also given to several of the problems that can occur with additional media as well as how to avoid them. The use of audio was discussed in detail as well. This included the main purposes of audio in a project and a few of the issues associated with each purpose. General issues with including audio in new media projects were also covered. Finally, this chapter addressed the addition of loading screens and the use of video over the Internet.

EXERCISES

1. On the Internet find an example of additional media used as content. Write a few paragraphs describing how the media was used, its effectiveness, and any benefits or negative aspects created by the addition of the media.

REVIEW QUESTIONS

1. Name two parts of a new media project that could be considered additional media.

2. Give an example of when it would be beneficial to replace text with additional media.

3. How can copyright and ownership affect the use of additional media?

4. What are the three purposes of audio in a new media project?

5. How can audio be used to give a viewer feedback?

6. What is a loading screen?

What Comes Next?

In this text, you have explored many of the concepts that influence the nature of new media and have studied the building blocks of design that can be used in this revolutionary form of communication. In hands-on exercises, you have worked with design elements at their most rudimentary levels and later assembled them into complex layouts and images. You now possess an understanding of what is required for successful visual communication. In short, you have what you need. What comes next is up to you.

What will you do with this knowledge and ability? Will you continue to refine your skills, or will you do nothing while this revolution in communication passes you by? As a new media designer, you have entered a field that has begun to change everything around us—entertainment, education, and even society itself. Will you be among the few that harness and guide the evolution of this change, or will you stand on the sidelines as a spectator? The choice is yours. But remember, the world will be watching— and the world wants to be impressed.

Glossary

abstract expressionism A style or artistic movement that relies on spontaneous reaction or self expression, through the use of a medium, to produce a nonrepresentational composition. Also known as action painting.

abstract formalism A style or artistic movement that makes use of formal design principles in a nonrepresentational manner. Commonly referred to as postpainterly abstraction.

abstraction The distortion or enhancement of certain qualities in an image, as opposed to a realistic portrayal.

actual line Any line that is actually drawn and remains visible. Opposed to implied or imagined lines.

additional media Any self-contained media (sound, video, etc.) that is included as a part of a larger media presentation.

additive color Method that produces a specific color through the mixing of light waves made from the three primary colors (red, green, and blue). This is the method used by computer monitors and television screens.

adjacency effect The relative appearance of a shift in value due to the proximity of another value. An example of this is a gray square that appears lighter in value when it is placed over a dark background.

art deco A decorative style based on geometric forms.

artist A person who works in any of the fine arts.

audio The reproduction of sound, usually through the use of technology.

background sound Sound used as secondary content in a media presentation. As opposed to foreground sound, which is the use of audio as primary content.

backlight In an image, an area that is lighter in value because of ambient or reflected light that does not come directly from a primary light source. An example of this is a lighter area within a shadow that is caused by light reflecting from a surface other than the main light source.

balance In composition, the visual equilibrium of all elements (value, importance, etc.) included in a design.

bit A basic unit of measure for data based on binary digits. Eight bits is equal to one byte.

byte The common unit of measure for digital data. One byte is made up of eight bits.

chiaroscuro The use of light and dark in the rendering of an image to create the illusion of depth in three dimensions.

color A property of light of a specific wavelength (e.g., red, orange, yellow, etc.).

compatibility In digital-based media, the ability to use a certain file format or file property, produced by one system, on another. An example of this is the .jpg file format for images. Not only is this sort of file compatible with most imaging software, but it can be viewed in most Web browsers.

composition The arrangement of different elements of design so that they work together as a whole in both layout and unity.

conceptual unity A comparative similarity of different visual elements based on a common idea or thought (e.g., seven circles, the numeral 7, and the printed word *seven*).

context The entire background or environment, whether visual or conceptual, relative to a specific element. An example of context in an image is a figure seated in a dark woods. The surrounding woods is the context for the seated figure.

contour   The outline of a figure or object.

contrast   The difference between elements based on principles of design, such as light and dark or color (e.g., there is a high amount of contrast between two areas of a circle that are black and white).

cool   In reference to color, one of several hues, such as blue, green, and violet that are associated with cool temperatures. These are seen as opposites of warm hues, such as red, orange, and yellow.

crystallographic   Arrangement of visual elements in a dispersed manner that emulates the growth of crystals, often a repetitive pattern.

cubism   A style and artistic movement that is characterized by the division of visual elements into cubes and geometric shapes within a composition.

dadaism   A style and artistic movement that purposefully makes use of incongruent and often nonsensical elements in design.

decorative type   Classification term used to refer to typefaces that do not fit in any of the more common groups of type or that are extremely stylized. Also called novelty type.

deep navigation   A navigation structure that requires a presentation user to follow one of several direct paths of content pages to view information. To change paths, the user must return to a page higher in the navigation structure. Opposite of shallow navigation.

delivery   In reference to media presentations, how the presentation data arrives at its destination. Examples of this might be over the Internet, on a CD-ROM, or through wireless transmission.

design   To produce an artistic unit through planning and execution.

designer   As differentiated in this text, a person that uses skill (often aesthetic) to plan and produce something that performs a function.

diffused   Something that has been spread out or dispersed. In reference to

lighting effects, illumination that does not appear as sharp in detail or contrast.

display   In reference to electronic media, the technology used to reproduce a presentation (e.g., a computer monitor or a projector).

dithering   The arrangement of different colored pixels in certain image formats to simulate a color that cannot be produced by the technology being used.

emphasis   The use of design elements to call attention or emphasize a certain part of an image or layout.

evolution   In design, the gradual change in some visual element over time.

expressionism   A style and artistic movement that is characterized by a distortion of reality to convey inner experience.

focus   In design, the direction of the viewer's attention through the use of visual elements.

font   A particular typeface in one size and style.

format   The circumstances and physical nature of a visual presentation. A large canvas and a computer monitor are examples of format.

futurism   A style and artistic movement that is characterized by the depiction of movement through elements of design.

gamut   In reference to color, the entire range of colors that can be reproduced by a specific system (e.g., the gamut of color that can be produced in print is different from the gamut of color that can be produced on a computer monitor).

golden spiral   A method of composition created by dividing a rectangle into three equal parts and then subdividing the last section into thirds again. The process is repeated for each smaller rectangle inside of the last. A line drawn through each of the rectangles creates a spiral.

grid   An area divided by equidistant horizontal and vertical lines. As a design tool, it is used to align elements within a layout or design.

hashing Slang term for hatching. The use of drawn lines to emulate value produced by lighting effects.

hatching The use of drawn lines to emulate value produced by lighting effects. An example of this is hatching that is used to create darker areas in an image.

highlight In design, the brightest, most reflective area of a figure or object.

hue A term used to refer to the base color of a color variation (e.g., red is the hue of pink).

illusionary space The portrayal of three-dimensional space on a two-dimensional picture plane. An example of this is a drawing of a room's interior on a flat piece of paper.

imaginary line A line in an image that has not been drawn but is created in the mind of the viewer through some pictorial means that indicates direction. An example of this is a figure that points toward an object. In the mind of the viewer, a line exists between the pointing finger and the object.

impressionism A style and artistic movement that is characterized by an attention to the effects of light and atmosphere intended to convey mood and impression.

information (phase) The first phase of the design process. The information phase is concerned with gathering information that will influence the rest of the design (e.g., purpose or goal, audience, and content).

intensity The amount of pure hue present in a specific color. Also known as saturation.

interaction (phase) The second phase of the design process. The interaction phase determines the arrangement of content, what controls will be given to the user, and how the content will flow.

interactivity The ability of the viewer to interact or influence content. An example of this is the ability of a user to select answers for scoring as part of a media-based quiz.

isometric perspective A method for displaying three-dimensional space on a two-dimensional picture plane. Isometric perspective is characterized by the use of parallel lines that do not recede to a vanishing point.

kerning In typography, the adjustment of space between individual characters in a word or line of text.

leading In typography, the adjustment of vertical space between two lines of text.

legibility How well text can be read.

line A thin mark made in drawing or design.

linear navigation Navigation of content that proceeds from one unit to the next in a linear fashion. An example of linear navigation is a slide show.

linear perspective Any one of several methods to portray three-dimensional space on a two-dimensional picture plane that uses guidelines for accurate perspective rendering.

medium In design, the material or technology used to create a graphic or image (e.g., paint, ink, a computer).

midtone The middle range of values in a graphic.

modern type Classification term used to refer to typefaces developed during the 1700s, characterized by a more mechanical appearance than other type families.

modular navigation Navigation of presentation in which content is segregated into smaller units or modules based on subject matter or other similarities. An example of this is a Web site that contains several short stories. The pages of each story are grouped together in navigationally structured units that prevent a reader from directly accessing pages of a different story while viewing another.

monochromatic Having only one color or hue. An example of a monochromatic image is one that uses only variations of red in the entire design.

motion The change of an object's position in space.

negative space The area of an image that exists around rendered objects. The opposite of positive space.

new media Any of several forms of evolving presentation that make use of technology and interactivity.

nonrepresentational abstraction Design that uses visual elements in a way that does not portray the representation of objects or figures from the physical world.

old style type Classification of type that has its roots in Roman stone carving and Renaissance script.

one-point perspective A method for creating the illusion of three-dimensional space on a two-dimensional picture plane. In accurate one-point perspective, the guidelines used for depth recede toward a single vanishing point.

open navigation Navigation that allows a user to view content in any order. An example of this is a presentation that permits viewers to access any page from any other.

pace The rate of change or evolution. An example of a fast-paced presentation is one that changes scenes or content quickly.

perspective The portrayal of an image in a manner that emulates a point of view. Usually associated with the illusion of three-dimensional space on a two-dimensional picture plane.

pixel The smallest unit of display for a monitor or video projector at a certain resolution. For example, a screen with a resolution of 800 by 600 will have a grid 800 pixels wide and 600 pixels high. A simple way to think of pixels is as the colored dots that make up an image displayed on a monitor. Because of this, the pixel is often used as a unit of measure for images and graphics. For example, an image is said to be 150 by 200. The numbers refer to how many pixels wide by how many pixels high the image will appear. Keep in mind that this does not translate to other units of measure, like inches or millimeters, since the size of a pixel can differ from one monitor to the next.

pixelation The alteration of an image or graphic that occurs when a device that makes use of pixels, such as a computer monitor, is used as a display. This usually occurs when elements of the graphic are smaller than the size of a single pixel.

pointillism A style and movement in art related to impressionism. Characterized by small dots of pure color used to depict objects.

point-of-view motion Illusionary motion in which the viewer seems to move through space. An example of this would be a flight simulator.

pop art A style and movement of art that typically uses techniques and imagery from advertising and mass media.

positive space The area of a design that is made up of a rendered figure or object. The opposite of negative space.

presentation (phase) The third phase of the design process. This includes designing the layout and the appearance of a presentation as well as the development of a working prototype.

psychic line An alternate term for an imaginary line. Also known as a psychic wire.

psychic wire An alternate term for an imaginary line. Also known as a psychic line.

radial In references to a pattern that branches out from a common center (e.g., a sunflower or star).

realism A style and artistic movement that is characterized by a portrayal of objects as they appear, without modification.

relativity A dependency of a property or attribute on another. An example of this is a square that appears darker when placed on a light background.

repetition In design, the repeating of a form several times within the same composition.

rhythm In design, the repetition of a form to create a pattern in space. Visual rhythm is often associated with an interval of space between the forms.

sans serif type Classification of type family characterized by the absence of serifs.

saturation In reference to color, the degree of a color's purity. Also known as intensity.

script type Classification of type that emulates handwritten script.

semiotics The general theories of signs, symbols, and communication through their use.

shade A degree of darkness of a color's value. An example of this is blue mixed with black. The new color produced is a shade of the original. This is the opposite of tint.

shadow   A dark area caused by an object blocking a path of light.

shallow navigation   A navigation structure that allows a presentation user access to all parts of the presentation from any other part. The opposite of deep navigation.

shape   In design, a form or contour of a body. Shape can also refer to one of several commonly recognized geometric forms, such as a square or triangle.

slab serif type   Classification of type family characterized by flat or thick rectangular serifs. Also called Egyptian type.

space   In design, an area allotted to some form or an entire composition.

streaming   In reference to media, the process of sending data in a continuous stream while the data is being used. An example of this is a video file that begins to play while later parts are still being received.

style   In design, the manner in which something is done or a reference to a particular movement of art.

subtractive color   A method for producing color that reflects specific wavelengths of light while absorbing others. An example of this would be an object that has been painted blue. The paint reflects the light waves in the blue range, but the other colors are absorbed. Because only blue light is reflected, the object appears blue.

surrealism   A style and movement in art that is characterized by the portrayal and interpretation of the workings of the unconscious mind and dreams.

symmetrical   In design, any element that can be divided into similar halves. An example of this is a circle.

tertiary colors   Colors that represent half steps between primary and secondary colors along the color wheel. An example of this is the color red-orange. This color is found between the primary color red and the secondary color orange.

texture   The arrangement of smaller elements to produce a specific appearance or feel of a surface. In design, tex-ture often refers to an association of the sense of touch with a purely visual element.

theme   In design, a repeated subject or idea that is used to give unity to a piece. An example of this would be a new media presentation that utilized imagery and graphics from the 1960s to present content.

thumbnails   In design, small rough sketches or drawings that are used for planning or to work out ideas in layout and composition.

tile   The continued repetition of a visual element in an arranged pattern. An example of this is a single image repeated as the background of a Web page.

time   In media, the duration or interval of change (or lack there of).

tint   A degree of lightness of a color's value. An example of this is the addition of white to a specific color. The new color produced is a tint of the original. This is the opposite of shade.

tracking   In typography, the adjustment of space between all of the characters in a word or line of text.

transition   The change of one state or condition to another. In new media, one of several visual effects that can be used to lessen the severity of abrupt changes in scenes, pages, or images. An example of this is an image that fades into view.

transitional type   Classification of type family characterized by attributes that form a sort of half step between the old style type families and modern type.

twisted perspective   A method of perspective in which several different views of an object are shown simultaneously. An example of this is a cave painting of a bull in which the main body of the animal is seen in profile but the horns are drawn as they would appear head on.

type   Printed or other reproduced characters, such as letters or numerals.

type families   Groups of type classified by similar attributes (e.g., old style, modern, sans serif, etc.).

typography   The art or process of arrangement, style, and appearance of type.

unity The arrangement of different elements so that a single harmonious design is achieved.

value In design, the relative property of light and dark areas attributed to light.

visible spectrum The full range of light frequencies that can be seen by the human eye.

visual pun In design, the use of two familiar but contrasting visual elements in an unexpected way that produces a different, sometimes humorous narrative or association. An example of this is an automobile rendered to look as if it was made from marshmallows.

volume An area of space in three dimensions (e.g., a vase has volume).

warm In reference to color, one of several hues (red, orange, yellow) that are associated with warm temperatures. The opposite of cool hues (blue, green, violet).

Web safe pallets A selection of standard colors provided by most imaging software applications that is limited to the 256 colors accepted as "Web safe" and that can be reproduced in most Web browsers.

Index

A

Abstract expressionism, 264
Abstract formalism, 264
Abstraction, 250–257
  altering the original, 253–255
  approaches to, 253–256
  changing the view in, 255
  defined, 250
  mixing metaphors in, 256
  nonrepresentational, 256–257
  reasons for using, 251–253
  style in creating, 255
Accessibility, global, 12
Actual lines, 77, 78
Additional media, 320–331
  legal issues with, 324
  presentation and, 324–325
  reasons for using, 321–322
  technical issues with, 323–324
Additive color, 141–143, 146
Adjacency effect, 113–114
Aesthetic value, 27
Animation, 320, 321
Antialiasing, 85–86
Application filters, 62
Art deco, 263
Artistic movement, style as, 260,
    262–263
Artists, 14
Ascender, 283
Association, 240–245
  comparative, 244
  sensory, 242–243
  symbolic, 241–242
Asynchronous communication, 12
Atmosphere, compensating for, 31–32
Audio
  choosing the right, 329
  as content, 327–328
  as environmental enhancement,
    326–327
  as feedback, 325–326
  general issues with, 328–329
  in new media projects, 325–329
  problems with looping, 327
Audio file, 320

B

Background sound, 326–327
Backlight, 108
Balance, 55, 194–209
  color and, 204–206
  crystallographic, 203
  emphasis and, 275–276
  focus in, 196–197
  golden spiral in, 202
  implied motion and, 207
  irregular elements in, 199–201
  lack of, in creating tension, 197
  radial, 203
  rule of thirds in, 201–202
  space and, 198–199
  texture and visual weight in,
    206–207
  value and, 203–204
  visual, 194, 227
  weight of elements by size and
    groups, 195–196
Baseline, 283
Bit, 20
Bitmap image, 20
Black, 106, 140, 144
Black and white, 106–107, 140
Byte, 20

C

Capline, 283
Captions, placement of, 187
Cave paintings, 7, 126
CD-ROMs, 320
CMYK color system, 146, 150
Color(s), 138–152, 156–173
  additive, 141–143, 146
  antialiasing and, 85–86
  balance and, 204–206
  CMYK, 146, 150
  complementary, 160–161, 162–163
  contrasting, 163–164
  in conveying illusionary space, 60, 73
  cool, 167, 168–169, 205
  defined, 139–140
  emotion and, 169–170
  informed choices in, 157–158

Color(s), *continued*
  intensity of, 148–149
  names of, 149
  perception and, 147–148
  primary, 143, 144–145, 146
  properties of, 146–149
  relativity of, 158–159
  rewriting history with, 161–163
  RGB, 143, 146, 150
  science of, 167–169
  secondary, 143, 145, 146
  subtractive, 143–145, 146
  symbolic, 171
  temperature and, 167–169
  tertiary, 145
  in texture, 207
  unity and, 159–160, 183
  value and, 104, 147–148
  warm, 167, 168–169, 205
  on the Web, 150–151
Color associations, 171
Color combinations, 157, 164–166
  alternate analogous, 165
  analogous, 165
  monochromatic, 166
  split complement, 166
  triad, 166
  value variation, 166
Color wheel, 144–145
Communication
  asynchronous, 12
  global accessibility of, 12
  interactivity and, 11–12
  synchronous, 12
  use of technology for visual, 17–20
Comparative association, 244
Compatibility, font, 295
Complementary colors, 160–161,
      162–163
  color temperature and, 168–169
Composition, 178–181
  layout in, 178, 183–189
  line and, 77
  unity in, 178, 179–183
Computer as design tool, 8–9
Computer monitor
  screen resolution of, 19, 50–51, 84
  size of, 19, 50
Conceptual unity, 180–181
Confusion, avoiding, 231–232
Consistency
  in layout, 40
  light source, 112
Content
  audio as, 327–328

evolution of, from user input, 12
  information flow in, 34–36
  in new media project, 34
Context
  creative, 262
  style as, 261–262
Contour, line as, 70–71
Contour drawings, 70–71
Contrast, 127
  color and, 163–164
  type and, 294–295
  value and, 115, 127
Control
  giving up, 311
  information flow and, 34–35
  viewer, 329
Cool colors, 167, 168, 205
  psychological effects associated with,
      168–169
Coppola, Ford, 96
Copyright, 324
Counter, 283
Creation, 17, 20–22
Creative context, 262
Crossbar, 283
Crystallographic balance, 203
Cube, 91
Cubism, 263

D
Dadaism, 263
Dark edge, 108
Decorative type, 286
Deep navigation, 315
Delivery, 17, 19–20
Depth perception, 57, 59, 61
Descender, 283
Design
  defined, 26
  defining, for the media designer, 27
  line as an element of, 72–73
  navigation, 36–37
  time as element of, 302
  type as element of, 291, 292
Designers, 14
Designer's block, 16
Design process, 26–42
  completing, 41–42
  information phase in, 28, 30–34
  interaction phase in, 28, 30, 34–38
  presentation phase in, 28, 30, 38–41
Design tool, computer as, 8–9
Detail
  attention to, 16
  texture as, 124

Developmental psychologists, 94–95
Diffusion, 109
Digital graphic, 16–22
    creation in, 17, 20–22
    delivery in, 17, 19–20
    display in, 17, 18–19
Dimensions, 91–92
Diptych, 53
Direction
    of light, 111–112
    line for, 77–81
Display, 17, 18–19
Distance, properties of, 60–61
Distraction, motion and, 306–307
Dithering, 151
Dodecahedron, 91

E
Ear, 283
Electromagnetic spectrum, 139
Elements
    irregular, 199–201
    weight of, by size and groups,
        195–196
Emotion
    color and, 169–170
    projection of, onto objects, 75–76
Emphasis, 272–278
    balance and unity in, 275–276
    making a difference in, 273
    in new media, 276
    through layout, 277–278
    through various elements, 273
Environmental enhancement, audio as,
        326–327
Evolution, 303
    as feedback, 304–305
    pace and, 304
Expression, line as, 75–77
Expressionism, 264

F
Feedback
    audio as, 325–326
    evolution as, 304–305
File size, 56
Filmmaking, 96
Filters
    antialiasing, 85–86
    application, 62
    texture, 129–130
Flat texture, 128
Flowchart, 37
Focus, 61, 196–197
Fonts, 282

compatibility of, 295
versus type, 283
Form, repetition of, 230
Format, 49
Format space, 49–53
    bending accepted rules of, 52–53
    getting knowledge about, 50–51
    size as concern in, 50
    using, 51–52
Freudian psychology, 263
Futurism, 264

G
Gamut, 149–150
.gif format, 20
Global accessibility, 12
Goal
    for new media project, 32
    for Web site, 31–32
Golden Rectangle, 51
Golden spiral, 202
Grid, 187–188

H
Habits, developing good, 16
Hashing, 82
Hatching, 81–82
Highlight, 108
Historical reference, type for, 293
Hue, 146–147, 156, 158, 160
Human factor, in defining new media,
        9, 11

I
Icosahedron, 91
Identification, shape and, 92–95
Illusionary space, 49, 56–61, 73, 74
    color and, 60, 73
    depth perception and, 57, 59, 61
    distance in, 59
    focus and, 61
    properties of light and distance in,
        60–61
    size in, 59
Images
    bitmap, 20
    monochromatic, 105
    raster, 21
    sharpness of, 61–62
    3D, 61–62
    vector, 21, 22
Imaginary line, 78
Imaging software, 21, 22, 111, 123
    guide features in, 188
Implied line, 77–78

Implied motion, balance and, 207
Impressionism, 263, 266
Information, references to additional, 187
Information flow, 34–36
Information phase in design process, 28,
    30–34
    defining the goal in, 31–32
    establishing the purpose in, 31
    identifying target audience in, 32–33
    planning information in, 33–34
Intensity of color, 148–149
Interaction phase in design process, 28,
    30, 34–38
    information flow in, 34–36
    navigation design in, 36–37, 38
Interactive projects, voice narration
    in, 321
Interactivity, 11–12, 310–316
    control and, 311
    navigation and, 311–316
Internet, video over, 331
Internet bulletin board, 311
Internet connection speeds, 20
Irregular elements, 199–201
Isometric perspective, 217–219

J
.jpg format, 20

K
Kerning, 290–291
Kiosk presentations, 320

L
Language, 90
Layout, 39–40, 178
    consistency in, 40
    emphasis through, 277–278
    evolution of, 183–186
    grid in, 187–188
    influence of print on, 186–187
    nongrid, 188–189
Leading, 291
Legal issues with additional media, 324
Legibility of type, 291, 293–294, 295
Light
    in defining value, 109–110
    direction of, 111–112
    properties of, 60–61
    reflected, 109
Lighting values, 112
Light source
    consistency of, 112
    effects of, 111–112
    position of, 110–111

Line, 68–87
    actual, 77, 78
    antialiasing and, 85–86
    composition and, 77
    as contour, 70–71
    in conveying shape, 69–70, 80, 91
    in conveying volume, 73–74
    in creating texture, 83
    defined, 69
    in depicting motion, 83
    as design element, 72–73
    for direction, 77–81
    existence of, 69–70
    as expression, 75–77
    imaginary, 78
    implied, 77–78
    kinds of, 77–81
    pixelation and, 84–86
    psychiatric, 78
    thickness of, 74
    unity and, 182
    as value, 81–82
Linear navigation, 312
Linear perspective, 212, 215
Loading screen, 330

M
Macromedia's Flash, 323
Media, 7, 108. *See also* New media
Media blending, 9
Metaphors, 189
    mixing, 256
Michelangelo, 161, 162
Midtone, 108
Modern type, 284
Modular navigation, 312–313
Monochromatic image, 105
Mood, value and, 116
Motion, 305–306
    distraction and, 306–307
    line in depicting, 83
    point-of-view, 305–306
Motion pictures, 8

N
Narrative, navigation as a, 311–312
Navigation, 311–316
    deep, 315
    design of, 36–37, 38
    linear, 312
    modular, 312–313
    as a narrative, 311–312
    open, 313
    paradigms in, 314–316
    shallow, 315–316

Negative space, 49, 69
power of, 54
prejudice against, 56
relationship between positive space
and, 55, 56
working with, 55–56
New media
additional media in, 320–331
as asynchronous, 12
asynchronous communication in, 12
color in, 143, 146–149
content evolution in, 12
defined, 7
differences in, 11–13
digital graphic and, 16–22
emphasis in, 276
evolution in, 7–9, 304–305
expectations in, 14
factors defining, 9–11
gamut and, 149–150
global accessibility in, 12
interactivity in, 11–12
job of designer in, 13, 14
layout and, 186–190
mixing, 13–14
mixing media in, 13
motion and distraction in, 306–307
navigation paradigms in, 314–316
perspective and, 220–222
pixelation in, 84–86
sharpness of image in, 61–62
style in, 266–268
virtual reality in, 58
visual vocabulary in, 230–231
New media designers, 6–23
defining design for, 27–42
development of good habits in, 16
goal of, 189
issues faced by, 6
position of, 13, 14
shape and, 94, 98–99
skills of, 15, 69–70
space and, 48
studying by, 15
target for, 16
tips for success, 14–16
tools for, 22
New media projects
audio in, 325–329
content in, 34
identifying target audience, 32–33
planning information in, 33–34
prototype in, 41
unity in, 81
New media software, 7

Nongrid layouts, 188–189
Nonlinear rhythm, 234–235
Nonrepresentational abstraction,
256–257
Novelty type, 286

O
Objects, projection of emotion onto,
75–76
Old style type, 282–283
One-point perspective, 214–215
On-line bulletin board, 12
Open navigation, 313
Original, altering of, in abstraction,
253–255

P
Pace, evolution and, 304
Perception, 93
color and, 147–148
depth, 57, 59, 61
Permission, getting, 324
Perspective, 212–223
isometric, 217–219
linear, 212, 215
new media and, 220–222
one-point, 214–215
rules of, 213
twisted, 220
two-point, 215–217
vanishing point in, 213–214, 217, 219
Photography, development of, 8
Phototype, 41
Pixelation, 294
Pixels, 18–19
antialiasing and, 85–86
size by, 19
Pixelation, 21, 84–86
Placement, rhythm and, 235
.png format, 20
Pointillism, 255, 263
Point-of-view motion, 305–306
Pop art, 264
Positive space, 49, 53–56, 69
power of, 54
relationship between negative space
and, 55, 56
working with, 55–56
Presentation, additional media and,
324–325
Presentation phase in design process,
28, 30, 38–41
layout in, 39–40
phototype in, 41
style in, 41

Primary colors, 143, 144–145, 146
Print, influence of, on layout, 186–187
Psychic line, 78
Psychic wire, 78
Purpose, establishing, 31

R
Radial balance, 203
Raster-based software, 21, 22
Raster images, 21
Realism, 264
Recorded sound, 8
Rectangle, 90
Reflected light, 109
Relativity, 113
    color, 158–159
    of value, 113–114
Repetition
    of basic shape or form, 230
    caution in using, 327
    creating, 227
    creating a visual vocabulary with,
        229–231
    in creating texture, 127, 128
    defining, 227–228
    rhythm and, 226–235
    shape and, 99
RGB color, 143, 146, 150
Rhythm, 55, 232–235
    altering, 233–234
    defining, 227–228
    nonlinear, 234–235
    placement and, 235
    repetition and, 226–235
    visual, 228
Rule of thirds, 201–202

S
Sans serif type, 285
Saturation, 148–149
Scale, texture and, 131–132
Scott, Ridley, 96
Screen resolution, 50–51
Script type, 286
Secondary colors, 143, 146
Semiotics, 241
Sensory association, 242–243
Serifs, 283, 291
Shade, 147
Shadow, 108–109
Shallow navigation, 315–316
Shape(s), 90–101
    association and, 98–99
    defined, 91
    grouping of similar, 97–100

grouping within, 99–100
identification and, 92–95
line in conveying, 69–70, 80, 91
repetition of, 230
subtle use of, 95–97
in two dimensions, 91
unity and, 182–183
Sharpness of image, 61–62
Simulation, texture as, 126
Single-medium barrier, 8
Sistine Chapel ceiling, 161–163
Site map, 37
Size
    balance and, 195–296
    depth perception and, 59
    format and, 50
    by pixels, 19
Slab serif, 285
Software
    imaging, 21, 22, 111, 123
    raster-based, 21, 22
    vector-based, 21, 22
Sound. *See also* Audio
    background, 326–327
    perception of, 57
    recorded, 8
Sound waves, length of, 139
Space, 48–64
    arrangement in, 198–199
    depth perception and, 59
    division of, 198
    format, 49–53
    illusionary, 49, 56–61, 73, 74
    kinds of, 49
    negative, 49, 53–56, 69
    positive, 49, 53–56, 69
    properties of light and distance in,
        60–61
    rhythm and, 227
    texture as, 124–125
    unity and, 182
    use of, 48
Speech, speed of, 321–322
Square, 90, 91
Static graphic, 320
Stereoscope, 58
Storyboard, 35, 37, 39
Streaming, 331
Stress, 283
Style, 41, 179, 260–268
    as artistic movement, 260, 262–263
    as context, 261–262
    creating, 266
    in creating abstraction, 255
    as in new media, 266–268

in new media, 266–267
philosophy and, 263
as technique, 260, 261–262
visual glossary of, 263–265
Subtractive colors, 143–145, 146
Surrealism, 112, 263
Symbolic association, 241–242
Symbolic color, 171
Symmetrical composition, 196
Synchronous communication, 12

T

Target audience, identifying, 32–33
Technical issues with additional media, 323–324
Technique, style as, 260, 261–262
Technology, use of, for visual communication, 17–20
Telecommunications, 9
Telegraph, 8
Television, 8
Temperature, color and, 167–169
Tension, lack of balance in creating, 197
Tertiary colors, 145
Text, 164
in creating flat texture, 128
texture and, 133
Texture(s), 122–134
balance and, 206–207
color in, 207
creating, 126–128
as detail, 124
flat, 128
line in creating, 83
repetition in creating, 127, 128
scale and, 131–132
as separate component, 125
as simulation, 126
as space, 124–125
text and, 133
unity and, 183
uses of, 123, 124–125
value in, 207
visual information and, 132–133
Texture filters, 129–130
drawbacks to using, 130
Third dimension, illusion of, 57–58
3D images, 61–62
Three dimensions, 91–92
Thumbnails, 39–40
Time, 302–307
as element of design, 302
Tint, 147
Titles, type for, 288–289
Tracking, 291

Transitional type, 284
Transitions, 303–304
Triangle, 90
Twisted perspective, 220
Two dimensions, 91
Two-point perspective, 215–217
methods for using, 216–217
rules for, 216
Type
adjusting, for design, 289–290
anatomy of, 283
combining different, 288–289
in communication of emotion, 292–293
compatibility and, 295
contrast and, 294–295
as design element, 291, 292
font versus, 283
for historical reference, 293
legibility of, 291, 293–294, 295
pixelation and, 294
readability and, 287
reader and, 287–288
standard adjustments in, 290–291
working with, 287
Type families, 283–286
decorative, 286
modern, 284–285
old style, 282–283
sans serif, 285
script, 286
slab serif, 285
transitional, 284
Typography, 282–295

U

Unity, 178, 179–183
color, 159–160, 183
conceptual, 180–181
creating, 179–180
emphasis and, 275–276
protraying, 81
tools for, 182–183
type and, 288–289
visual, 180–181
User input, content evolution from, 12

V

Value(s), 104–118
aesthetic, 27
balance and, 203–204
black and white in, 106–107
color and, 147–148
contrast and, 115, 127
defined, 105

Value(s), *continued*
    defining different areas of, 108–109
    direction of light and, 111–112
    light in defining, 109–110, 112
    line as, 81–82
    mood and, 116
    relativity of, 113–114
    strength of, 106–107
    in texture, 207
    unity and, 183
Vanishing point, 213–214, 219–220
Vector-based software, 21, 22
Vector images, 21, 22
Video clips, 320, 323
Video demonstrations, 320
Video files, 323–324
Video over the Internet, 331
View, changing, in abstraction, 255
Viewer control, 329
Virtual reality, 58
Visible spectrum, 139
Visual balance, 227
Visual communication, use of
    technology for, 17
Visual pun, 256
Visual rhythm, 228
Visual unity, 180–181
Visual weight, 206–207
Voice narration in interactive projects,
    321
Volume, 69, 92
    conveying with line, 73–74
    in three dimensions, 91, 92

W
Warm colors, 167, 205
    psychological effects associated with,
        168–169
Wavelength, 142
Web browser, 20
Web design, 50
Web-safe pallets, 150–151
Web site(s), 320, 322–323, 327
    colors on, 150–151
    defining goal for, 31–32
    design of, 28
    format issues in, 50–53
    goal for, 31–32
    information phase in, 28, 30–34
    interaction phase in, 28, 30, 34–38
    navigation in, 36–37
    negative space in, 57
    presentation phase in, 30, 38–41
White, 106, 140, 143, 144
Work habits, developing good, 16
Working progress, 27
World Wide Web, choosing media over,
    329–331
Wright, Frank Lloyd, 73

X
X-height, 283